Dancing on the Edge:
Chaplaincy, Church & Higher Education

DANCING ON THE EDGE:
Chaplaincy, Church & Higher Education

EDITED BY PETER MCGRAIL
AND JOHN SULLIVAN

MATTHEW JAMES PUBLISHING LTD

© 2007 Peter McGrail & John Sullivan

This book is sold subject to the condition that it shall not, by way of trade or otherwise, be lent, resold, hired out, or otherwise circulated without the publisher's prior consent in any form of binding or cover other than that in which it is published and without a similar condition including this condition being imposed on the subsequent publisher.

The moral rights of the authors have been asserted

First published in Great Britain 2007 by:
Matthew James Publishing Ltd,
19 Wellington Close,
Chelmsford,
Essex CM1 2EE
www.matthew-james.co.uk

ISBN 9781898366881

Cover design by Gill England

Printed and bound in Great Britain by Biddles Ltd, Norfolk

CONTENTS

Preface	9
Introduction	11
Chapter 1 *Dancing on the Edge* -A Report into Catholic Chaplaincy in Higher Education	15
Introduction	16
Part One: Chaplaincy and the Changing Profile of UK Students	20
1. Introduction	20
2. The Changing Patterns of Student Life	21
3. Student Relationships with Chaplaincy	23
4. Sunday Eucharist	30
5. Catholic Societies	31
6. Conclusion	34
Part Two: Relationship with the Institution: Operating within an Ambiguous Set of Parameters	36
1. Introduction	36
2. Sitting On The Edge': The Distinctive Nature of HE Chaplaincy	37
3. The Closest and Most Remote Relationships	40
4. Chaplaincy in a Secular Institution: the Blurring of Boundaries?	44
5. Formal and Perceived Relationships	47
6. Conclusion	50
Part Three: Relations with Other Religious Bodies within the Institution Ecumenism and Interfaith Engagement	51
1. Introduction	51
2. Ministry to a Denomination or to the Institution?	51
3. Ecumenical Plant	57
4. Worship in an Ecumenical Context	59
5. Interfaith Chaplaincy	60
6. Conclusion	64
Part Four: Supporting and Managing the Work of Chaplains: The Relationship with the Catholic Community	65
1. Introduction	65
2. The Appointment Process for Chaplains	66
3. Support and Supervision of Lay Chaplains	71
4. Support and Supervision of Catholic Priest Chaplains	77
5. Conclusion	84
Recommendations	86

Chapter 2	*Interstitial Interventions: The Workplace Ecology of University Chaplains* John Sullivan	89
Chapter 3	*A Spiritual Presence on the Frontier* Kevin Egan	109
Chapter 4	*A Seat at the Table? Chaplaincy and Student Services in a Church University* Steven Shakespeare	125
Chapter 5	*Chaplaincy and University Student Services* Sheila Aynsley-Smith	139
Chapter 6	*Student Composition, Chaplaincy Clientele, and Channels of Communication* Simon Robinson	151
Chapter 7	*Chaplaincy: The View from the Other Side* Gemma Simmonds	175
Chapter 8	*Chaplaincy with a Parish Link* Roberta Canning	191
Chapter 9	*Beyond the Campus: Chaplains fostering outreach activity and community service* Gerard Devlin	205
Chapter 10	*Chaplaincy in Ecumenical and Inter-Faith Contexts* Stephen Williams	225
Chapter 11	*Reimagining the Chaplaincy for the 21st Century - An American Perspective* Monica M Manning	249
Appendix	*Reflecting on University Chaplaincy*	269
Annotated Bibliography		273
Index		284

ACKNOWLEDGMENTS

Grateful thanks are due to the following organizations for funding this project:

- The Theodore Trust
- The Catholic Fund for Chaplaincy in Higher Education
- The Catholic Student Trust
- Liverpool Hope University Catholic Studies Research Group

We wish to thank also the many people who co-operated so willingly and helpfully during the research – chaplains, college and university staff, students, and parish clergy. Chaplains in particular kindly provided both welcome and hospitality during the fieldwork period.

Rev. Dr Paul McPartlan and Ms Ursula Leahy read the report in various stages of draft, made numerous helpful suggestions, and saved us from many errors. Those that remain are of course our responsibility.

LIST OF CONTRIBUTORS

Sheila Aynsley-Smith is Head of Student Services at Manchester Metropolitan University

Roberta Canning is the Roman Catholic Chaplain to the University of Bangor, North Wales.

Gerry Devlin is Chaplain to St. Mary's College, Strawberry Hill, London.

Kevin Egan is Director of the Leadership & Pastoral Care Postgraduate programme at All Hallows College, Dublin.

Monica Manning is an independent educator and executive officer of The Nova Group, www.novalearning.com

Peter McGrail is senior lecturer in Catholic Studies at Liverpool Hope University.

Simon Robinson is Running Stream Professor of Applied and Professional Ethics at Leeds Metropolitan University

Gemma Simmonds lectures in systematic theology and spirituality at Heythrop College, University of London.

Steven Shakespeare is Anglican Chaplain to Liverpool Hope University.

John Sullivan is Professor of Christian Education at Liverpool Hope University.

Stephen Williams is Senior Anglican Chaplain to the University of London.

Preface

We are indebted to Professor John Sullivan and the Reverend Dr Peter McGrail for making available to us who are involved in various areas of university life, this rich collection of essays. This book is prefaced by the report that the editors undertook recently on chaplaincy in higher education called 'Dancing on the Edge'. In that report, in an ordered and thoughtful way, we heard of the complexities around the contemporary university chaplaincy.

The secularisation of the academy has outpaced the secularisation of contemporary western societies. Needless to say, the media and intellectual elites have been in the vanguard of that process acting often as prophets of a self-fulfilling prophecy. Nevertheless, there is a gap between the perceptions of these academic elites and many of the students and communities they serve. Undoubtedly, the vagaries of the secularisation process has made religion increasingly unfashionable. It is more difficult today within the academy for westerners to articulate their religious affiliation or spiritual persuasion. The nature of this psychological restriction means that it is much easier for many to leave discussions of spirituality or religion (even of purpose and meaning) outside the door of the laboratory or the lecture room. For a whole generation or two, this has meant that any talk of being part of a religious community is more difficult and sometimes even embarrassing.

However, the university itself changes with its new existence in the global village and many other religious followers who join the university community do not carry the same inhibitions as those adrift from their former Christian moorings. Whatever we make of doctrinal or institutional orthodoxy, an individual's life in the modern university takes unimaginable twists and turns, not only when there are national or community crises, but also when life itself presents its challenges and surprises. The pursuit of intellectual ideals does not free any of us from the burden and excitement of important personal choices.

It is at the level of the personal, this interface between the mundane and the academic, that windows into the human soul and the human personality are opened. They are not as easily identifiable or philosophically describable or discrete as modern academics may think. It is in these unexpected, even vulnerable, human moments in the midst of serious academic pursuit that the university turns to its counselling services and health support services and, if they are privileged to have good chaplains, its chaplaincy. I have become more convinced of the indispensability of the chaplaincy as I come to understand better the requirements to support individuals within learning communities and to nurture personhood and vocation, even for those who have no religious commitment.

Naturally, chaplains today have to work with greater cultural sensitivity and are often burdened by all manner of misconceptions as representatives of religious faith. Yet there is a correlation between a university's health, safety and counselling services, which normally deal with those in crisis already, and the establishment of a nurturing university community. The chaplaincy, in my view, is not an ambulance service but, as these essays indicate, helps to raise the ideals of the university. It is, and should be, part of creating wholeness, establishing community in the midst of rank individualism and helping the university achieve its real purpose of enabling its scholars and students to pursue their particular area of disciplinary expertise while establishing a humane and 'whole' community. To be 'whole' fundamentally means that the pursuit of the mind cannot be undertaken at the expense of the wholeness of persons (body, mind and spirit) whatever the materialists among us think. At its best the chaplaincy plays a vital role of helping to fulfil the mission of the university.

This is a difficult view to articulate. However, in a foreword to such a stimulating collection of essays, may I suggest that the challenge for us at Christian foundations must be to help chaplains not to remain 'dancing on the edge' but to inform the broader purpose of creating a healthy academic community; agents of change affecting the centre while 'dancing on the edge' as the report describes.

These essays not only spur us on to think again about the role of the chaplaincy but may even cause us to reconsider the role of modern universities, especially for those among us who treasure their Christian foundations.

Professor Gerald Pillay
Vice-Chancellor & Rector
Liverpool Hope University
August 2006

Introduction

PETER MCGRAIL AND JOHN SULLIVAN

The decades that bridged the twentieth and twenty-first centuries have witnessed a remarkable growth in the British Higher Education Sector. The explosion in the number of students and universities, the changing profile of new students, and the impact upon student life of the progressive introduction of student fees have all been major influences upon life in HE. At the same time, the increasingly competitive edge of factors such as the publication of annual university league tables and the periodic Research Assessment exercise have brought new pressures to staff – academics and administrators alike. Any sense that our universities and colleges were oases of academic tranquillity characterised by lengthy stretches of free time has long been lost. Instead, for both staff and students the pace of campus life continues to accelerate, and each academic year brings new pressures.

The impact of these changes has been felt in every corner of the sector – not least at the point at which the Christian churches seek to engage with HE institutions and offer support to their members. There has never been a single model of HE chaplaincy in this country. Rather, the churches have adapted their presence on campus to the particular circumstances of each university or college. In some places there has been a tradition of welcome, and chaplains have been viewed as valuable institution-wide resources. In other places, a strongly secular institutional agenda has made their presence more marginal. However, by the beginning of the twenty-first century the relative stability that had marked chaplaincy life – whatever the model adopted – had been lost in most places. Alongside the institutional changes mentioned above, a key factor driving many establishments to reconsider their relationship to chaplaincy has been the growth in the numbers of students coming from a non-Christian background. This growth has been due in no small part to the economic drive to recruit from beyond Europe. Changing geo-political concerns, particularly since 9/11, have fed into a widespread repositioning in the approach of universities and colleges to the presence in their midst of students and staff from various faith traditions.

All of this has placed particular pressures on the work of Christian chaplains as they have sought to negotiate their way through a nexus of shifting relationships and expectations – with regard to their students, their institution, their ecumenical colleagues and their sponsoring denomination. It was with a wish to gain a clearer understanding of how those pressures play out on the ground that the Roman Catholic Conference of Chaplains in Higher Education approached Prof John Sullivan and Revd Dr Peter McGrail, both of the Theology and Religious Studies Department of Liverpool Hope, in 2004, asking that a qualitative study be undertaken of life across a range of representative chaplaincies. In response, Peter McGrail conducted fieldwork in a number of institutions across England and Wales between June 2004 and January 2005. The written report of his findings, *Dancing on the Edge*, was presented to the annual meeting of English and Welsh Catholic chaplains in March 2005, and then to the Roman Catholic Bishops' Conference of England and Wales.

The chaplaincy community as a whole responded very positively to the findings of the Report. John Sullivan and Peter McGrail therefore sent it out to a number of people drawn from the academy, university administration and chaplaincy, inviting them to a Colloquium at which a number of issues raised in *Dancing on the Edge* could be explored further. Subsequently, an international ecumenical group met at St. Deiniol's Library, North Wales, in May 2006 to discuss a series of papers. This book is the result of their preparation, dialogue, and reflection.

The book opens with the original report, *Dancing on the Edge*. One of the key characteristics of it is the lively manner in which it permits different parties on campus to speak for themselves. This methodological approach permits the key issues to surface quickly and directly. These issues are then taken up and discussed further in the following essays, which are based upon the papers presented at the 2006 Colloquium. These essays bring out the multi-faceted and complex interaction, in university chaplaincy, between historical legacy, human chemistry, institutional politics, management structures, internal and external communication networks, social factors, theological perspectives, denominational sensitivities, individual gifts, gender issues and surrounding ecclesial cultures. A spectrum of approaches from the academic community to chaplaincy is revealed, ranging from outright and explicit suspicion and hostility, through indifference or benign neglect, to different types of support and hospitality. Student responses to chaplaincy offer a parallel range – from enthusiastic commitment to deliberate avoidance. In these essays there are examples of personal story, theoretical interpretation, social analysis and spiritual exploration, the whole collection being an exercise in practical theology. Insights are offered from lay men and women, religious and clergy; from academics, chaplains and student services professionals; from different Christian denominations. They take into account contexts from the United Kingdom, Ireland, and the United States of America. Chaplains and those who work with them engage in dialogue. The needs and responses in relation to chaplaincy provision of students, staff, management, the local community and church, all receive attention.

In the first of these essays, John Sullivan sets the scene by exploring the ecology of the workplace in which chaplains operate. The next essay, by Kevin Egan, examines distinctions between spirituality and religion, and suggests that the chaplain can be a real and significant spiritual presence on the frontier. Steve Shakespeare explores the interaction between chaplaincy and student services in a Church university, and the opportunities, dangers and ambiguities that the setting presents. In the following essays Sheila Aynsley-Smith brings a complementary perspective from her position as Head of Student Services, and Simon Robinson examines the make-up of the increasingly diverse student body and the resulting challenges in communication. Gemma Simmonds' essay opens out many issues around gender and power in a chaplaincy context. A move outwards of the focus begins with Roberta Canning's examination of chaplaincy in a setting with strong links with the local parish, and this is taken further by Gerry Devlin's examination of how chaplaincy can foster outreach activity and community service beyond the campus. A different relational aspect is addressed by Stephen Williams, who explores the increasingly important ecumenical and interfaith issues. Finally, the perspective widens again as Monica Manning's essay, written from an American context, invites a re-imagining of the chaplaincy for the twenty-first century.

We believe that the book offers a realistic assessment of many of the challenges facing chaplains in HE, as well as evidencing a committed engagement and sense of hope. Chaplains will find here mapped out crucial features of their work environment. Senior managers in HE will find themselves surprised, challenged and comforted in different proportions as they see their institutions described from the chaplains' perspective. Members and office-holders in the Church, too, should experience both discomfort and encouragement as they ponder the Report and the essays contained in this book.

Chapter One

'DANCING ON THE EDGE':

A REPORT INTO CATHOLIC CHAPLAINCY
IN HIGHER EDUCATION

*BY PETER MCGRAIL
AND JOHN SULLIVAN*

*This chapter was originally published in 2005
as a Report for the Conference of Catholic
Chaplains in Higher Education*

INTRODUCTION

BACKGROUND

This report concludes the second phase of a major review of Catholic chaplaincy provision in Higher Education (hereafter HE) in England and Wales. The review was initiated by the Conference of Catholic Chaplains in Higher Education. The first phase was a questionnaire addressed to all Catholic HE chaplains, which resulted in an initial report to the Bishops' Conference of England and Wales at the Low Week meeting of 2003.

Following this a recommendation was made that a further, qualitative, study should be undertaken, involving a small but representative number of HE institutions, and with the student body as the principal focus. A number of names were suggested as research partners. These included John Sullivan, Professor of Christian Education at Liverpool Hope University College. The Committee of the Conference approached Liverpool Hope to initiate discussions with Professor Sullivan. Rev. Dr. Peter McGrail, Lecturer in Catholic Studies at Liverpool Hope, and Director of Pastoral Formation in the Archdiocese of Liverpool, was identified as the potential principal researcher. In the ensuing discussions it was agreed that the remit of the study should be broadened out to include, in addition to students, chaplains, HE institutional officials, and ecumenical partners. The ecumenical dimension was further strengthened in response to a stipulation by the major funding organization, the Theodore Trust.

MODE OF WORKING

After taking initial soundings among the chaplains as a whole, the Committee identified and made initial approaches to the Catholic chaplaincies in eleven HE institutions. (Henceforth the term institution will be used alone, unless ambiguity might result.) For different reasons two of these declined to participate in the study; the other nine all agreed. An overview of the nature of the participating institutions is given below.

The project consisted initially of fieldwork, in which Dr McGrail visited each of the participating institutions either once or twice between June 2004 and January 2005. The heart of the research was a series of interviews. These were always complemented by informal observations of chaplaincy life; he attended chaplaincy events where possible, including celebrations of the Eucharist and other services, and was shown round the plant, ecumenical and Catholic. It was normally the responsibility of the chaplain (or senior chaplain in the larger institutions) to make all the arrangements for all these activities; in this they were most co-operative and helpful, as also were all those interviewed, who included students, ecumenical partners, and institutional staff at various levels, including some very senior.

In total the following interviews took place:

- Catholic Chaplains – fifteen (the nine lead chaplains and six assistant chaplains). All these were one-to-one.
- Ecumenical Chaplains - three groups (from two to five); eight individuals
- Students – twelve groups (from two to twelve); twelve individuals. All these were chaplaincy users or residents; by the nature of their selection most were practising Catholics, but not all.
- Institutional personnel – seven, all one-to-one.

The interviews varied in length, the average being around 40 minutes. All those with the chaplains were longer – 60 to 90 minutes. All were recorded, by agreement. Apart from one or two brief asides, no interview respondent asked not to be recorded. All respondents were assured of confidentiality for themselves as individuals, and as far as possible for their institution.

The interviews were 'semi-structured', with a framework of standardized questions designed to open up a dialogue. No attempt has been made to convert the responses into statistical data, such as would be appropriate to a quantitative study. Rather, this report attempts to capture the voices, to reflect on them, and to analyse the key issues. It thereby identifies areas of interest and concern which require further consideration. Recommendations are made to act as the basis for such further consideration.

OVERVIEW OF INSTITUTIONS

Because of the special nature of Oxford and Cambridge a conscious decision was taken to exclude them from the study. The selection of the institutions was based on three interlocking parameters - geographical location, the nature of the institution, and the chaplaincy set-up. The goal was to achieve a balance of different aspects of all three parameters.

GEOGRAPHICAL LOCATION

The nine institutions are located in Wales, and in the Midlands, North-west, South, South-east and South-west of England.

NATURE OF INSTITUTION

One is a Catholic College; the others are all universities. They include one constituent college of the University of Wales; three Russell Group universities; one 1960's university foundation and three former polytechnics/technical colleges. Several operate across multiple campuses, and one comprises a number of constituent colleges.

CHAPLAINCY SET-UP

The selection was influenced by the desire to include both priest and lay chaplains, both male and female, working alone and with assistant chaplains, and in different types of partnerships, both ecumenical and parish-linked.

ANONYMITY OF INSTITUTIONS

The numbering system used is encoded and does not correspond to any of the above classifications. (The interview references are the code for the institution followed by a differentiator between the various interviews conducted at that institution.)

OVERVIEW OF REPORT

It became evident as the research proceeded that the life and work of chaplains and their chaplaincies have to be carried out within a nexus of four separate but interlocking patterns of relationships and spheres of activity, each of which at the present time is in a state of flux. The chaplains must negotiate their ways through the ambiguous and ill- or un-defined terrains that comprise their field of work. In each of these terrains they are, in varying degrees, in a situation of liminality – hence the report title 'Dancing on the Edge', a phrase used by one chaplain to describe his work. The four parts making up the report deal with these areas. In brief:

PART ONE: CHAPLAINCY AND THE CHANGING PROFILE OF UK STUDENTS

The enormous growth in student numbers and the radically changing patterns of how universities and student life operate has had a major impact on the whole traditional understanding of chaplaincy, and on the parameters in which chaplains can work.

PART TWO: RELATIONSHIP WITH THE INSTITUTION: OPERATING WITHIN AN AMBIGUOUS SET OF PARAMETERS

Most chaplains find themselves working on the very edge of the – usually secular - institution. This is not always entirely negative, but creates major ambiguities and uncertainties with regard to their status, boundaries and even the recognition of the validity of their presence.

PART THREE: RELATIONS WITH OTHER RELIGIOUS BODIES WITHIN THE INSTITUTION: ECUMENISM AND INTERFAITH ENGAGEMENT

The need to function ecumenically is a positive element of chaplaincy work, but again relationships and working patterns are often undefined and ambiguous, with resulting tensions. The growing thrust within institutions towards an interfaith rather than specifically Christian vision of chaplaincy presents further new and difficult challenges.

PART FOUR: SUPPORTING AND MANAGING THE WORK OF CHAPLAINS: THE RELATIONSHIP WITH THE CATHOLIC COMMUNITY

The sense of isolation felt by many chaplains is most painfully experienced in their relationship with the institutional church that appoints them. Individual support varies, and can be good, but there are very few systems in place for sustained supervision and support of chaplains and chaplaincy.

Recommendations are given at the end of the report, and an Appendix containing material intended to stimulate further reflection appears at the end of the book.

PART ONE

CHAPLAINCY AND THE CHANGING PROFILE OF UK STUDENTS

1. INTRODUCTION

The most recent Report into Trends in Higher Education maps the startling growth in the numbers of students in Higher Education (henceforth HE) in recent years, and identifies a number of developments that have impacted significantly upon the life of Chaplaincies.[1] Across the eight years covered by the Report (academic years 1994-5 to 2001-2), the number of undergraduate students increased by almost a third across the UK. The number of full-time students increased by only 13%, while the number of part-time students almost doubled. By the last year of the study over a third of all undergraduates were part-time students, as against less than a quarter at the start. The report did not analyse the numbers of mature students separately, but comments that there is correlation between the figures relating to them and those for part-time students. At the last year of the study, region-by-region mature students made up between 20% and 40% of all undergraduates. Finally, across the eight years of the study the number of international students (from non-EU countries) increased by over 50%.

The senior Anglican chaplain at one of the institutions considered in this project commented on the change in the composition of the student body:

> It's certainly a fantasy that perhaps older generations still have that people at university are called 'undergraduates,' that they're mainly male and between the ages of eighteen and twenty-one, and they come from Guildford and they're white. This has been a numerical minority for about 30 years. (6.2)

Instead, the current student body across the HE sector as a whole is characterised by a rich diversity in terms of racial and socio-economic origin, nationality, age and patterns of study. In this chapter we will use data gathered during the research to discuss the impact such an extraordinary process of change has had upon the life and ministry of chaplaincies in HE. We will first explore in more detail the changing patterns of student life, before considering the relationship between the chaplaincies and the student body. We will then

---

[1] Universities UK (2004) *Patterns of Higher Education Institutions in the UK*. Fourth Report. Available at http://bookshop.universitiesuk.ac.uk/latest/

briefly consider how these changes are reflected in student participation in the Sunday Eucharist, and finally discuss the role played by Catholic student societies in the institutions studied.

2. THE CHANGING PATTERNS OF STUDENT LIFE

2.1 FRAGMENTATION WITHIN THE ACADEMY

One of the consequences of the increase in student numbers has been pressure on physical space within institutions. Simply meeting the classroom requirements for the proliferating number of courses has rendered timetabling a complex issue. This has been compounded by the development of modular courses, packaging student-tutor contact into discrete parcels of time that differ between programmes, and even within them. As a consequence, there is very little shared timetabling across an institution; even the long-standing tradition that Wednesday afternoon was held clear of lectures for inter-varsity sports is fast disappearing. Life on campus has, therefore, become very fragmented; it is increasingly difficult to find times at which students from across an institution are able to gather together. As we shall note below, this development has had a profound impact on the operation of chaplaincies.

2.2 STUDENTS IN PAID EMPLOYMENT

The process of fragmentation has been intensified by student response to the radical changes over the past twenty years or so in the systems of financial support offered to them. Very many full-time students now hold part time jobs, typically in the retail, leisure and care sectors, to supplement their income from the very restricted grants now available and from student loans. The Students' Union Welfare Officer in Institution 8 underlined the demands that such working made upon them: 'The University would like to say that they're not working more than 15 hours a week. I know a lot of them who are working 30 hours a week in their second year.' The consequences of this engagement with work outside the university were not, in her opinion, entirely negative, as it prevented the students from becoming entirely absorbed in university life. There was, however, the potential for tension and even conflict:

> I think while they're working hard they are very torn. They are often quite resentful that - how can I put it, they're glad they've got a place at university, and resentful how hard they and their parents have got to [work]. And sometimes they feel quite guilty that they're not contributing anything to the home economy, though some of them are. (8.3)

From the institution's perspective, there is also an understandable concern that the academic work of students is likely to suffer as a result of their working long – and frequently late – hours in other sectors.

2.3 Part-time Study

A further consequence of the financial burden now placed upon students is the already noted growth in the numbers of part-time students, many of whom commute from home rather than residing on or near the campus. The modular delivery of programmes facilitates flexible approaches to learning and teaching. Many students integrate part-time HE involvement into lives that have their primary focus outside the academy. The Student Welfare Advisor quoted above reckoned that in her institution over 50% of students now lived at home. Many of these commuted into the university from distances of over thirty miles, and tended to remain on campus only for periods of academic contact time and to use the library facilities. This pattern of engagement increases the fragmentation of institutional life.

2.4 Consequences for Chaplaincy Life

These changes have had considerable impact on the life of chaplaincies. In the past chaplaincies were able to use the considerable common free time enjoyed by a small and largely resident student population to arrange meetings, events and time away. The fragmentation of the timetable, the growth in the number of part-time students commuting from home, and the pressure of paid employment, has severely disrupted the stable pattern of life that once facilitated the chaplains' engagement with students. Summarising the effect of such changes on his ministry, one chaplain said:

> I think the impact is devastating, because there's not the freedom. And I think that the Chaplaincy particularly needs not just free time, but a whole lot of common free time – when people are not going to be required to be somewhere else, and those who want to can be there. And there is no such thing as common free time left. Lectures and seminars go on to seven, eight, nine – right into the evenings now. The pressure, on Sundays they go back to the lab, to finish this that and the other. [...] People haven't got the freedom. They haven't got the times to associate and to go away together, to learn things together. And such time as you have got, you can only do one or two things – so you can't be involved in this that and the other, in a whole wide range of things. (9.1)

3. STUDENT RELATIONSHIPS WITH CHAPLAINCY

Despite the restrictions created by the changing patterns of academic life, chaplaincies continue to offer a raft of activities and liturgical celebrations that are taken up by students. There are still week-ends away, regular sessions for faith sharing, courses such as CaFE, and of course the celebration of the liturgy. Students still – within the increasing constraints placed on their time – continue to use the chaplaincies as drop-in places. The primary difference between the situation today and that in earlier years lies in the reduced numbers of students involved. This final factor could become increasingly significant for the life of the chaplaincy as time goes on; chaplains will always be called upon to provide one-on-one care to individual students who approach them for advice, prayer or sacramental ministry, but if they are to continue to animate a sustained community of faith within the institution, the engagement of a committed core of students will be essential. As one chaplain put it:

> There has to be a critical mass at an event or whatever's going on for the students to feel comfortable there themselves. When I started as a chaplain I used to say, 'Right, it doesn't matter how many people come,' but I don't believe that now. It does matter how many people come. It doesn't have to be lots and lots, but it does have to feel full enough and alive enough for those students to come back and feel main-stream in what's going on there and so on – with a party or a discussion group or with anything else. (7.1)

The interviews with students suggested that the chaplaincy still served a broader community role that complemented their personal engagement with the chaplain. (This is borne out by the findings of a student-led survey of chaplaincy users carried out by the students in Institution 7. They asked whether the respondents thought that chaplaincies helped people, and if so why. It was striking that friendship, support and community building were the commonest reasons cited, followed by faith development and opportunities for faith sharing.)

In this section the research-project student interviews will be used to identify the needs that students felt the chaplaincy was serving; we shall differentiate between home and international students. We will then consider the potential for chaplaincies in which students are resident to help form a faith community in the heart of the institution – flagging up a couple of concerns that arose from the fieldwork. We will conclude by discussing a concern, raised a number of times, whether chaplaincies are becoming identified with too narrow an element within the Catholic student body.

3.1 Home Students

Practising Catholic students coming into HE found that their faith stance was likely to be challenged in a number of different directions. The first challenge was from those fellow students who either did not understand their faith or were hostile towards it. Not surprisingly, several students expressed relief at being able to freely express their faith in the chaplaincy without suffering mockery. Many of the students arriving at university would already have encountered a similar hostility whilst at school, but in Catholic Schools and Sixth-form Colleges they would have been in an environment that at institutional level at least was supportive of their Catholic faith. Moving to a secular university, however, they now found themselves in a setting institutionally at least indifferent to their faith, if not itself hostile. Catholic students could thus feel quite marginalized in matters of faith, and the chaplaincy could provide an essential safe haven for them. One student explained:

> They can walk in and know what's going to be the common link with everybody. I think for a lot of people that's probably the nice thing about it. Somewhere they can feel they haven't got to explain themselves – just be themselves. And they are with people who don't necessarily think the same, but you know, have got a similar outlook on life (2.4)

Whilst the first challenge may be an intensification and institutionalisation of a hostility that many students may experienced prior to their move to HE, the second challenge would be new for many who had attended Catholic schools. This came from the evangelical wing of the Christian community:

> You've got friends and acquaintances – and you're walking down to the pub, and somebody says, 'Are you saved? And if you're not, you're going to Hell!' You kind of think, "Well, why should I defend my faith so strongly to these people?" That was one of the reasons why I was so pleased to find the chaplaincy, because no assumptions are made by any of the people here that you need to do something. We meet people where they're at, and we don't try to force anything on people. (5.4)

Once again, the chaplaincy provided a safe place in which nobody had to 'prove' anything. Yet several students expressed a sense of appreciation that their engagement with the chaplaincy permitted them to grow and develop in their faith:

Because my actual knowledge of the faith that I have is not really extensive, I find it a practical way for me to keep improving and increasing my knowledge of the faith that I'm in. I find that the Catholic chaplaincy is a good way of grounding me in the main areas of my faith. (5.4)

3.2 INTERNATIONAL STUDENTS

The growing number of non-EU students in British universities (resulting from major international recruitment on the part of universities over the past decade) has been noted. These students bring their own needs, and it became evident from several student interviews that the chaplaincy provided a lifeline for many. Several international students spoke of the culture shock of coming to Britain. One African student said, 'Before I came to Europe I thought Britain was one strong religious country. But when I came, I found it was quite the opposite – that was very shocking to me.' (5.4) Adjusting to the secularised nature of life here – often institutionalised within the academy – was for some very disorientating:

> I come from a country and culture where it's not secular – God is a normal part of your conversation. I have found that wherever I've studied I tried to find myself in an atmosphere where I can have that as well, and that's one of the reasons why I'm so happy here in the chaplaincy – just to say the word 'God' in a conversation and not have people looking at you oddly. Because it does feel like a very secular culture here, and it does feel very – there's a completely different world-view around you. (5.4)

To such students, access to a community of faith within the chaplaincy not only softened the shock of being away from home, but also provided a vital moral framework within which they could continue to live with integrity in an alien environment:

> I was really, really lost when I first got here [from Nigeria]. And just being here I managed to dampen the shock, the discomfort. Of course I still felt away from home. It's a small community, truly, so initially when you come in here, you're far away from home, nobody knows you and truly you could just go on and do whatever you wanted to do – be a different person from the one person you were at home. But when you come into this community, there is a moral effect of keeping you in check. So the smallness of the community is a good thing. (9.4)

This support could also be expressed in practical ways. A mature Brazilian student spoke of his frustrations in attempting to place his children in schools through the local authority:

> I almost gave up and returned back in that first month. The chaplains helped me – at least I could to talk to someone about it. I could sort of express my feelings. And that is very, very helpful because it seems that nobody understands you, everybody has solved their problems. [...] You're almost in despair, sometimes. But here, at least, the chaplain phoned the Catholic school, and they arranged an interview, and after that I got a place for my son. This support in the beginning was fundamental. Just to have someone to talk to is important – you know you're not on your own. (9.5)

Other international students spoke of the difficulty in adjusting to British student life – in particular to the drinking culture they encountered among students here. One American exchange student explained:

> I live [in the student hall] across the road, and when you go back there it's like a romper room sometimes. I get back on a Sunday, and they ask, 'Where have you been?' And I say, 'Mass.' And they're, like, 'Yeah!' Some of my flat mates think that because I don't go out and drink every single night – I am sometimes seen as a sort of 'shut-in.' (7.8)

Even home students, coming to a large university town, found this aspect of student life difficult to cope with:

> I got the same shock when I got here. In comparison to where I come from, people don't fall drunk in the streets at that age. It is amazing. The first night I was here, they were all going to 'Double Vision,' or something. The whole idea of the night is to ensure that you have double vision – that's the name of the disco. So that means that you're going to get that drunk or whatever. And there's police marching up and down the street taking people home. What's the point? (7.8)

For such students the Catholic chaplaincy was a safe haven, where their values were shared and where they felt able to be themselves:

> This is a place where I've got a nice niche right now. It's okay for me just to be myself, and not have to be worried about being pressured to do things that I just don't want to. [...] This is a place where I can come, and I don't feel that everyone's trying to shove liquor down my throat. (7.8)

3.3 Chaplaincy Residencies

Five of the chaplaincies provided accommodation for a number of students, ranging from seven in one institution to sixty-three in another. Patterns of community life varied considerably. In one chaplaincy the residents and chaplain ate dinner together each evening, while in another, they ate together once a week. Other residential chaplaincies operated even more informally, with no prescribed common meals. There were likewise differing expectations about the engagement of these students in the spiritual life of the chaplaincy.

Having resident students could have a positive impact on the life of the chaplaincy. At the very least, the rents raised in each case made a considerable contribution to the running costs. A group of committed Catholics within the chaplaincy also could provide the chaplain with a core group of students who helped to facilitate the liturgical life of the chaplaincy and around whom other projects could be developed. In two chaplaincies they also provided an important informal ministry to other students, forming a welcoming community within the chaplaincy.

The operation of residential chaplaincies did, however, raise two concerns. The first was over the considerable amount of the chaplain's time and energy required in running and maintaining them. One chaplain described his sense during his first few months that he was 'more a clerk of works than anything else.' (2.1) In the smallest chaplaincy, the chaplain found himself maintaining as well as running the building:

> It's enormously time consuming. I reckon I could work full-time running this place partly because in general we can't afford to use tradesmen for minor stuff. Like there's one of the sinks which persistently leaks in one of the student rooms. I can't go and get a plumber out and waste sixty quid for a guy to come and tighten it with a monkey wrench, so I'll go and get the monkey wrench and tighten it myself. (4.1)

The most common strategy used by chaplains to address the problem was to form a management committee of local people who had expertise in relevant fields. Generally speaking this appeared to work well, and their advice was welcomed. However, there was evidence in one chaplaincy that the chaplain still needed to put considerable energy and leadership into the Management Committee itself: in this case there was a strong sense that of still having to make most of the running. Moreover, the fact remains that as the person on-site, the day-to-day running of the plant and the responding to immediate crises inevitably fell on the chaplain. We found only one chaplaincy in which a full time administrator had been employed to completely manage the building. This was only possible because as the largest residence it generated sufficient income from rent. It is doubtful whether any of the other chaplaincies visited would be able to afford a similar arrangement.

The second concern lies around the need for appropriate guidelines, and transparent systems, that would ensure the operation of current good practice with regard for the protection of vulnerable adults. Whilst none of the resident students was technically a minor, instances were related of residents who had suffered mental health or emotional problems that would have left them potentially vulnerable to abuse. Chaplains living in and managing residential chaplaincies are placed in a position of considerable trust, and are themselves vulnerable to allegations of misconduct. We found little evidence that this issue had received the serious consideration it needs, nor that chaplains in charge of residences had been given any specific training in their legal responsibilities to their residents. We recommend that this be addressed as a matter of urgency.

3.4 Meeting the Needs of All Catholic Students?

A concern was raised in five institutions (2, 5, 6, 7 and 9) that the chaplaincy was increasingly meeting the needs of only a small group of Catholic students. At one level, this simply reflects a natural risk of the chaplaincy being focussed around a peer group to the exclusion of other students. One chaplain located this tendency within a broader framework: the way young people construct their personal identity through their relationship with a peer group:

> Take this year's Cath Soc Committee. Lovely people [...] And some of them have formed very close relationships. But that has its dangers, and people will meet one or two others, and they'll go and live together in the same house, from the same year. So that [the Committee] becomes a group of friends. But they're not branching out and making other friends. And so that kind of peer group culture actually militates against the Chaplaincy working properly. (9.1)

A concern was also expressed that chaplaincy was identified in the student mind with a particular stereotyped student personality – 'people who are socially inadequate, can't make friends anywhere else, and [for] whom this is a kind of crutch.' (7.1) This narrow identification could present a vision of the chaplaincy as standing at the edge of student life and experience – whereas a common concern among chaplains was that all Catholic students should perceive chaplaincy life and activities as open and welcoming to all.

The issue was compounded by a sense that the core of students most likely to be involved in chaplaincy were committed to a very traditional expression of Catholicism that risked alienating other students:

> When one stands back, if one has eyes to see, it is a conservative agenda. And I would say that on the whole our students are conservative. [...] They're not young fogies. There's also the balance to that – there are a handful with a more radical agenda. But when I came here I expected a much more radical agenda from students – justice and peace, 'Let's change the Church.' They want Rosary and Benediction. The liturgy is quite formal, and if you try to do something different, there's hell to pay – the moans and the groans, and 'What was that all about?' 'Did we have to sing that hymn?' It quite often comes down to music and hymns. I change the sexist language [in the presidential prayers] – and you don't get people coming to say 'thank you.' It's, 'What are you on about? It's bloody obvious that "man" means everybody.' And you can sort of feel, 'My goodness!' (6.1)

Reflecting on the same phenomenon a mature student (Institution 2) suggested that at this point in the Church's life the traditional students were the ones who were most likely to have a sense of commitment to Church institutions such as chaplaincy. This finely focuses the dilemma in which some chaplains appear to be caught. Their desire is to provide a chaplaincy service for the Catholic community in its broadest sense – providing a place in which individuals with vastly differing faith perspectives and degrees of commitment to the institution can feel at home. However, given the pressures on students' time, there is a real risk that only the most committed will invest to a significant degree in the chaplaincy. This in turn establishes a vicious circle through which others whose approach would be more tentative might feel excluded. This would be equally true if the committed core represented a more radically liberal vision of Catholicism. The chaplain has to perform the very delicate duty of encouraging the faith of those who come, whilst creating an all-embracing chaplaincy environment. Within the constraints of contemporary HE this is becoming an increasingly difficult task.

4. SUNDAY EUCHARIST

The changing patterns of student life outlined above, alongside growing trends towards secularization in society as a whole, have also impacted upon the participation of students in the Sunday celebration of the Eucharist. The need of students to work in paid employment at weekends and the growing numbers of part-time students result in a generally low percentage of Catholic students attending chaplaincy Eucharists. This was as true in Institution 1 (the Catholic College) as it was of the secular universities. As a consequence, most of the institutions reported that the bulk of their Sunday congregation was made up of international students.

Attendance at Sunday Eucharist is one of the key indicators the Catholic community use to measure levels of participation in the life of the Church. Although the Church would eschew any sense that the figures for people attending Mass were in any way a performance indicator for the effectiveness of individual ministry, there was nonetheless a sense among priest chaplains (as among many other clergy) that the numbers were one of the few tangible signs of whether or not they were doing a 'good job:'

> You're always worried whether you're doing a good job. A lot of the obvious things – one of the obvious things is actual Mass attendance, which is critical really because that's where the Church comes together. And if they're not coming together, nothing's happening is it, really? And I'm always wondering why the attendance is as low as it is. It's not increased since I've been here. In fact, it's probably decreased. Yes, it has decreased. When I first came I used to reckon that both the morning and evening Masses averaged about fifty-five [...] Currently, they're running more in the forty to fifty-five range. Fifty-five is the more upper one. Last Sunday we were about forty-five or forty-eight in the morning, and thirty-eight or so in the evening. (9.1)

There was a sensitivity on the part of some chaplains that the low numbers of students attending chaplaincy Eucharist would be used by hard-pressed parish priests to question the effectiveness of their ministry; this will be considered further in Part Four.

We also found evidence that some students attended the Eucharist in local parishes. This may be explained in part by a certain wariness on the part of other students about the role of a dominant group within the chaplaincy.

Restricted Sunday bus timetables were also cited as a motivating factor. In two institutions there was no distinct 'chaplaincy' Eucharist, but students took part instead in the Sunday worship of the local parish to which the chaplaincy was closely linked. These cases will also be considered in Chapter Four.

5. CATHOLIC SOCIETIES

In several of the institutions studied, a key element in the relationship between the chaplain and students was the Catholic Society (generally referred to by chaplains and students alike as 'Cath Soc.') Catholic Societies are student-led organisations formally affiliated to the Students' Union of their institution. As such, they receive funding from the Union and access to Union facilities. They are nominally independent of the Chaplaincy, and elect their own student officers. In practice, however, wherever Catholic Societies existed, they operated in very close association with the chaplaincy, with their official structures tending to merge with those of the chaplaincy itself. In this section the Catholic Societies in two institutions will be briefly examined. In Institution 9 the society is closely integrated into the chaplaincy structures, though there were questions as to how effectively its Committee were engaged in the pastoral support of students. The Catholic society of one of the constituent colleges of Institution 6, on the other hand, illustrates the difficulties faced by Catholic associations in highly secularised institutions. We will then consider the case of Institution 4, in which there is no Catholic Student Society, as it raises broader questions of student engagement and of ecumenical partnership.

5.1 INSTITUTION 9: A SEAMLESS WEB?

The Catholic Society in Institution 9 was very closely identified with the chaplaincy. Some of its members sat on the Chaplaincy Committee, and also on the university committee that oversaw the running of the ecumenical Chaplaincy. (See further Chapter Two.) Student members of the Society's Committee were interviewed, and this makes it possible to bring alongside each other the perspectives of both students and the chaplain. This juxtaposition highlights a gap between the two positions with regard to the role played by the Committee.

The Treasurer to this Society's Committee was asked to explain the nature of the relationship between the Society and the chaplaincy. He replied:

> We're not independent here, we're in-house. I'd say we were almost a sub-set, like an individual group of the in-house. Because, strictly speaking, we're probably individual, but in no way do we work individually. We've got a position on the Chaplaincy Committee. We like to get involved in all the things that happen in the chaplaincy. Everything that the chaplaincy does, Cath Soc does, and most things that Cath Soc do, the Chaplaincy will have some financial backing or try to get people along to it. (9.4)

When asked about the role of the chaplains in the life of Cath Soc, the student replied:

> A very important role. The chaplains are constantly in the meeting. And we're constantly going to them for things – for everything, basically, but even if not for support, then they will either help at events or they will be at events. [...]They're almost like members of the Catholic Society. They're kind of our overseers. (9.4)

The chaplain, however, expressed concern that the Catholic Society risked becoming a closed peer group (see above, section 3.4). The detrimental effect of a narrow-based Catholic Society on the life of the chaplaincy was, in the mind of this chaplain, compounded by the constraints upon student time:

> I hoped that we could work a little more at getting the Cath Soc Committee to have more of a commitment - which it used to have in the past, before my time – of being there before the Mass, being welcomers and things like that. It's more difficult. We find it very difficult to get the Cath Soc Committee to come to the morning and evening Mass, and to be around before or after. And although we try to plan various things for the beginning of term, I think you're always up against this thing that people really haven't got the time. We've been lucky in arranging Cath Soc meetings, but in other years it's been impossible to find any time when they could all be together. [9.1]

There was no doubt on the part of either the chaplain or the Committee that the Catholic Society performed a significant social role. However, the constraints of contemporary university life had limited the potential for it to play the broader pastoral role desired by the Chaplain.

5.2 Institution 6: A Catholic Society in a Secular Institution

One of the colleges of Institution 6 was a late eighteenth century foundation that from its inception had espoused Enlightenment values. These included an institutional hostility towards religion. A number of student religious associations were, however, affiliated to its student union. These included a Catholic Society. During the academic year prior to this project an attempt was made by a pressure group within the Students' Union to disassociate all student religious societies. If successful, this would have removed their funding and also the already tenuous position they occupied within the institution. One of the students described what happened:

> Last year, a motion was put forward – it must be said, it was slightly dodgy – by the union who wanted to see all religious societies in the College disassociated. Of course, this produced a sort of really, really strong response from people who went to the next meeting and had to actually vote on this issue. Overwhelmingly, the motion was just kind of shot to the ground, basically. [...] And it just shows that while the College officially thinks one thing, in practice the people who study there actually have their own religious views. They do exist. It was kind of extraordinary – three hundred against the motion, eight for. It was quite a nice motion actually, because it had just got in on the sly: not a lot of people had heard of it, but the meeting was just packed. (6.3)

This incident reflects broader tensions that predate the recent shifts in the make-up of the student body; it highlights the tension between faith organisations and secular institutions that will be more thoroughly explored in Part Two.

5.3 An Alternative Approach

In Institution 7 we found a different approach. Here there was a student forum whose members were the chaplains and a small body of students, invited to participate by the chaplains. It was in its third year of operation. The forum met regularly to discuss and review chaplaincy matters, particularly events: as one of the student members put it 'We collect the ideas that other students have about what they would like to do and what they would like to see in the chaplaincy, discuss it with the chaplains, and then try and organize a way to make it work.' (7.10)

This clearly gave the students a sense of ownership of the life of the chaplaincy; it was this body which initiated, conducted and reported on the outcome of the survey about chaplaincy use and benefits referred to under Section 3 above.

5.4 INSTITUTION 4: WITHOUT A CATHOLIC SOCIETY

When asked if there was a Catholic Society, the chaplain replied:

> I've floated it on a couple of occasions with them, and said, 'Wouldn't you like a Catholic Society?' 'No. We don't want a Catholic Society. We don't need a Catholic Society.' I mean, students today are not joiners, you know, full stop. The culture is not one of joining, and nobody gets a buzz out of having a Cath Soc T-shirt, you know. So places that inherit that ethos, yes, maybe, you know, because it gives people a peg on which to hang their identity. But here it would be quite disruptive. It would be too strongly Catholic. (4.1)

The final words suggest that the establishment of a Catholic Society would not be welcomed by all within the university. This suggestion was borne out by the University Chaplain, an Anglican priest, who regarded denominational societies – indeed, denominations themselves - as a 'dying breed'. Moreover, he understood denominational student societies to express and possibly ferment Christian disunity – to him of great symbolic importance, given the ecumenical front that he sought to present to this very secular university:

> When I came here in '89 there was a Methodist Society and a Catholic Society and an Anglican Society. And I said to my friends, 'Why don't we scrap this. You know they are dying. They're not very nice. They're all snooty. They all defined themselves by being better than the others. They're just our tiny tribes. Why don't we throw in our lot?' (4.2)

These and related issues are considered further in Part Three.

6. CONCLUSION

Changes in the patterns of student and university life have eroded the traditional model of chaplaincy. The lives of the institution and its students alike are fragmented. The chaplaincy needs to adapt to operating with short discrete bursts of activity which come and go, with little long-term engagement on the part of most students – even those who do use the chaplaincy as a base in the more traditional manner.

Chaplains are increasingly having to re-invent their work, re-establish relationships, and be proactive in seeking fresh ways to engage within a disengaged culture. This can often be energy-draining, and provides very little from which the chaplains can draw their own spiritual and emotional nourishment. Part Four will give further attention to the needs for support and encouragement for chaplains.

PART TWO

RELATIONSHIP WITH THE INSTITUTION: OPERATING WITHIN AN AMBIGUOUS SET OF PARAMETERS

1. INTRODUCTION

In the United Kingdom the Churches provide chaplains to a range of non-ecclesial institutions, most notably hospitals, prisons and the armed forces. Whilst in each of these sectors actual provision may vary from institution to institution, the relationship between chaplain and institution is generally set within a nationally-agreed framework. Consequently military, hospital and prison chaplains generally have a sense of their location within the organisation, and an awareness of the formal channels through which they relate to their institution. They also, at least in theory, are responsible, in varying degrees, to the institution as well as to their sponsoring denomination for the way they carry out their work.

The relationship between HE chaplains and the institution they serve is far less clearly determined. This is largely because HE institutions enjoy considerable autonomy in determining their own systems of governance and day-to-day management. They are under no statutory obligation to provide chaplaincy, and, indeed, the avowedly secular nature of many universities presents some with a difficulty in even accepting chaplaincy as playing any formal role in its life. As a result, the fieldwork revealed a striking divergence in the ways in which the relationship between chaplaincy and institution was played out. The extremes were, on the one hand, an institution in which the chaplain was securely embedded within student welfare structures and even sat on the principal decision-making body, Academic Board, and, on the other, one in which the chaplains struggled for any formal recognition at all of their contribution to the life of the institution.

With the exception of the first example, the relationship between chaplaincy and institution was always characterized by a degree of ambiguity. For the most part chaplains were, as one put it, 'dancing on the edge.' (7.1) The fieldwork revealed a range of strategies by which chaplains – acting alone or as part of an ecumenical team - sought to raise their profile within the institution and to formalise their relationship with it. Such strategies included gaining access to degree ceremonies, or, in one case, attempting to negotiate a formal service agreement with the institution. At the same time, interviews with institutional staff suggested that the clarity desired by the chaplains was problematic from their perspective. This was due mainly to the perceived need to balance respect for the secular milieu with the increasing presence of non-Christian faiths on campus, largely as a result of the drive to recruit international students. The resulting ambiguity placed chaplaincy in a potentially precarious position. Positively, outwardly secular institutions could prove surprisingly supportive of chaplaincy life, providing premises and, in some cases, budget allocation. Yet, in the absence of a formalized arrangement, such provision could at any time be reviewed and, perhaps, revoked. Again and again, everything came down to the quality of personal relationships, and to the building up of good will. Consequently the appointment of a new Chaplain, Vice-Chancellor or Head of Student Welfare could significantly impact upon the status and operation of the chaplains.

This part explores the different relational patterns identified in the fieldwork. It opens by clarifying the distinctiveness of HE chaplaincy vis-à-vis other institutional chaplaincies, by drawing on interviews with two chaplains who had previous experience of military and hospital chaplaincy respectively. It then contrasts the two institutions in which the relationship was the closest and the most remote, before going on to examine the different ways in which universities interpreted their secular status. It then uses one institution to explore the differing perceptions of their relationship held by chaplains and institutional staff. Finally, Part Two examines a number of structural issues that operated across all the institutions visited.

2. 'SITTING ON THE EDGE': THE DISTINCTIVE NATURE OF HE CHAPLAINCY

Two respondents in the same institution had previous experience as institutional chaplains, in different sectors. One was the Anglican chaplain, who came from a background of military chaplaincy. The other was a post-graduate student who had spent several years as chaplain to a large hospital. Looking back at their former posts, they were able to identify with great clarity the ambiguous nature of university chaplaincy – whilst also recognising how that ambiguity could at times serve the chaplain's interests.

The former military chaplain characterized the difference in these terms:

> Army chaplaincy is a little different in that you are actually a part of the establishment, whereas [at] university you are very much on the edge, looking in. No matter how welcoming the university is, you're not actually part of the set up as such. [...] At university there is actually the expectation that you will just be sitting on the edge and you're there when they need you. (8.2)

The former hospital chaplain similarly positively expressed the integration of chaplaincy into the institution he had served:

> You're in the same boat as the staff. You share the same pressures that they have, that you're there in terms of complete equality with them and that they can't pull rank over them, and they can't pull rank over you. (8.4)

At the same time, both recognised that there were advantages in enjoying some distance from the institution of the university. Thus:

> It's very easy for someone to get caught up in the lifestyle and ethos of the army and to become very much, perhaps too much, part of it. In this situation you can't because you sit on the edge of it and you can actually look in an awful lot easier. It's much more objective to see what's going on and probably to spot where the problems are much more than in the forces. (8.2)

The former hospital chaplain further expanded on this theme. The independence of the university chaplain from the institution permitted him/her when necessary to criticize the university in a manner that would have been unthinkable in the more closely regulated setting of the hospital:

> [In the hospital] were the chaplain to say something which would have been regarded as controversial for the institution, not only would the institution have the power to stop it, but the institution would stop it. Now, that doesn't happen here. The university does not have the power to stop the chaplaincy speaking out if necessary. The corrective would come from the Bishop, but it would not come from the university. (8.4)

He understood the hospital's corrective power, which he described in terms of 'interference,' to arise from the contractual, 'economic' relationship it had with the chaplain. Without this direct element of control, the relationship between chaplain and university was more nuanced, and offered the chaplain greater freedom of movement and action.

The themes introduced by these two respondents resonated with a number of comments made by chaplains of all denominations. Thus, a Lutheran chaplain spoke of his sense of being constrained even by the very nominal link between the Ecumenical Chaplaincy of which he was a member and the Student Welfare Services department of the university:

> I don't want to be part of the institutional, hierarchical system of the university. [...] We are belonging to welfare services. I don't want to belong to welfare services. It's more like you're coming from outside the university than having to work in the university, with the university. But still having the freedom – and therefore not being in the hierarchy – to say things that won't please people. (2.2)

The chaplaincy assistant in the same institution echoed these sentiments by stating that the chaplains could 'feed things into the university [...] – sometimes almost as an advisory body.' This freedom of expression was understood by some university chaplains as creating the opportunity for them to act as 'honest brokers.' (2.2) Thus, in two universities the chaplains met regularly with senior staff – in one case, once a term with the Vice-Chancellor. When asked how useful those meetings were, one Anglican chaplain replied:

> It varies. It's a chance for him to get stuff off his chest, but he doesn't really. There's a sense that we can be honest brokers and we bring issues to him that others perhaps wouldn't want to because he's in charge – and we've nothing to lose. (2.2)

At the same time, that respondent recognised that such meetings were becoming a formality as better consultative processes were introduced into universities at all levels: 'I think the world has moved beyond that kind of model. If people have got something to say to their boss now they're much more likely to say it.' (2.2) This sense of a culture change in the academy towards better formal channels of communication was reinforced by the very different experience of the one chaplain who was thoroughly incorporated into the institutional structures. She felt that it was precisely her place at the Board table that permitted her to feed back to management 'some of the way it looks from the other side.' (1.1) The sense of the free-acting chaplain, therefore, as the effective voice of conscience within an institution, may not be as realistic as some may wish to believe. Once again, any effectiveness almost entirely depends upon the quality of the relationships. Indeed, the situation in Institution 1 suggests that it does not necessarily follow that one needs to stand entirely outside the institution in order to confront it: this chaplain was employed precisely to speak the truth. At the same time, her position on the highest committees does raise a number of concerns that will be noted below.

With one exception that will be examined shortly, all the chaplains surveyed were 'sitting on the edge' of their institutions. It was nevertheless possible to identify different degrees of their peripheral state. Sometimes, the most secular universities proved remarkably open to facilitating the work of the chaplains, whilst a blurring of the parameters of the relationship and the reluctance to enter into formal agreements could, surprisingly, prove to be in the chaplains' favour. In exploring this range of positions, we begin by drawing out the contrast between the two institutions which held the closest relationship and the most remote between formal structures and chaplaincy. We then consider the range of positions between these poles.

3. THE CLOSEST AND MOST REMOTE RELATIONSHIPS

The closest relationship between institution and chaplaincy was, not surprisingly, in Institution 1, the Catholic College. The most distant in structural – though not necessarily in personal – terms was in Institution 5. The Catholic chaplain in each case was a woman. However, whereas the chaplain to Institution 1 was entirely employed by the College, the local diocese employed her counterpart in 5. In both cases the diocese also ensured that the local clergy were available for the celebration of the Eucharist; in Institution 5 this was achieved through the establishment of a close formal link between the chaplaincy and the local parish. The two chaplaincies further differed in that whilst a Catholic chaplain alone served Institution 1, in Institution 5 the chaplain worked closely with ecumenical colleagues. Indeed, as will be seen, a proliferation of denominational chaplains presented Institution 5 with a particular set of difficulties. Each institution will be considered in turn.

3.1 'THE BREATH OF GOD IN AN INSTITUTION:' CHAPLAINCY AT THE HEART OF THE HE INSTITUTION

The Chief Executive of Institution 1 understood the Chaplaincy to be an integral part of the College's identity, 'the representation of our mission.' (2.1) The chaplain, in the Principal's view, was to be 'the breath of God in an institution, just bringing the Spirit into the institution in a way that then makes everybody reflect on their role in doing the same things.' (2.1). This remarkable vision was translated into action by fully integrating the chaplain into the College's institutional structures:

> We wanted to [...] ensure that Chaplaincy was represented through institutional structures, so the chaplain sits on ... Academic Board, and also has right of access to any of the school meetings, and is on the Students Services Committee, and various other committees; we would involve her or him, (whoever it is) to be at those points, you know, the academic year or the academic structures.

It was envisaged that the chaplain's presence on these various bodies would allow him/her 'to just speak a word in various settings that helps the institution's connectivity' – effectively, to play the 'honest broker' identified in the previous section.

There was evidence from the interviews that suggested that this system did work in practice – largely through an interplay between the chaplain's formal status as committee member and her informal contacts with, for example, the leaders of the Students' Union. Such interplay can only be successfully negotiated within a small institution. Even there it creates the potential for conflict between the chaplain's institutional role and her personal ministry. This was acknowledged by the chaplain – for example, she suggested that conflict could emerge in the event of her being party to a decision of Academic Board to close courses. It is very doubtful whether the degree of institutional integration enjoyed by this chaplain would be either possible or desirable in a larger secular university. At the very least, the independence so valued by the former military and hospital chaplains in Institution 2 would be severely compromised. Nonetheless, whilst no other chaplain in an institution visited attained membership of Academic Board, many regarded membership of university committees as a useful means of relating to the institution and as a sign of the perceived regularity of their role. This aspect will be further explored in section 5 below.

3.2 'We Don't Really Designate these People:' Chaplaincy on the Outer Edge of the Institution

At first sight Institution 5 might appear to have one of the broadest-based chaplaincy provisions in the country. It officially recognises no fewer than 12 different chaplains, drawn from the major Christian denominations and from the largely autonomous congregations represented in the local area.

This apparently generous provision, however, masks a series of structural difficulties that currently present both university and chaplains with a number of serious problems. These were beginning to come to a head at the time of the fieldwork visit, as the university sought a way of formalizing a complex situation without compromising its commitment to its secular status.

The question turned around the understanding of 'recognition.' For the university this entailed no more than the allocation of an annual honorarium of £100 to each chaplain and the inclusion of their contact details in the Welfare section of the student handbook. The university provided no physical plant. Chaplains were not afforded staff status, nor were they automatically issued with library cards or email addresses. Indeed, the institution felt some unease about the designation 'chaplain':

> Is it really legitimate to call them 'chaplains', and is it legitimate for us to have anybody as chaplains at the university – because we don't really designate these people. We designate them as chaplains, but what does 'chaplain' mean? (5.2)

This coupling of a conceptual institutional recognition with disengagement in practice created a situation of considerable ambiguity. Whilst the university had effectively established a relationship with the chaplains, it was extremely cautious about formalizing that relationship, not least because of previous experience: 'Everybody who has tried to tackle that in the past,' reported the Head of Student Services, 'has just in the end left well alone.' Her preferred option was for the university to eschew any formalization of the relationship, and to offer students no more than a list of contacts in the area:

> I mean, ideally what I would like, what I would personally like to see is the provision of information to all our students on the faith opportunities that are around within the area. [...] we just direct them to what's available in the locality and we don't have anything else to do with it – and that's one way of dealing with it. Then we don't have any responsibility whatsoever. (5.2)

The situation was further complicated by the uneven understanding held by the different chaplains of their role with regard to the student body. Two denominations (Anglican and Catholic) had appointed full-time chaplains to the university – an Anglican priest and a Catholic lay woman. These denominations also maintained their own chaplaincy buildings, with a limited number of places for resident students in each. Both chaplains invested considerable energy in networking within the university, developing informal contacts with administrative and academic staff. Furthermore, the Anglican chaplain, who had been in post longer, had taught courses in the university and currently served as a member of the Student Welfare Coordinating Group – an unofficial committee of the university, but chaired by the Head of Student Services. For him this was indicative of the ambiguity of the university's position:

> So there is a recognition of chaplains as being significant figures when dealing with welfare problems, but that's fairly universal – I mean an ambulance service, basically – a kind of safety net, particularly useful when someone dies.

These chaplains also met regularly with their Methodist and Orthodox colleagues, with whom they made an informal ecumenical team. All other recognised chaplains were effectively local ministers who provided support to individual students as and when required within their congregations. Whilst the ecumenical team were pressing for the establishment of more formal links with the university, both they and the university perceived the other, very much part-time, chaplains to prefer the status quo.

There was evidence, however, that the status quo could not continue, for two reasons. First, the university was becoming uneasy about the activities of some of its recognised chaplains. There was a concern that the university might find itself held responsible for any serious failings on their part, particularly in regard to the spiritual advice given to vulnerable students or those with mental health problems:

> I mean, we have some hearsay, do you know what I mean? I'm not talking about inappropriate behaviour, but perhaps a particular way of looking at things, which are detrimental to a student's actual – [...] So there are all sorts of issues here, which we have been lucky to get away with, that could potentially be quite – put us in a difficult position where things go wrong. We don't know what these individuals are doing, how they approach this responsibility. But would any of them agree with that? Nobody. (5.2)

The second reason was the growth in the number of students with non-Christian faith allegiances – due, largely, to the recruitment of international students. Whilst the university could not countenance any increase in funding for the current system, it recognised that an argument might be made for increased funding if the emphasis were to be shifted to an inter-faith chaplaincy. There was no conviction, however, that even that would be required of a secular institution that already provided substantial student support through its existing welfare department:

> We provide a range of services, a range of support services for students that they not be linked to anything other than some specific needs. So if we were to say, well, we would make a room available and those of you who wanted, and those faiths that wanted to have a part in some sort of spiritual exploration, I don't even know whether we have a duty to do that. I couldn't say for me it is necessary. (5.2)

The starkness of the structural distance between university and chaplaincy in this institution highlights a number of issues that were less immediately evident but were nonetheless present in other settings studied. These issues are, first, how important it is that the churches recognise the genuine difficulty avowedly secular academic institutions have when asked to enter into a formal relationship with religious groups. Second, many chaplains occupy a liminal position relative to the institutions in which they minister. Third, networking within the institution is essential for all chaplains – as is also the seizing of opportunities to engage with whatever unofficial committee structures become opened. Finally, ecumenical collaboration is not an add-on, but in many institutions may be necessary for survival.

4. CHAPLAINCY IN A SECULAR INSTITUTION: THE BLURRING OF BOUNDARIES?

If Institutions 1 and 5 present the two extremes of the chaplaincy-institutional relationship, then consideration of a series of other institutions highlights the different ways in which officially secular institutions can co-exist with ecumenical chaplaincies. There is no single model; indeed in Institution 6 we can recognise a number of very different approaches being taken by different colleges of the same institution.

4.1 INSTITUTION 4: THE UNIVERSITY CHAPLAIN

The Catholic chaplain described the original ethos of Institution 4, founded during the 1960s, as 'escaping from Oxbridge and escaping from religion while keeping the comfort zones.' (4.1) This vision, however, had been subverted almost at the start of the university's existence by the endowment there of an ecumenical chapel and university chaplain, by a prominent local figure outside the university. Consequently, this most secular of institutions had found itself with a significant religious building at the centre of its main campus, and in its midst an ordained minister with the title of 'University Chaplain', reporting directly to the Vice Chancellor. The university preserved at least the outer appearance of its technically secular nature by insisting that the chaplain should be engaged as a lecturer in one of the university departments.

Whilst the relationship between the University Chaplain and the university was set out formally, the denominational chaplains did not enjoy the same clarity of status. Designated as 'Associate Chaplains,' they had offices inside the Ecumenical Centre, but enjoyed no formal relationship with the institution – save through the ecumenical chaplain, who was effectively regarded by the institution as the head of a chaplaincy department. This, in practice, was unrealisable, not least because of the very different concepts of chaplaincy that underpinned the ministry of the various Associate Chaplains. Most parties – the University Chaplain especially - had experienced considerable pain over the years as a consequence.

4.2 INSTITUTION 6: THE COLLEGIATE EXPERIENCE

Institution 6 includes a number of Colleges founded in very different circumstances. Several are avowedly secular in nature – even to the extent of forbidding the posting of religious notices. Others have since their foundation embraced a more visible religious presence. Both the Anglican and Catholic churches deploy a number of chaplains across the institution, each being responsible to some degree to a senior chaplain of their respective denomination.

One of the Colleges has employed a senior Anglican priest as Dean since its foundation. However, a recent development in this institution has been the agreement of several other colleges to co-fund their Anglican chaplain. The senior (Anglican) chaplain explained how this would work in practice:

> They'll be dovetailed in – usually to Student Services, because that's where the budget holder usually is. And I'm very happy to work with people in that situation – because this hasn't just happened. This has been the product of many years of networking, of confidence building. (6.2)

There are currently four Anglican chaplains who are jointly funded with academic institutions in England.[2]

4.3 Institution 9: A Formalized Committee Structure

Institution 9 was originally founded with an explicitly secular ethos. All the chaplains are still paid by their respective denominations, but the university now maintains a well-equipped base in the heart of the campus, in which the two Catholic chaplains and their Anglican and Free Church colleagues have offices. The building is also used by other faith groups – most notably for Friday prayers by Muslim students. The manner in which the building was managed offers a striking example of how an institution can adopt a nuanced position. It protects its secular status by not employing chaplains itself. At the same time, it is able to facilitate faith provision without attempting to replicate its normal departmental structures and thereby avoids mapping unrealisable line-management structures onto the collaborative work of chaplains. This situation will, therefore, be explored in a little more depth.

A committee chaired by a university academic of professorial rank manages the ecumenical chaplaincy. The committee Chair is directly appointed by and reports to the Vice-Chancellor; minutes are also circulated to key university administrative departments. The committee meets three times each year. It consists of representatives of the chaplains, of the student societies, and of other faith groups present in the university, and two or three people nominated by the Vice-Chancellor. The committee oversees the running of the Chaplaincy Centre, and is the channel through which the relationship between the chaplains and the university is negotiated. Chaplains are officially recognised by the university through a formal letter from the Vice-Chancellor on the recommendation of the Chaplaincy Committee Chair. In addition to the formal budget for the running of the centre, the Chaplaincy Committee Chair has access to an endowment fund that yields around £6,000 per annum. This he uses to support student-initiated projects across all the faith groups present in the university.

In this university we found one of the most comfortable and flexible relationships between secular institution and chaplaincy. The Chaplaincy Committee provided a framework that at the same time permitted representatives of

---

[2] See Board of Education: Aiming Higher: Higher Education and the Church's Mission – a new (2005) Anglican report on HE chaplaincy, available from Church House Bookshop, and on-line at www.cofe.anglican.org/

various faith groups to receive recognised status within the university and the university to show itself as even-handed in its treatment of all faith groups. The interfaith dimension of the chaplaincy will be considered in greater detail in the next chapter.

4.4 INSTITUTION 3: THE CHAPLAIN CO-ORDINATOR

Institution 3 demonstrates the extent to which some of the more recent HE foundations are far less hostile to religion than those founded earlier. This post-1990 university had a long-standing arrangement with the Anglican Church by which they collaborated in the appointment of an Anglican Chaplain, and shared responsibility for that chaplain's maintenance after appointment: the diocese provided a stipend, the university a house. The chaplain's status within the university was further secured by his acting as a member of the teaching staff – currently engaged to teach on two days per week. This formal position had been strengthened in recent years by the university conferring upon him the title of 'Chaplaincy Co-ordinator'. He explained what this entailed:

> [The university] didn't want actually to call somebody the University Chaplain, which I think was good. They wanted to recognise all the denominations as being chaplains, so the sort of title they came up with was Co-ordinator. That basically means I represent the chaplaincy at university committee level and management level. It means that, I mean I suppose I head up the chaplaincy team and chair chaplaincy meetings – and really I suppose I ultimately decide the sort of policy in chaplaincy, but we do it together. The development plan we have at the moment was written by me, but after discussion with the other chaplains. (3.2)

The chaplaincy was formally nested within the university's Student Services Department, and the Chaplaincy Co-ordinator sat on its management group. Consequently, he was involved in general student services policy-making. This engagement with the institution at committee level, he said, not only offered an opportunity to represent the interests of the chaplaincy, but also proved to be invaluable in terms of networking.

5. FORMAL AND PERCEIVED RELATIONSHIPS

Institution 7 offered an opportunity to engage with a number of interested parties and to compare their differing perceptions of the relationship between the chaplaincy and the university. Two issues emerged from these discussions.

First, the development of relationships over a period of time may create an impression of greater formality than in fact is the case. Second, whilst the desire of chaplains to move from the ambiguity of their role to a more secure formal position is understandable, it could, if pressed for, potentially lead to a diminishment rather than improvement of their role

5.1 'Who's the University?' Clarifying Recognition

The conceptual difficulties surrounding the notion of a university's 'recognition' of chaplains were highlighted in section 3.2 above. Less sharply, it became apparent at Institution 7 that the official status the chaplains spoke of themselves having was, once again, dependent rather more upon the perspective of senior management than upon a formal process of recognition; the formal processes encountered in Institution 9 (section 4.4 above) were completely absent. The informality of the relationship became clear as the Head of Student Services mused on whether or not the chaplains were formally recognised by the university as institution:

> Well how would you define 'recognise'? It accepts them. They had to push for this but they are invited to awards, degree ceremonies and special events. So it acknowledges that we have the support from the churches but there's no... you know, as I said, who's the university? (7.4)

In other words, there was an implicit acceptance of the presence and activity of the chaplains in the university, but the impetus for that had come from the chaplains rather than from the university. Furthermore, the final question is telling; in the absence of a formal agreement, there is no mechanism by which the university can officially 'recognise' its chaplains. Their position, therefore, depends upon the personal attitude of significant figures in the university, and on patterns of working that have become regarded as established:

> The Vice-Chancellor certainly recognises them. Other members of the senior management team, their sort of understanding is, 'Oh yes we have chaplains and [her name] deals with that.' That's the way things are, 'Oh well that's in [her name]'s area,' and that's the way things work here. [7.4]

The relationship, therefore, was completely informal and built upon trust rather than a formal process by which chaplains were recognised and granted official status within the university. There was a shared sense between the Head of Student Services and the Catholic chaplain that the current relationship worked. Each recognised its ambiguities, but felt that there was no need to press for further clarification: working along blurred edges, the chaplain felt, offered opportunities for flexibility.

5.2 University and Chaplaincy – Dancing a Pas-de-Deux on the Edge?

Not all the ecumenical chaplains, however, shared that positive sense of their current relationship with Institution 7. There was a real concern, particularly on the part of one of the Anglican chaplains, that the relationship ought to be set into a more formal framework. He had therefore proposed that the Ecumenical Chaplaincy should enter into a Service Level Agreement with the university. This Agreement would, he believed, help to clarify the official status of chaplains within the university and set out the expectations of both the university and chaplaincy. It would thus make the lines of responsibility and communication plain whilst avoiding the controlling element of the institution feared by the former hospital chaplain (section 2 above). A formal arrangement would also depersonalise the relationship of the chaplaincy to the university, reducing the dependence of the chaplains upon the goodwill of senior staff. Lifting the relationship beyond the level of personal contacts and goodwill would, in turn, promote continuity in the relationship despite changes in senior personnel.

From the university's perspective, however, attempts to regularize the relationship were perceived as potentially creating more problems than they solved. By not granting official status to the chaplains, this secular institution was able to defend itself from the accusation that it was actively promoting religion. The blurring of boundaries actually permitted a delicate balance to be maintained: chaplains were able to sit on informal university committees, be included in student induction processes, and generally exercise a presence in the university. That balance, however, would be jeopardized the moment the spotlight of formalization was brought to bear upon their status:

> I think it's one of those things, once you start unpacking it, it becomes painful picking at it. I mean we have had a few tensions with the counselling team, some of whom have felt we should be a completely secular institution and shouldn't be giving out any kind of faith message. (7.4)

It is not only the chaplains, therefore, who are 'dancing on the edge.' Their entire ministry may depend upon a delicate pas-de-deux with university academics and adminstrators of good will in the face of institutional criticism within a secularist perspective.

6. CONCLUSION

The variety of attitudes that institutions have to chaplaincy reflects the prevailing attitudes of the very different eras in which they were founded and in which their statutes and basic ethos were set down. The institutions visited date from very different periods, and they were founded with very different aims. There are even contrasting attitudes to chaplaincy between the 1960s foundation and the newer universities. The 'Spirit of the Age' can change rapidly, but arrangements once put in place tend to remain as relics of bygone times, without review or updating. Of course, the founding ethos of a given institution may well still be highly relevant today. At the same time, religious affiliation and practice is clearly important to a significant minority of university students and staff, providing for many a sense of purpose and motivation, a framework of values, a sense of personal and communal identity. Acknowledging the role of chaplains need not commit a university to any particular creed or code, or jeopardise its secular nature. Facilitating the free expression of religious life on campus by university recognition of and support for chaplaincy does not entail endorsement of any particular religion. For example, university support for student unions does not entail endorsement of student union positions on many issues.

PART THREE

RELATIONS WITH OTHER RELIGIOUS BODIES WITHIN THE INSTITUTION: ECUMENISM AND INTERFAITH ENGAGEMENT

1. INTRODUCTION

As Part Two identified, the institutions featured in this study showed a common preference for relating to their chaplains as an ecumenical group rather than as individuals. In arranging future chaplaincy provision this preference cannot be ignored; it is recommended that a broader ecumenical engagement about HE chaplaincy between the churches at national level should be pursued. However, there are a number of important issues that need to be addressed if a more ecumenical model is to operate successfully on the ground. These touch directly upon the question of how Catholic chaplains can balance their duty to Catholics in the institution with working in what, for their ecumenical colleagues, is becoming increasingly a more ecumenically collaborative chaplaincy structure.

Part Three begins by exploring whether the work of chaplaincies is seen as being ministry to the whole of the institution within which they are located, or to the members of the denominations who sponsor them. It identifies a number of factors around this issue. It then goes on to examine the various places visited where premises were shared ecumenically. Finally it broadens out to consider the developing thrust for interfaith rather than ecumenical chaplaincies touched on previously.

2. MINISTRY TO A DENOMINATION OR TO THE INSTITUTION?

It was apparent that in several institutions two very different perceptions were at play of the scope of the chaplains' ministry. Were chaplains of various denominations deployed in the university to minister to the institution as a whole, or primarily to those members of the university whose denominational allegiance they shared?

2.1 DIFFERING POSITIONS

Generally speaking, whilst in each setting Catholic chaplains were engaged in ecumenical, university-wide ministry –frequently to a significant degree - the primary focus of their operations was within the Catholic community. This approach was succinctly explained by one chaplain who operated from two bases – a residential Catholic chaplaincy, and an ecumenical centre:

> I always see my role [...] my primary task here is the running of this chaplaincy; it's the worship of God, it's the nurturing of people in the faith – and all those sorts of things. A slightly secondary role is how you relate to other people in the university, in the ways that you might support non-Catholics. And the university is a huge institution and you could bury yourself in that and find all your time taken up running around, sitting on this, going to that – which may be all very wonderful, but is it really doing the primary function of what the chaplaincy should be doing? (9.1)

This view-point, which was widely shared among Catholic chaplains, differed markedly from the general Anglican position, which was one of ministering beyond denominational boundaries. The senior Anglican chaplain in Institution 6 suggested that the broader Anglican focus was an extension of the understanding an Anglican priest would have of parochial ministry from within the Established Church:

> [The Anglican approach to parish ministry] is a territorial, rather than a congregational, strategy. And by extension that's the same attitude and same understanding that Anglican chaplains have in a university setting. They're there for everybody, whether they're of faith or no faith. They're there for everybody – staff, support staff, administrators, teachers, caterers – whoever it may be, It's a holistic and entire stance towards ministry. (6.2)

This position was echoed by the institution:

> Now when it comes to the institution, how do they perceive us? They see the Anglican Church as the recognized Church, and they recognize that we offer a service to the whole community, not just to a tendency within it. (6.2)

It was his experience, he said, that Free Church chaplains had generally come to share the Anglican sense of a ministry to the institution as a whole – even though that 'may not be in the mindset of the people who are paying for them.' As a result, he felt, there was a willingness in those parties to work not within a denominational focus, but as equal members of an ecumenical chaplaincy team.

This was certainly borne out at a number of other institutions, as can be illustrated by a closer examination of Institution 7. The ecumenical chaplaincy there was also engaged with two other HE institutions. Rather than each denominational chaplain seeking to reach his or her students across the three institutions, responsibility for the different institutions was shared among the chaplains. Thus one Anglican priest was described as 'Anglican and Free Church chaplain in effect' to one of the institutions. (7.2) That she was not also described as 'Catholic chaplain' is, however, an indication of the limited way in which Catholic chaplaincies are able to engage with this model of university-wide chaplaincy operating across denominational boundaries.

The situation was complicated in the first place by the fact that the local Catholic diocese deployed two chaplains across the three institutions, each of whom had been given a specifically institutional brief. Only one of these chaplains was observed during this project, and a complete picture cannot be drawn, as the two chaplains appeared to relate to the ecumenical centre in different ways. Nonetheless, a brief consideration of how the chaplain interviewed engaged with the vision of ecumenical colleagues, whilst retaining a clear focus within the Catholic community, demonstrates the subtlety of Catholic engagement with such ecumenical endeavour. He worked closely within the institution alongside the Anglican priest cited above. He and she shared responsibility for representing the chaplaincy on the student welfare committee, rotating the committee seat annually. Responsibility for providing a chaplaincy presence in each of the university halls of residence was divided between them, on geographical rather than denominational grounds. Both played an institution-wide role in the induction processes for new students. Yet, whilst the Anglican/Free Church chaplain was based in the Ecumenical Chaplaincy centre, the Catholic priest maintained his own chaplaincy base, which was the highly visible focus for Catholic life in the university. The chaplain had, therefore, arrived at a balance between his commitment to work ecumenically and his denominational responsibilities. The arrangement worked because of the good relationship he enjoyed with his Anglican colleague.

2.2 Tensions over Perceived Catholic non-Participation.

However, there was also evidence that a perceived semi-detached stance on the part of denominational chaplaincies could damage the ecumenical witness to the university. Speaking in terms broader than the institutions he engaged in, one ecumenical partner in Institution 7 said:

> It's not helpful when one chaplain comes up to people and asks what their religion is every time they meet them. That's not really helpful, is it? And so from that level of what I would call rudeness, you go to people whose vision of Catholic chaplaincy is, 'If I gather ten good Catholics around me and improve their lives then that's my chaplaincy job done.' That's fine, but then that means that it's got nothing to do with the institution, which is part of how we see chaplaincy. (7.2)

In another institution, a strong sense was encountered that the independent existence of a Catholic chaplaincy with its own base diverted student energy and attention away from the ecumenical base. A Lutheran chaplain, contrasting the different patterns of use made by students of the ecumenical chaplaincy on the one hand and the Catholic chaplaincy on the other, said:

> [...] the relationship between us and the Catholic Chaplaincy is a kind of envy – and the tradition which is standing in the way. Envious because there's a Catholic tradition and there's a full Catholic chaplaincy. If we set up - and we set up a mid-week worship, there's hardly any students coming. This may be partly because we advertise it badly, but the other side is that there is no tradition of church-going, going to Mass. So there's this part of envy and misunderstanding that (how can you speak about it?), it's working: everyone is coming, and there's a full chaplaincy and lots of work. (2.2)

A chaplain in a different institution, this time an Anglican priest, expressed a concern that ecumenical co-operation was not a natural Catholic response. The Catholic community, he felt, had more than enough going on within its own ranks to occupy a chaplain's energy and attention:

> The great strength of the Roman Catholic community is solidarity. The chaplain can depend. He is secure. He'll have all kinds of home-grown domestic difficulties: people who denounce him, people who want him to be more liberal or more conservative, people who don't even see him as a proper priest. [...] He doesn't need any other colleagues or any other communities. And it takes a lot of largesse for a Roman Catholic chaplain to make the other members of the Christian community feel they are wanted, welcomed. It's not a reflex action. It's not a Catholic cultural part of the air they breathe. (4.2)

Catholic chaplains were not insensitive to such comments. One chaplain felt that the negative portrayal of their position was unfair, and argued that a totally non-denominational approach risked representing an inauthentic experience of ecumenism.

> Anglican Chaplains tend to parody the Catholic position: 'All the rest of us get on very well together, but the Catholics tend to stand apart.' Well, there is reason for that, in that we see our priority as gathering students and providing pastoral care for students. [...] I insist on my commitment to the ecumenical task. We want to work ecumenically, but that does not mean being answerable to the Anglican chaplain. So the Anglicans get in a huff, and say, 'The Catholics don't want to be involved.' So you can either withdraw and confirm that view, or you can radicalize it and become more involved, but keep them on their toes, and say that the ones who are not being ecumenical are in fact the Anglicans. (6.1)

The chaplain did not develop he meant by 'radicalization.' However, if ecumenism is truly to be constructed on the basis of bringing together the best of the different traditions, then it must be built upon the establishment of a shared space within which all can be authentically themselves, but with real friendship, mutual respect and a willingness to learn from each other. A genuinely ecumenical chaplaincy, therefore, would build positively on the strengths of all of its participants: it would, in effect, hold a vision and a mode of working that embraced unity in diversity.

2.3 THE ANGLICAN CHAPLAIN AS SENIOR CHAPLAIN?

As the last quotation suggested, in many institutions the Anglican chaplain frequently exercised a role as senior chaplain, or was understood as doing so by the university. This was the case even in those universities that had avoided establishing formal patterns of relating to the chaplains.

There appear to be three primary reasons for this. The first is the sheer historical and cultural weight of establishment. The second is the above-mentioned broad remit within which Anglican ministry is understood. These two factors come together in the third, which is the preference of institutions such as universities to think in terms of departmental structures. Therefore, even where the position of the ecumenical chaplaincy within the institution is ambiguous, there is a tendency on the part of the institution to map a departmental structure onto chaplaincy and to treat the chaplain who is most visible to the institution as its head. The way this works in practice was expressed by one Catholic chaplain:

> He would be seen as a contact point for a lot of people, I suppose: the Head of Department is how you would be viewed. So a lot of people in the university who want to be in touch with the chaplains would do so through him – which is fine if the information is passed on: more or less it usually is. Invitations to preach at certain events or organise memorial services – they would always go to him. Again, I suppose he's seen as the Head of Department, and someone's got to have that position; it wouldn't work otherwise. (2.1)

However, whilst the university might effectively regard the Anglican chaplains in these terms, in practice they were often not at all in a formal ecumenical arrangement that enabled them to exercise the managerial role that would normally fall to a departmental head. With the exception of Institution 3, where a matrixed system of line management was in place, there was little sense in any of the institutions that a senior chaplain exercised line management over chaplains of other denominations. This was even the case in Institution 4, in which the university's expectations were most clearly set into an institutional framework. The University Chaplain there explained that during the first ten years of his time in post, his experience of managing the team of chaplains had been positive: 'It was all about inclusion and forward planning and shared chairmanship and joint projects that would work and avoiding joint projects that wouldn't work.' However, more recently this model had proved unsustainable, as despite his attempts to maintain efficient management, personal relations between the chaplains had deteriorated to the point at which the weekly meetings became strained – 'rather bad group therapy sessions.'

> I came really to quite a severe personal crisis [...] where actually I thought the gap between good management practice and bad personal co-operation was so great that it would show. So there came a point where I began to loosen the ties, and they are very loose at the moment. (4.2)

This last case reintroduces a discourse that flowed through Part Two. As was noted, the role of chaplaincy within most universities was secured by the chaplains building up of a network of good relations with key personnel, rather than by the existence of formal structures. Similarly, the smooth operation of an ecumenical chaplaincy depended upon the maintenance of good relations between the chaplains. When mutual trust and good will deteriorated, as appears to have been the case in Institution 4, then the nominal existence of a clear internal management structure was insufficient to maintain a sense of unified direction.

It should be noted that in neither of the two cases in which an Anglican priest was formally recognised by the university as either 'Coordinating' or 'University' chaplain (Institutions 3 and 4 respectively) was that position automatically tied to an Anglican appointment. The current University Chaplain in Institution 4 is the first Anglican to hold that post.

3. ECUMENICAL PLANT

3.1 OVERVIEW OF PROVISION

Shared ecumenical facilities were found in all but two of the institutions studied. (Institutions 1 and 5). In three the ecumenical base was located within other buildings of the university – on the ground floor of the Students' Union (Institution 3), in the basement of the Student Welfare Office (Institution 2), or within the circulation space of a teaching block (Institution 8). In Institutions 2, 4 and 9 the ecumenical base was sited in a separate building owned by the university – though the situation at Institution 4 was complicated by the unusual way the University Chaplaincy was founded there. In Institution 7 the Ecumenical Centre was located not within university property but within the premises of a Local Ecumenical Project at the heart of the university area. Various arrangements were in place for the constituent colleges of Institution 6.

The range of facilities provided varied enormously. The best-equipped and most spacious were in Institutions 4, 7 and 9; these provided not only individual office space to all the chaplains, but also large meeting rooms and gathering spaces. In Institutions 4 and 7, the ecumenical centres also incorporated sizeable dedicated chapels. The space allocated to the chaplains in Institutions 2 and 3 was far less lavish. In Institution 2 there was only one large office, shared by all the chaplains. The plant there, however, also incorporated a large student common room/meeting room, a kitchen and a small chapel. A similar arrangement was provided in Institution 3.

In the main campus of Institution 8, the chaplaincy plant was divided into two sectors. Located in one was the common space, consisting of a large meeting room, which doubled as a chapel; kitchen; and an office for the Anglican chaplain. A short distance away within the same building, the Catholic chaplain had an outer and inner office and a very small chapel, primarily for the reservation of the Blessed Sacrament. The university also provided the ecumenical team with an office in each of the two other campuses; in practice these were used by the two assistant Catholic chaplains as their bases.

3.2 ECUMENICAL CHAPLAINCY OR CATHOLIC CHAPLAINCY?

For two of the institutions (3 and 8) these shared facilities were the chief focus of Catholic chaplaincy activities. In the remaining cases the Catholic Church also maintained a distinct Catholic chaplaincy centre. The use made of the ecumenical plant by those chaplains who had a Catholic base differed from institution to institution. Thus, the main office of the Catholic chaplain in Institutions 4 and 9 was located in the Ecumenical Chaplaincy, and the Masses in Institutions 4 and 8 were celebrated in the shared spaces. In Institution 9, however, weekday Masses were celebrated in the Ecumenical Centre whilst Sunday celebrations took place in the Catholic chaplaincy. There was a sense that Catholic students in these institutions identified to differing degrees with the Ecumenical Centre. In Institution 2, however, all Catholic activity took place in the Catholic chaplaincy building – which was, as has been noted, a source of concern to other chaplains. This pattern of use accentuated a sense among the chaplains there that the Ecumenical Centre, slightly off the main campus, was underused by the student community. Each chaplain committed him/herself to spending one day per week there to receive callers and deal with phone calls. The Catholic chaplain was uncertain about the value of the time he spent there:

> We're underemployed. There's an office and there are four or five at a time, hanging around, and no-one really pops in, or whatever. The rest is surfing time on the internet or emails or reading. [...] There isn't really much to do – it's almost like trying to find work. (2.1)

This sense that the chaplaincy was not a natural drop-in point for students was echoed by another chaplain:

> In this setting here in an institution, and without the traditional background of church-going, you have to actually set up things. You have to go out of the Chaplaincy in order to get people in. And it's far more going out than sitting in and waiting for people coming in. (2.2)

The presence of a separate Catholic chaplaincy was also a bone of contention in Institution 4. The University Chaplain felt that the construction in the early 1990s of the present Catholic chaplaincy had disturbed an ecumenical pattern of work that had been carefully built up around the University Chaplaincy:

> Quite a considerable change came when the Roman Catholic chaplaincy was first [established] without any consultation, without any warning, really, the Roman Catholics built their own building and called it the chaplaincy. So I have two chaplaincies and in one sense it doesn't matter in the slightest, but in another sense it was a terrible affront to the kind of living together that this place had got as one of its gifts. (4.2)

This comment does not acknowledge that a Catholic chaplaincy had existed off-campus elsewhere in town for many years. However, the construction of a new building on the edge of the campus had accentuated the distinct nature of the Catholic presence.

The Catholic chaplain in Institution 7 appeared to operate almost entirely out of his denominational chaplaincy base.

4. WORSHIP IN AN ECUMENICAL CONTEXT

Given the tensions around the provision of separate Catholic chaplaincies, we were surprised that the issue of Eucharistic hospitality did not emerge as a strongly-expressed theme. We were struck by a general sense of respect – albeit tinged with sadness – for the Catholic position on the part of ecumenical colleagues. This is reflected in the following comment from an Anglican chaplain, though it is noteworthy that he understood the regulation of Eucharistic participation in the Catholic Church as a responsibility of the local rather than the universal Church. This misunderstanding in itself demonstrates the conceptual gap between different denominations on the issue:

> I think the problem comes at diocesan level, not actually from the Anglican perspective because we very much take the view that everyone's welcome to receive who's in communion with their own church. But I think I'm right in saying that the Catholic diocese here is not in favour and the Catholic chaplain, of course, would uphold that [...] So if I attend the Roman Catholic Mass which is on tomorrow night I will not receive in sensitivity to other people. Not because I wouldn't want to, but out of sensitivity. (3.2)

A note of tension did emerge when there was a conscious ecumenical desire to celebrate a single Sunday Eucharist embracing the entire university community. This desire would always be frustrated by the Catholic Church's position on intercommunion and the desire of Church-going Catholics to attend Mass. The widespread practice that was reported in many institutions of non-Catholic students focussing their Sunday worship on a particular local church would also militate against the notion of a single university Eucharist each week.

In none of the institutions studied was there a current practice of simultaneous celebrations of the Anglican and Catholic Eucharist, though that had been the custom at one stage in at least one institution. The nearest approach to it was the weekly 'Wednesday Worship' at Institution 9, which was led by the three denominational Student Societies (Anglican, Methodist and Catholic) present in the university. Worship opened with a highly participative and occasionally creative Liturgy of the Word at which all are present. Then the assembly divided along denominational lines (Catholic; Anglican and Methodist together), moving into separate spaces for the Liturgy of the Eucharist.

There was broad evidence across the institutions studied of joint planning of worship events such as carol services, of pulpit sharing, and of a willingness to engage ecumenically in a broad range of non-Eucharistic worship such as Taizé prayer.

5. INTERFAITH CHAPLAINCY

As was noted in Part One, the almost universal policy of active international recruitment in recent years has led to the arrival of large numbers of students from non-Christian backgrounds. The most significant element within this group has been Muslim. Their arrival has coincided with the raising of the international profile of Islam over recent years, and with a growing sense of Muslim identity on the part of young British Asian people. As a consequence, several chaplains said that the Islamic Society was the largest student society within the university, drawing down significant funding from the Student's Union. The various institutions represented in the survey demonstrated a range of responses.

At one extreme, Institution 4 – avowedly secular in nature - was reported by its Catholic chaplain as being extremely wary about extending its engagement with religious groupings on campus to non-Christian religions:

> The university really doesn't want to go there regarding other religions. I mean it's hostile. It doesn't have the hostility it has towards Christianity, but it doesn't know what the hell to do, and it's scared witless of inter-ethnic conflict and/or Jewish and Muslim societies. (4.1)

Other institutions went to considerable lengths to accommodate the growing number of Islamic students. Thus the Ecumenical Centre in Institution 9, which was managed and funded by the University, had been modified to provide permanent ritual washing facilities, and was used each week for Friday prayers by large numbers of students. The need to provide such interfaith facilities was evidently being prioritised by some universities as they planned for their future. Thus, Institution 8 was building a new interfaith centre on one of its campuses that incorporated provision for Muslim prayer. Similarly, in at least one of the constituent colleges of Institution 6, a new L-shaped multi-faith worship space had been provided; the Anglican chaplain there spoke warmly of the experience of celebrating the Eucharist in one leg of the space, whilst Muslim prayers were taking place in the other.

A combination of the institutional tendency to move towards interfaith provision, and a genuine desire for meaningful engagement across faith divides, has led a number of ecumenical chaplaincies to consider broadening their self-understanding to embrace an inter-faith dimension. This was expressed most clearly by one of the non-Catholic partners at Institution 2:

> Our plans, or our dreams, work out along the lines of a centre where different faiths can have different areas, but shared under the same roof. So we have separate praying and worship places because we're all doing different things, really – doing different kinds of worship. But we're all under the same roof, we're in constant dialogue. We see each other - there is a common currency even though what we do is separate. (2.2)

Institution 9 was the only one observed in which significant steps had been taken to formalise the relationships between the Christian chaplains and those of other faiths. The life of the chaplaincy within the university was articulated through a highly complex series of concentric teams of chaplains that moved outwards. The centre was a team of four full-time Christian chaplains, moving to a team of five that included them and the full time Jewish chaplain. Beyond that came the broader ecumenical team, comprising the four full time and a number of part time Christian chaplains, and finally, broader still, the all-embracing 'Multi-Faith Chaplaincy Team' that included two Muslim, a progressive Jewish and a Buddhist chaplain. This team met once a term as a sub-committee of the Chaplaincy Committee. The structure does, at least, provide a mechanism through which the university can formally recognise a broad range of chaplains, and through which if necessary it could also refuse or withdraw that recognition. It is a very flexible system, but it is difficult to escape the sense that it represents an extension outwards of a typical Christian approach (albeit with a significant Jewish element) rather than something radically different which would be a completely integrated interfaith chaplain. In this model the Christian churches still occupy an enormously privileged position.

Establishing genuine multi-faith chaplaincies will not be an easy task, and there is a real danger that if short cuts were taken they could have damaging consequences for all. One Catholic chaplain interviewed, who had wide experience of interfaith dialogue, reflected this concern. He was anxious that interfaith modes of life and work should not be set up unless they were underpinned by sound theological reflection and a clear understanding of the purpose, modalities and parameters of interfaith work and dialogue:

> Well, there seems to be a certain confusion. I've found that a lot of ecumenical things, it's kind of, where it comes from a sense of falling numbers there's a sense that we have to change, we have to leave a lot of our own stuff behind and meet people in the middle. I found, - and certainly with inter-faith dialogue as a Catholic it's deepened my sense of Catholicism, as I would hope it would deepen an Islamic, a Muslim sense of Islam. That's my kind of understanding of interfaith dialogue: we're not looking to convert one another but we're looking to diversity and to understand each other better and to understand ourselves. (2.1)

The complexity of the issue was highlighted by the senior Anglican chaplain at university 6. He was already engaged in interfaith work as one of the constituent colleges had a Muslim chaplain, and there was a possibility of another being appointed elsewhere within the institution. Contrary to the opinion that chaplains (Catholic and otherwise) had expressed elsewhere during the research, he insisted that Muslims were happy with the title of chaplain and with the concept of chaplaincy. However, a Muslim understanding of the role of chaplain, he said, differed markedly from that of Christian chaplains:

> I'm in conversation with my colleagues in the NHS and prison service where they already have Muslim chaplains [...] The

expectations are very limited. The Muslim chaplain will lead worship and that will be it. They won't take part in any pastoral activity. They won't take any referral for pastoral care – for example if prisoners find they've got difficulties at home. Within the NHS there will be some visiting, but it will be limited. And again, it's a very tightly focused expectation of leading worship and perhaps a bit of teaching of the Qu'ran, or study in that way. So they don't have the broad remit, and the engagement, and the positive engagement that I would expect my own chaplains to have. (6.2)

Creating an interfaith chaplaincy on a sound and workable footing would call for significant reflection and dialogue. What was observed in the fieldwork appeared largely as attempts to extend the current models and expectations of ecumenical chaplaincy to include provision for members of other faith groups. This seems unlikely to be successful unless it goes further and deeper than just mapping current expectations of (a) the role of chaplain and (b) the concept of a shared ministry to the institution as a whole onto an interfaith setting.

The Anglican chaplain in a different institution further illustrated the day to day complexities of moving from an ecumenical to an interfaith chaplaincy model. He was concerned that his university was planning to transform its current provision without proper consultation, and for very practical reasons felt that for the university to impose a single multi-faith base would be 'the worst possible case:'

> Everyone would want to use it, and you'd obviously want to have, folks would want to have a daily Mass, I run my Eucharists twice a week, the Moslem group would want to come in and say their prayers [...] Not least, providing a space from a Christian point of view where one would want to have imagery. It would be a case of putting it up and pulling it down all the time because obviously you couldn't leave it around because it would offend other faith traditions. I think there are practical difficulties. If they're talking about a multi-faith centre with some shared space and still some small dedicated space that's a different matter. You could still have your Christian prayer room which is ready for use, and so on. But because we've not been consulted we don't actually know what's proposed. But the best case scenario is that things remain as they are. (8.2)

There is, therefore, a general movement on the part of institutions towards replacing their current ecumenical approach to chaplaincy with an inter-faith perspective. This helps universities in their legal responsibilities of care, and supports recruitment. However, such a development may have a profound impact upon the current patterns of chaplaincy life. It would further impact upon Catholic chaplains who already have to negotiate a delicate pathway between ministering to their Catholic students and collaborating ecumenically. Consequently, the emergence of a new structure for faith provision in HE risks further isolating Catholic chaplains within the institutions they serve. The Catholic Church's response, therefore, needs to be carefully developed in close collaboration with the other denominations, and requires some engagement at national level. Above all else, the Christian churches need to extend to the university setting the clarity of thought that they bring to interfaith issues at the highest level and represent that clearly to the universities. Otherwise, unsatisfactory and uniformed arrangements may be made, entirely in good will at the local level, that fail to respect the integrity of the various religious parties.

6. CONCLUSION

It is virtually impossible now for chaplains to work without being engaged in close collaboration with their ecumenical partners, and this is increasingly the expectation of the institution. These creates many opportunities – for example, enormous benefits in sharing resources, plant, ideas and support. However, there may also be problems for the Catholic chaplain – not least misunderstandings of the primary focus of the chaplain's work. Chaplains often find themselves sailing in uncharted waters with very little to guide them, and little sense of their being supported.

At times, for various reasons, the situation on the ground may not be entirely consonant with the shared theological principles that inform good ecumenical dialogue and practice. Many decisions are made on the ground that might have benefited from a more sustained engagement with the churches at a higher level.

A framework for interfaith working has much less experiential foundation on which it could be built, but is even more urgently needed.

PART FOUR

SUPPORTING AND MANAGING THE WORK OF CHAPLAINS:
THE RELATIONSHIP WITH THE CATHOLIC COMMUNITY

1. INTRODUCTION

The complex sets of relationships outlined earlier underline the ambiguity of the chaplain's role. He or she has to find a way of ministering to a body of students, in a rapidly changing academic environment, within an institution that may be at best ambivalent in its attitude towards chaplaincy, whilst at the same time forging a relationship with ecumenical chaplains who may have difficulty over the Catholic chaplain's primary focus on the Catholic community rather than on the institution as a whole. All of this needs to be managed against the background of slow but inexorable institutional progression towards interfaith approaches. If chaplains are to exercise a fruitful and happy ministry in this constantly shifting landscape the question of their support and supervision becomes urgent. With this in mind we move in Part Four to considering the fourth relational dimension, that of the chaplain with his or her sponsoring denomination.

As we have noted in previous parts of this report, it can be difficult to disentangle the different relational strands that form the nexus of the chaplain's ministry. The question of support and supervision also relates to issues that touch upon the institution and upon ecumenical relations. Consequently Part Four begins by considering how these operate (or sometimes do not) as fora for support and supervision. We will thus begin with the institution, and then focus more specifically on the relationship between Catholic chaplains and their dioceses. With regard to the second issue, we shall first examine two aspects that demonstrate the ambiguities within which chaplains are required to operate in regard to their ministry and their sponsoring denomination. The first is the manner of their appointment, where a range of practices is identified and analysed - some highly commendable, others more problematic. The second aspect relates to appropriate support and supervision.

2. THE APPOINTMENT PROCESS FOR CHAPLAINS

2.1 Non-Catholic Chaplains

Not surprisingly, it was the places where the structural relationship between chaplain and institution was most explicitly articulated that demonstrated the most unequivocal involvement of the institution in the chaplaincy appointment. This is seen most clearly in the appointment of the University Chaplain to Institution 4, though his account of his appointment points up the tensions inherent in the situation. As was noted in Part Two, his appointment was subject to his securing acceptance as a bona fide academic and member of the teaching staff.

> I proposed teaching a course on the psychology of religion and was sat down and given a very aggressive interview by people who were determined to prove I didn't know what I was talking about and shouldn't be trusted to teach. It was quite an exciting occasion but it was aggressive, uncompromising, unkind. But perhaps it was just par for the course of an academic institution but I mean that all happened when I arrived. But I survived. (4.2)

Where the relationship between institution and chaplaincy was more informal, the involvement of university staff in the appointment of chaplains was perceived by the chaplains as an important element in formalizing the relationship. However, as with the question of recognition explored in Part Two, so also the official status of university representatives on appointment panels was more ambiguous than chaplains' accounts at first suggested. Once again, a close examination of the data from Institution 7 reveals the complexity of what at first sight might appear a significant involvement of the institution. In discussing their appointments, the ecumenical chaplains insisted that institutional representatives had played a role in their appointment. However, as the discussion progressed it became clear that such university staff were present only in a personal capacity – even if they came from the highest echelons of the institution:

> The last person who sat on our panel was the pro-Vice-Chancellor, but she was there not as a university appointee as such. It is an ambiguous role that they play, because obviously you've invited someone from the university – a bit odd. (7.2)

There was a conscious attempt by chaplains to involve significant members of the university staff in appointment panels and management committees. The clearly-stated aim was to draw the university into a sense of ownership of the decisions made by such bodies, and therefore also of the work of the chaplaincy. This, as one chaplain put it, could be a 'win-win situation.' (7.3) However, there was evidence of a rather more cautious interpretation of the significance of these events by those university personnel who took part. The Head of Student Services highlighted the ambiguity of her position on such bodies:

> I mean I am invited to all sorts of things – as a lot of my colleagues are, not just in relation to the chaplaincy – where I guess I am representing the institution, but without any real mandate. (7.3)

Once again, the real driving force here was not, in fact, a progressive formalization of the chaplaincy-institutional relationship, but the exercise of mutual good-will built up through the development of personal relationships. This apparent muddle, nevertheless, often produces good results. Attempts to clarify it might destroy something beneficial, as individual good-will might be eroded. In this sense, therefore, ambiguity may not always be a bad thing. Although ambiguity may cause discomfort, some realities and relationships defy formalisation, and are resistant to any simple clarification.

Even more informal engagement of the institution in the appointment process was cited by the Anglican chaplain to a different university. He began by saying that the university had been involved in his appointment; its representatives included the Registrar and the Student's Union Welfare Officer. However, once the process was elucidated it became clear that whilst these people had met with all the candidates ahead of the interview process and had indeed fed opinions into the interview panel, it was the local Diocese that had been finally responsible for making the appointment, and their decision was then communicated to the university:

> So before I arrived the Vice Chancellor knew who was coming. So the first time I saw him he must have done his homework because he just came right out and said, 'Hello, [name]' So he'd obviously been informed officially who it was, and knew who it was. (8.2)

A similar informal process of consultation was carried out with the ecumenical chaplains in another institution over the appointment by the sponsoring denominations of a Free Church chaplain:

> As chaplains we met all the candidates. We didn't formally interview them, but at the end of the day after the formal interviews were completed we fed our impressions into the interview panel. (2.2)

The potential problem presented by all these situations lies not in the involvement of university staff in the appointment process per se, but in the differing interpretations given to that involvement. In a secular institution without a formalized relationship between university and chaplaincy, the engagement of key personnel in the appointment process is probably best understood as consultative or as an expression of personal interest. This, in itself, is to be welcomed. It would be a mistake, however, to see such engagement as a sign of the university's validation of the role and purpose of the chaplaincy. The clear distinction visible in the last two quotations between consultation of ecumenical partners and key officials and a formal interview process may reflect more accurately the relationship between the various parties.

2.2 Catholic Chaplains

The appointment of Catholic chaplains generally contrasts with the process used for their ecumenical colleagues. A mixture of practices exists for the appointment of lay chaplains; in the case of clergy the traditional pattern of direct appointment by the Bishop without a formal procedure remains the norm.

2.2.1 Lay Chaplains

In line with its declared intention of placing chaplaincy at the heart of the institution, the Catholic College made a policy decision to employ a chaplain on a fully formal basis; this was seen as being in contrast with other institutions:

> I think a number of places have chaplaincy on the cheap, and what we had to do was to put our money where our mouth is and invest in chaplaincy by paying somebody a reasonable salary, by offering them good conditions of service, and by ensuring that they got a decent budget. (1.2)

The chaplain was therefore to be fully employed by the institution and given a formal full-time contract involving 37.5 hours per week. After a twelve-month probationary period, the position became permanent. The post was filled through a formal interview process that involved both institutional staff and student representatives.

> The post was advertised [...] Application, standard application – called for interview and presentation. So [we] had a day here when it was a 15-minute presentation with questions. So it was over half an hour. Then there was an allotted hour for an interview.

> Because it was July there were no students involved in it, so there were about ten members of staff at the presentation and six at the interview, and only one overlapped. They interviewed four candidates (the other three were male, just for the record), and rang me that evening. (1.1)

This full formal process was unique among the lay chaplains interviewed; more informal processes were common. In Institution 5 the appointment mirrored that of clergy appointments. The chaplain was already working in a voluntary capacity for the Diocese, and was approached directly by the Bishop. No formal contract was drawn up, though the outlines of the role were agreed informally. The chaplain receives an honorarium of £4000, equal to the diocesan clergy stipend, for which she writes herself a monthly cheque on the chaplaincy account. The Diocese does not pay National Insurance. This was not unique; in another case intervention (by a Catholic priest-chaplain) was required to ensure that National Insurance was paid for the religious sister employed by the Diocese as chaplain (Institution 3). Normally, however, as with the clergy, National Insurance contributions are paid.

The arrangement in Institution 5 is able to succeed because of the existing relationship between the chaplain and the Bishop and the evident good will of all parties. It also depends to a large extent upon the fact that the chaplain is not dependent upon the honorarium as her sole source of income. It is difficult to project this situation beyond her term of office; the Diocese has neither the available clergy to replace her with a priest, nor sufficient funds to employ a lay person at a professional rate.

Headhunting on the basis of existing relationships also came into play with the appointment of assistant chaplains. This potentially raises issues of compliance with employment legislation:

> He created this position for, not for me, but he had me in mind creating it. If I had said no the job would have been made public so I had a certain date to see and make my mind up - because he was going to take a Chaplaincy Assistant on anyway - but he did me first because [...] he knew what I was like. (7.5)

2.2.2 CLERGY CHAPLAINS

Such legal issues do not arise when the Catholic chaplain is a diocesan priest; his appointment mirrors any other clergy appointment. The stipend received and payments of National Insurance contributions follow general diocesan clergy guidelines. As with placement in a parish, the appointment is completely internal and is generally made by a direct approach from the Bishop to a priest. Several of the clergy chaplains found their appointment a surprise:

> I'm the sort of person who thinks, 'Well, if they ask me to do something, I'll probably just say "yes".' And I went in, and there were two things put to me. One was a parish, and the other was what was described as a 'change in ministry.' 'Would I accept a change in ministry?' And I assumed it would be a hospital. [...] So I sort of groaned inwardly, and said 'Yes.' [...] And they said, 'University Chaplaincy,' and you could have knocked me over with a feather. (8.1)

In other cases, there was a clear sense that the appointment followed logically on from previous working experience. Thus, one chaplain, who had had considerable work experience with young people before beginning seminary formation, was told of his forthcoming appointment even before his ordination to the priesthood:

> I think, you know, to be fair to the Diocese they were looking at my background, saying, 'We want somebody like that, who's got experience, to work in this sort of setting.' (7.1)

There was no evidence from the fieldwork that the Catholic reservation of the appointment process as a purely internal matter generated conflict between Diocese and institution. This, we believe, is because academic institutions actually prefer not to formalize their relationships with denominational chaplains; as was noted in the case of non-Catholic chaplains, there has been a reluctance of institutions to become officially involved in appointment processes. The maintenance of a formal distance and the blurring of relational parameters thus actually safeguards the canonical right of Catholic Bishops to reserve to themselves the appointment of clergy, and of lay people with pastoral responsibility. However, there was evidence that in an institution where ecumenical structures were strong, a perceived lack of consultation in the timing and manner of appointments could be felt as weakening the carefully constructed profile of the ecumenical chaplaincy. A common mind and way of working that had been generated across years of hard work could be put at risk. It should be noted that this concern applies across all denominations.

> Much more important is the way in which someone is appointed – they bring in an external culture that doesn't fit and work, carries with it all the paranoia, power plays, anxieties, external forms of culture. And they get plonked here, and then some period of time, some kind of rubbing along together, and inevitably there are projections about what they want, what they stand for. [...] I dread the idea of [the current Catholic chaplain] going, partly because I respect him, and partly because God knows how I am going to find the energy to start with somebody who will come in and start from the beginning again. (4.2)

2.2.3 PREPARATION FOR THE POST

Most of the priest chaplains interviewed themselves had experience of HE. One had studied at both Oxford and Cambridge, one had spent several years in residential youth ministry, whilst at least one other had been a teacher before applying to seminary. One of the assistant chaplains had extensive prior experience of working as a chaplain in other HE institutions. These experiences were reference points to which they returned in conversation – drawing comparisons or contrasting different approaches to working with young people that they had encountered. However, it was uncertain whether they regarded such experience alone as sufficient preparation for taking on the role. Speaking about his appointment, one chaplain reported:

> The Bishop said to me, 'So what do you think?' I said, 'I don't know how to be a university chaplain.' And he said, 'Well, you've been to university, haven't you?' So I said, 'Yes.' He said, 'What did you find there?' And I talked about a few things. 'Well, have a go.' And, I'm afraid, that's it. (8.2)

We asked all the chaplains if they had received specific training for the post before they began their term of office. There was only one affirmative response – and that was a chaplain responsible for a student residence who had taken a food hygiene course. One chaplain, upon her appointment, took the Chaplains' Course given by Ushaw College. Others spoke warmly about the sessions offered to recently-appointed chaplains by the Conference of Catholic Chaplains in H.E. The personal on-going support given by the Conference co-ordinators was greatly appreciated.

3. SUPPORT AND SUPERVISION OF LAY CHAPLAINS

The ambiguous position of chaplaincy within the institution can generate difficulties at a personal level. Without a clear sense of the parameters within which they are working, chaplains are thrown back on their own resources to define their role, set goals and monitor their progress towards those goals. This is particularly true of Catholic priests, for whom there is no detailed job description, and who arrive in the institution from a parish ministerial culture that rarely fosters clear processes of supervision and line management. However, even for those chaplains with job descriptions, the blurred lines of responsibility to Church and institution often resulted in uncertainty about line-management, support and supervision in their work. A number of practices emerged, ranging from very clear structures down to the chaplain being more or less completely unsupported in his/her work.

3.1 'It's Fantastic': Institution 1

The situation of maximum support was, once again, found in Institution 1. Here the chaplain was line-managed directly by the Chief Executive, meeting for an hour every two to three weeks. A system was also being put into place for annual appraisal. This system reflects the high value that this Catholic institution placed upon chaplaincy, and represents a significant commitment in terms of time on the part of senior management. No parallel system was encountered during the fieldwork. It raises questions concerning the quality of support and supervision given to chaplains elsewhere – either by the institution itself or by their sponsoring dioceses.

3.2. Matrix Line Management: Institution 3

The position of the Catholic chaplain in Institution 3 offers a particularly interesting example of the interaction between institutional, ecumenical and denominational strands of management. As was noted in Part Three, the Anglican chaplain to the university was officially recognised as Chaplaincy Co-ordinator, which, in the university's eyes, created a formal relationship between him and the other chaplains – Catholic included. However, the religious sister who served as Catholic chaplain was employed not by the university but by the Diocese, which had entrusted responsibility for her line management to an experienced priest chaplain at another HE institution in the same town. This complex arrangement could have generated considerable tension, but appeared to work quite smoothly. This undoubtedly was due to the good-will of all parties involved, the university included. Both the Anglican Co-ordinator and the Catholic line manager evidently held the Catholic chaplain in high regard and were supportive of her work.

In practice, detailed, hands-on line management was provided by the priest. He and the chaplain drew up her targets together at the beginning of each academic year. They met at the beginning or end of each term for a full day's evaluation, and briefly each week. The chaplain described the experience positively:

> For myself I say what I accept in terms of the chaplaincy, what I'm working towards – whether it's setting up CaFE as a parish-type course, how you do that. Whether it's what you're going to do with students. How I'm coping myself – physically, emotionally and everything else. I find that is excellent. (3.1)

The Co-ordinator respected this formal process, and understood his role as being 'more supportive.' He would not, he said, 'try to influence policy of [the Catholic] chaplaincy and pastoral work because the day to day stuff is, really, it's largely informal and one-to-one networking.' (3.2). Rather, his aim was to ensure that the chaplain was kept in the loop about general developments within the university, and through regular contact with the line-managing priest to check that her work-load was maintained at a reasonable level:

> I mean, a big concern with her is that she won't stop – and you can see that she's full of energy. And I think, you know, we both worry sometimes that she needs to slow down a bit and perhaps think of herself. So those are the kind of issues we talk about and sort of share with each other. (3.2)

The relationship and support was appreciated by the chaplain:

> We get on very well, we have a good working relationship and whatever I think of initiating he will support one hundred per cent as long as I get it up and going. [...] We're in contact every single day either before - in one way or another, we do that. So we do know everything that's going on and he will inform me – he's very good about that, about informing me about any things that are happening at Student Services and that, excellent at doing that. [...] I do know everything that is going on, that is: I can say that, and it's a big, big plus. (3.1)

That this triangular arrangement succeeded was largely due to the mutual good understanding of the parties involved. It should be noted, however, that previous occupants of the posts had not enjoyed the same relationship of trust, and difficulties had ensued. It is clear that a change in any one of the post holders could easily jeopardize the smooth working of the system; for example, the introduction of a Co-ordinating Chaplain who wished to exercise a more direct line management role would upset the careful balance of responsibilities that currently generated a highly supportive environment for the work of the chaplain.

3.3 THE CO-EXISTENCE OF INDEPENDENT MANAGEMENT COMMITTEES: INSTITUTION 2

By way of contrast to the remarkable synergy found in Institution 3, Institution 2 demonstrates how different chaplains, whilst working within an ecumenical structure, were managed (or not) quite independently by their sponsoring denominations. As in the previous case, this managerial structure could potentially have proved problematic at the level of ecumenical working - had, for example, a clear line been given by a committee that took the chaplain's work in a radically different direction. However, it became apparent from the interviews that there was a degree of obscurity concerning the extent of the supervision and oversight even where this formal management structure was in place. Thus, whilst the Free Church chaplain was certain that his Management Committee was his employer, he was unclear as to whether or not the Chair of the Committee could in any way be regarded as his line-manager.

The Anglican chaplain too had identified a lack of appropriate oversight in the systems he inherited upon appointment. He had taken steps to ensure that a suitable management structure was set in place with the aim of ensuring proper resourcing and support from his Diocese for the work of the chaplaincy:

> Soon after I came here, realizing that being directly accountable to the Bishop wasn't necessarily always a very workable arrangement, we established a Higher Education Chaplaincy Group within the Diocese which is chaired by the Dean of the Cathedral, who sits on the Bishop's staff. And the reason for that group is twofold. One, for us to provide accountability to the Diocese via the Dean – and the Committee also includes people from the university, and people from the Bishop's Council. But also – and more important from our point of view – to get resourcing and support from the Diocese to support the work that goes on here. So, in terms of formal structure, that's where my accountability lies. (2.2)

3.4 THE PRIEST CHAPLAIN AS LINE MANAGER

In three institutions (6, 7 and 8) the Catholic Chaplaincy comprised a team in which lay chaplains – some of them religious sisters – were led by a priest. These teams met regularly to discuss policy issues and, in one case at least, determine how the chaplaincy budget was to be spent. When asked about line management and appraisal, one of the lay chaplains answered:

> A Yes, he does, yes. We take our time to go in at the end of each term and sit down and have a chat.
>
> Q So you know at the beginning of term there's a clear sense of what you need to do? You set targets?
>
> A Oh, yeah (7.?)

The line management role of the priest chaplain in another team was less clear. This may reflect the fact that he 'inherited' assistant chaplains who had much longer experience than he of working in the institution, and who had established a clear sense of their own role and ministry. In this place, indeed, there was a sense that meeting with his co-chaplains gave the priest an opportunity to critically evaluate his own ideas, rather than providing a vehicle for him to manage their work.

> I think primarily, here, at the moment, I think my two co-chaplains gently would definitely tell me if there was something going awry. I think we've had one instance this term where we've had to have a very frank discussion. You know, whilst that's not easy I was heartened that we could have it. (8.2)

The management of religious chaplains by a secular priest also presented a structural complexity, as the religious already had lines of support and responsibility within their congregations. The delicacy of working within these pre-existing relational patterns became apparent in Institution 6. The senior Catholic chaplain there – a diocesan priest -was responsible for the management of ten chaplains, of whom the majority were members of religious orders, both men and women. The senior chaplain was reluctant to impose a further level of structured support, and preferred a more informal approach to line management, describing his method as 'not hugely interventionist,' and drawing a parallel with the relationship between parish priests and their dean:

> I like to think of myself as working collaboratively, so I see them as independent in their institutions, and I'm there to support them as and where necessary. And any issues that they have would come back to me. I think the easiest way to see it is as a dean in a deanery. In effect, there's a deanery of chaplaincies in this university, and I would be the dean. And if they have any

> questions or issues I would try to resolve them. I'm the one they relate to as the next step up. (6.1)

This informality also extended to the issue of annual appraisal:

> I looked at the Bishops' Conference documents, and thought of taking those up. But a lot of what happens is informal. So I use in my head the model I've looked at. I don't give them forms to fill in, and go through the forms, but I do sit down with each of the chaplains in turn, and it's up to them – they take it up or don't. It's more difficult with some than with others because they're just not interested. And if they're not doing any damage, that's fine. (6.1)

His final point raised the question of how good practice was maintained, and whether there might be call for a more structured system of accountability. On this matter he evidently experienced a degree of tension. On the one hand, the nature of the pastoral relationship between chaplain and student did not sit comfortably within the provider-client relationship developed in secular systems of accountability (for example in a counselling model). On the other hand, he exhibited some unease at the risks that too light an oversight could pose:

> As I've been speaking to you today, I've been very aware of the fact that everything is quite unprofessional – it just happens. And I suppose I'm acutely aware of that, but I don't want to completely change it because it would take too much energy away from other things that I think are more important. (6.1)

3.5 THE SELF-MANAGED LAY CHAPLAIN

The lay chaplain in Institution 5 had enrolled on the Chaplaincy Course at Ushaw on being appointed. A prerequisite of the programme had been that during the period of study she should be supervised by the priest of the local parish, to which the chaplaincy was closely linked. However, whilst the two enjoyed a good working relationship, and she felt supported by him, his engagement in her work did not amount to supervision in a formal sense:

> Technically he was my supervisor when I did my chaplain's course in Ushaw but in practice, it largely consisted of saying 'Oh, thank God, somebody's looking after the students.' (5.1)

The priest himself had insisted that his own skills did not lie in the direction of student chaplaincy, and that he was happy to leave its running completely in her hands. She was, therefore, entirely responsible for the management of her own work:

> I set the programme, I devise the targets. There is no mission statement. There's a vision. The vision is of an open, outward welcoming, Catholic community which is distinctly working in an ecumenical framework, making all people welcome, offering hospitality particularly to those who are particularly in need of it. (5.1)

Continuing to work on the basis of her existing good relationship with the Bishop, she submitted an annual report to him and the Trustees outlining the work that had been done and identifying current needs.

4. SUPPORT AND SUPERVISION OF CATHOLIC PRIEST CHAPLAINS

The situation outlined with the last mentioned chaplain very closely approximates to that of those Catholic chaplains who are diocesan priests. In a very real sense chaplaincy is an extension of the general mode of operation of parish clergy, who act with considerable autonomy and without direct line management or supervision. Whilst efforts have been made recently in a number of dioceses to introduce voluntary systems of clergy appraisal, these have generally seen a very low take up rate. The notion of supervision has been met by some clergy with suspicion and even hostility. It may be that the introduction of such systems – no matter how supportive – into a ministry such as the Catholic priesthood, which is understood as an intense mixture of personal vocation and ecclesial service, is a culture shift too far, at least for the present. By no means all the priest chaplains interviewed expressed a need for the type of support that supervision or appraisal would offer. However some at least felt that the ambiguities of the situation in which they were working presented a pressing case for some system of structured support.

A number of factors fed into this conviction. The first is the complexity of the institution – the multiple strands already explored across this report. The second is that chaplains are working outside the boundaries of 'normal' priestly activity. The third is the uncomfortable truth that their brother clergy do not always appreciate their work and ministry. The first of these has already been considered in detail. The second and third will be explored in the following sections, before we turn to the experiences of diocesan support related by the priest chaplains.

4.1 DOING A GOOD JOB OUTSIDE A PARISH

The work of most priests is generated for them by the routine of parish life. Congregations may be falling in numbers, but there is still a demand for the celebration of Mass. Parish and deanery schools can create a heavy burden of work, especially for their governors. Funerals and baptisms, and their preparation and follow-up, continue to make considerable demands of most priests. The common experience of HE chaplains, however, was that there was very little demand made of them, so unlike their counterparts in parishes they were constantly engaged in initiating work, much of it with a relatively short life span, in contrast with the longer rhythms of parish life. Several chaplains explained that each year they had to begin, as it were, from new. This impacts particularly upon their liturgical ministry; one chaplain, whose Sunday assembly was chiefly composed of international students, said 'I lose seventy percent of my congregation each year.' The short, intense time-span within which chaplains work exacerbates the difficulty of establishing priorities, and of being able to assess accurately either the value of work done, or – more crucially – the overall impact of their presence in the institution. Students may continue to benefit for the rest of their lives from what they received at the chaplaincy, but they are not around to express that to the chaplain. All chaplains, clergy and lay alike, may, therefore, have a sense of expending, and perhaps dissipating, energies without receiving long-term appreciative feedback.

4.2 Relations with Other Diocesan Clergy

The other factor to be considered is that in some cases the validity of a chaplain's role outside parish ministry is not fully understood or appreciated by his own peers. A number of excerpts from interviews illustrate this point. One suggested viewpoint was that parish clergy simply did not understand the work of a university chaplain:

> I mean my general impression has always been, you know, 'I think it's great what you're doing. I couldn't do it myself.' 'I don't know what you're doing.' There's a sort of - there's not a real - neither questioning of what I do nor any real attempt to use it. Occasionally a Head of Sixth Form or something from another Diocese - it will occur to them that it might be useful to get the university chaplain in to talk about going to university. But even that comes as a surprise, you know. (4.1)

This sense that there was little understanding within the Church of chaplaincy ministry today was shared by one of the Anglican chaplains. He linked difficulties over external perceptions to the question of funding:

> I think we have a very good idea of what we're about. I'm not sure people in the wider Church do. In fact, I know they don't, and you know, I spend a lot of time, particularly when I'm preaching in other Churches, making a point of saying something about the chaplaincy, trying to knock the point across, because at the end of the day they're the one's that are paying, but they don't really have an understanding of what we're about, what we're trying to do. (3.2)

It was the experience of some Catholic chaplains that matters had deteriorated to a point worse than just misunderstanding. They felt that their ministry was viewed with active hostility by other clergy – for which one felt that chaplains themselves had been partly responsible:

> I should think not many unless they were confident enough would probably voice to my face that they thought it was a waste of time, but I'm sure some do think it's a waste of time and think that we have big long holidays. Of course chaplains shoot themselves in the foot because if they go around saying that they do take all the big long holidays and they're just doing their doctorates, and not many people come to Mass, then what sort of publicity does that give us? So we pick up a legacy of, you know, of past times where things have been - not always been good at publicity ourselves so we deserve some of it. (7.1)

Another chaplain suggested a source for clergy ambivalence towards chaplaincy that ties in with the current broad structural changes in the Catholic community. He imagined the reaction of other priests to his appointment as chaplain in an institution in which around twenty students would come to Sunday Mass:

> 'My God! We've deployed a priest, a young priest, to serve that number of Sunday worshippers! He could be running a big parish. He was running a big parish!' Raised eyebrows, because they're probably thinking, my God – is that all that's going [to Mass]? (8.1)

This perception taps into four anxieties running though the Catholic community at present: the reducing number of clergy, the reducing numbers of regular Church goers, the widespread disappearance of young people from parish life, and the increasing inability of many dioceses to maintain the network of parishes intact. The Catholic community thus finds itself on the horns of a dilemma. The instinct of many clergy is that parish life should be prioritized – that, after all, is the focus of their own life and experience. The impact of a commitment to placing priests in HE institutions may be felt in another part of the Diocese, by a priest being asked to assume responsibility for two parishes, or even for parish closure. However, through university chaplaincy the Catholic community engages with young people – a group with whom the Church has less and less meaningful contact within the parish system. Chaplaincy, therefore, may be prioritized as at least one opportunity – perhaps the last opportunity – for engagement with young people:

> And I think that would apply to the Diocese in general and I think it would apply to the Diocese in general to youth work. We know we're crap at it and we're very convinced we're crap at it. We know that we're not keeping the affiliation of young people. And the university chaplaincy is the last chance saloon really. You know, if we've got a university chaplaincy in place we're still doing something for the young. (4.1)

If, as the current Government intends, up to 50% of the UK population will pass at some stage in their life through HE, then the numbers of people with whom the Church could engage through chaplaincy are growing, rather than shrinking. Having chaplains in post to engage with this growing body is an opportunity to be seized, and should be recognised as a mainstream element within individual diocesan strategic planning.

4.3 Diocesan Lines of Support and Responsibility

The last quoted priest went on to suggest that because his Diocese understood his work as the 'last chance saloon' in engaging with young people, it gave him considerable latitude for action, and did not enquire too closely into the numbers of people at the Masses he celebrated on campus. Yet is this diocesan hands-off attitude as supportive as it might first appear? Several priests expressed uncertainty or disappointment about how they linked into diocesan structures. Thus, when asked to whom in the Diocese he was responsible, one priest replied:

> I've absolutely no idea. I haven't had one phone call from the Diocese asking how I'm going on. The Dean's very good – but that's more by luck than anything. The provision of junior clergy in this Diocese doesn't really take into account supervision, or appraisal – which is non-existent in our Diocese. (8.1)

Where chaplains spoke of a supportive relationship with the Diocese, it was frequently because they had built up a good relationship with senior diocesan personnel – either with the diocesan Bishop (as in the case of Institution 5), or with Financial Secretaries or Vicars General. The value of these relationships is not to be doubted, though at times they cut across the presumed lines of diocesan responsibility. Thus, one chaplain felt that his work was closely supervised and supported by one of the auxiliary Bishops who was also a good friend – even though that Bishop was not responsible for the diocesan department that had formal oversight for chaplaincy matters. This situation raises the question of the implications for future oversight of the chaplain if the Bishop changed.

There were mixed reports of the impact of the pastoral visitation of diocesan Bishops to the chaplaincies. The students particularly valued such visits, not least because they provided an experiential point of contact with the universal Church. This was stressed by a student who had spoken about the risk of the insularity of student Catholic life:

> Recently the Bishop came on a Sunday evening and I think that's one of the best events we've had. He came and talked, absolutely brilliant and really good to see someone from outside – you know, someone coming inside and saying, 'We're interested in the Chaplaincy.' And talking about politics and religion, and education and religion. (9.4)

However, several chaplains feared that such visitations did not generally prove to be opportunities for real engagement about the direction that the chaplaincy was taking, or about crucial issues over the institution. One chaplain described such visits in the following terms:

> Benign neglect is the best description. You know, 'Young Mr Grace' walking across the set of *Are You Being Served,* and he says 'you're all doing very well' and then disappearing for another year. There's no-one to have a conversation with about how I'm doing ministry here. [...] Yeah, I would think there's a blank incomprehension by and large. (Unattributed!)

This presumably is not a universal experience, as several current diocesan bishops were once university chaplains themselves. Nonetheless, given the rapidly changing nature of the HE scene, it would be easy even for them to underestimate the differences between their own previous experiences and those of chaplains today.

4.4 Direct links with Parishes

Two of the chaplaincies studied were formally linked to parishes (Institutions 5 and 7). In neither of these did the parish priest act as line manager to the chaplain. However, there were evident benefits in the relationship for both parish and chaplaincy that included a level of support to the chaplain. In the first of these the relationship was formalised on the appointment of a lay chaplain who was herself a long-standing member of the parish. The parish priest recognised that as such she was able to relate both to students and to the parish. He felt that the relationship would not have been as comfortable if it had been attempted whilst a priest chaplain was in post:

> Maybe the fact that there is a lay chaplain there has helped us to gel better, whereas if you had a priest he'd tend to do his own thing, and he might want to keep as far away as he can from the parish priest! I just want to encourage her; she's the perfect person for it. (5.5)

This priest was very clear on the division of labour. As parish priest and local hospital chaplain he already had a full work load, and felt no desire to be more directly engaged with work with students: He 'wouldn't touch the university with a bargepole':

> There's no competition. We both do our own thing and help and sort of complement one another. I don't do anything to do with the chaplaincy – she does all that. From a priestly point of view I'll help out, and it seems to work out very well, you know? (5.5)

This 'helping out' consisted primarily in welcoming around fifty students each week to the weekend Masses, and being available to individual students should they wish to speak with a priest – a service of which he said they did avail themselves. There was also some sharing of resources – for example, lacking a parish hall, he would hold parish meetings and events at the Chaplaincy. The parish would reciprocate by occasionally buying resources – such as the CaFE material – which were then also available for chaplaincy use.

The parish to which the chaplaincy in Institution 7 was linked is located in an area of considerable socio-economic deprivation. In terms of the number of parishioners it would have been a prime candidate for some form of amalgamation or sharing of clergy. Therefore the current chaplain was initially appointed, as was his predecessor, with both parish and university responsibilities. However, shortly after his appointment the Diocese agreed that the positions of parish priest and chaplain should be separate, and that a Priest in Charge should be appointed from among the clergy working at diocesan level. This separation of responsibilities, nonetheless, did not result in a divorce between parish and chaplaincy; indeed, there was a sustained attempt to integrate the students into the life of the parish, with benefits to both. Two priests had since held the position of Priest in Charge, and the first of these explained how after some initial reservations the parishioners had come to recognise that to no small degree the continuing existence of their parish was bound up with its relationship to the chaplaincy:

> There was a feeling, I think, [...] that all the focus was going to be on the chaplaincy. It was going to be a chaplaincy church and the parish side would be forgotten about. And that hasn't happened. And I think most of the parishioners now would see that the future of their having a parish in this part of the city is also the focus of the Chaplaincy. (7.7)

A range of social activities were held across the year (for example, 'Murder Mystery' evenings, parish 'Generation Games') that engaged both students and parishioners. More importantly, the fact that the Sunday celebrations of Mass attended by the students were held in the parish church meant that there was a continuity of liturgical celebrations across the summer vacation. In many universities chaplaincy life effectively closes down outside term time – a factor that risks leaving the many international students who remain at the university across the summer without the chaplaincy focus for their faith on which they have come to rely. The fact that in this institution they could continue to worship with a parish community with whom they were already identified provided this growing number of students with a vital line of support.

The experiences of these chaplaincies suggest that where possible, direct links with parishes can prove highly positive. For the students they address to some extent the sense of isolation from the broader Church expressed in section 4.3 above, and they can ensure continuity of sacramental provision upon the appointment of lay chaplains. With careful handling such arrangements can, where appropriate, be considered in overall strategies for deployment of clergy and parish reorganisation, to the benefit of parishioners. Finally, the close links with parish clergy can provide the chaplain with support and also with a stronger sense of being tied into the life of the Diocese. The chaplain at Institution 7 sounded a note of warning that it was extremely difficult for one person to perform both roles. As with so much else therefore, a great deal depends on there being a good working relationship between parish priest and chaplain – a factor that would need to be carefully considered at the appointment of both.

5. CONCLUSION

All the relational complexes within which the chaplain must work have inherent ambiguities within them. There is thus a significant risk that chaplains experience isolation in all of them. This can be felt as a sense of remoteness from the institution, as misunderstanding on the part of ecumenical colleagues, and as a lack of appreciation of the chaplain's work within his/her sponsoring denomination; they may fall into the gap between Church and institution. We have been concerned at finding too many chaplains, of all denominations, emerging from this study as not having a clear role that is understood and owned by all the parties with whom and to whom they work; as being answerable to no-one for the hands-on aspects of their work; and as not experiencing the adequate support and supervision that their frequently lonely work requires.

At the same time, we believe that there is an important lesson that dioceses can learn from the experiences of their HE chaplains. All the chaplaincies studied have made, or are making, a transition from the relatively stable situation that prevailed in previous generations to a far less secure way of working. Rather than waiting for people to come to them, they need to engage in constant networking, forging strategic alliances with ecumenical partners and individuals of good will of no particular faith within the institution. They increasingly have to engage with non-religious aspects of university life (committees of various student associations, for example) in order to establish a credible presence on the ground. Their patterns of working are constantly being adapted and changed.

In its negotiation of this shifting scene, the HE chaplaincy may prove to be a microcosm of the broader Church. The breakdown of stable patterns of chaplaincy life and work that we observe there may reflect or fore-shadow a slower but no less real transition at parish level. The sense of scale will be different, but the imperative for the future mission for the English and Welsh Catholic community is also to break out of the self-enclosed world of traditional parish life into a more willing engagement in partnership and in dialogue beyond its own confines. Examples for the way forward, and warnings of some of the difficulties, can be taken from the current experience of chaplaincies, their students and their chaplains:

I think we are somewhere between fifteen and thirty years ahead of the rest of the country. Not prophetic in an, 'Aren't we clever, we're prophetic…' Prophetic in a sense that they are going to take longer to get there. (4.2)

RECOMMENDATIONS

1. Chaplaincy provision for HE should be made a mainstream element within individual diocesan strategic and pastoral planning.

2. Annual sharing at diocesan clergy gathering of principal developments/issues for chaplaincy work, not only in HE but in other sectors too, to promote more effective communication and understanding within the local Church about ministry. This should lead to proposals about how best to build on the work of chaplains in order to integrate students and ex-students into the local Church.

3. National guidelines are needed to cover formal agreements between universities, the Church and chaplains (similar to guidelines developed for school chaplains). These should cover rights and duties (including a job description), arrangements for remuneration, resources, accommodation, access, reporting and appraisal. These guidelines could be drawn upon when chaplain appointments are being considered. Such formal processes would help to ensure continuity between appointments, that equal opportunities issues are addressed, that effective communication between all parties is secured (with appropriate ecumenical sensitivity), and that lessons are learned from the previous incumbent. However, entry into formal arrangements should be carried out with discernment, and a recognition that the ambiguities inherent in relationships between the chaplaincy and the institution may sometimes be beneficial.

4. Where possible, priest chaplains should be identified early and given an extended period of preparation time (ideally several months) in which induction and training could take place.

5. Proper systems should be set in place for the support and supervision of the chaplains. Where appropriate consideration should be given to setting up a chaplaincy steering group, which would include representatives from the student body, university staff, local Church – both clergy and lay, both Catholic and ecumenical – and chaplaincy. Its functions could be similar to that of a school governing body, providing direction, accountability, support, advice and liaison; serving as a critical friend; and encouraging development plans for chaplaincy work.

6. Parish links can be a fruitful source of support and synergy for students, parishioners and chaplains alike. These should be fostered wherever possible.

7. An ecumenically agreed understanding of underlying principles relating to ecumenical chaplaincies, as expressed in the current state of HE, would be an enormously useful basis on which local agreements and local practices could be soundly built. Consultation should be initiated at the level of Churches Together in England, and Churches Together in Wales (Cytûn) to establish such an understanding.

8. Ecumenical and interfaith dialogue at national level is needed to address the wider issues relating to interfaith chaplaincy.

9. All resident chaplaincies should be reviewed to ensure that procedures for the protection of vulnerable adults are fully reflected in their systems

10. Chaplains managing resident chaplaincies should be given formal focussed initial and in-service training about their legal responsibilities.

Chapter Two

INTERSTITIAL INTERVENTIONS: THE WORKPLACE ECOLOGY OF UNIVERSITY CHAPLAINS

JOHN SULLIVAN

The focus of this chapter is on university chaplaincy as a workplace. A major theme in the report, *Dancing on the Edge* is the liminal nature of the work of chaplains, both in relation to much of what goes on in universities and also in relation to much of what goes on in the church that chaplains represent. Such liminality can carry negative overtones of uncertainty and lack of direction (and support), of marginalisation and lack of effectiveness. It can also, however, suggest something more positive: in contrast to so many other workers who find that they are over-managed, over inspected and under-appreciated, chaplains might avoid the prospect of excessive regulation, experience freedom to operate independently and creatively and enjoy the benefits of being able to spend much time helping people to focus on matters of enduring worth and on issues which have deep personal significance. In response to this reading of the burdens and (potential) benefits of liminality, I will explore the notion that one way of understanding the work of university chaplains is that it entails (in addition to whatever else it entails) the making of interstitial interventions. That is, university chaplains can do much good work in the crevices and gaps that can be found in any large organisation. If my use of 'interstices' refers to spaces that open up and opportunities that occur which must be recognised and responded to quickly, my use of 'interventions' acknowledges the fact that a great many activities of chaplains are often episodic, short-term experiments and initiatives, that fall short of attracting the label of strategy or policy, but which validly give expression to a long-term vision. Often such interventions cannot carry large numbers of people along with them; they are necessarily relatively small-scale efforts. However, such interventions can make a positive difference, helping people, and institutions, either to change direction, or to stay on course in the face of temptation or pressure to do otherwise.

I come at this chapter from a number of angles, each of which offers certain kinds of access to the work of university chaplains, yet each of which simultaneously limits what I see. First, there is personal experience of being a beneficiary of the work done by chaplains. Second there is professional contact, past and present, with and on behalf of chaplains. Third, there is the wider perspective on chaplaincy brought about cumulatively as a result of the blending of my professional experience - as a senior manager, as an institutional leader and as a management consultant - with long-term academic reading in the fields of theology, education, philosophy, leadership and staff development. These three angles of vision lead me to adopt an eclectic approach, one that draws upon personal, professional and academic dimensions of my own experience.

With regard to the first angle, as a full-time undergraduate student, in the very different university world of the 1960s, I felt then, and continue to believe now, that I derived enormous benefit from the work of chaplains, in terms of their example of how to be a thinking, caring, creative and committed Christian in an increasingly secular culture. The chaplains I encountered offered me inspiration, guidance, comfort and challenge. Leisure and social life, community worship and personal spiritual development, study and opportunities to exercise the responsibilities of service – all were extended by chaplaincy activities. As a part-time research student a decade later, I experienced university chaplaincy as a place where liturgy transcended what was available in a normal parish while displaying a creative fidelity in relation to tradition. The chaplaincy also provided a place of hospitality and welcome that allowed me to adjust to the atmosphere of university without denying or leaving behind me the worlds of work, home and wider family. Visiting speakers and ecumenical events widened my perspectives in various non-threatening ways.

As for the second angle, many years later, as a university professor, I enjoy various collaborative endeavours with chaplains, appreciating the leaven effect they have on my own institution. I had the privilege of being closely involved in their initial appointment, and I continue to play a key role in their appraisal. In addition to first-hand experience of drawing on the services of and collaborating with university and college chaplains, I have been involved professionally with various groups of school and university chaplains, providing in-service training or teaching them on Master's courses. In a previous appointment in higher education I came to know well and very much admire the special role developed by the chaplain, observing his influence on the Principal, tempering institutional requirements with humane responses, sometimes mediating in disputes between staff or students, sometimes operating as a catalyst of change that was needed, as well as being impressed by the way he constantly was a source of good news, pastoral care and inspiration for students and colleagues.

Three things on the third angle need to be said. First, my professional experience in leadership and management has shown me the huge range of factors that impact upon institutional life and the types of responses people make within their work context, from resistance, to compliance, to commitment. Second, leaders have to be guardians of the vision and changing the culture is one their principal tasks, as they bring together people, purposes and practices. One might say that, like teachers, leaders have to be realistic, in seeing how things are now, but also idealists, in seeing what is not yet but could be, and effective, in bridging the gap between the two. Third, I have a special interest in clarifying, for myself and for others, the interaction between the factors that are being brought to bear on the context one is in, the purpose of an organization, a role or a project, and the match (or mismatch) between the approaches adopted and these contexts and purposes.

Each of these three angles of approach has important limitations. First, as a beneficiary of chaplaincy, I must acknowledge that there are many student experiences for which I cannot speak, most obviously those of women, international students, students without religious affiliations, those less interested in intellectual exploration and those of a younger generation than myself (though a few aspects of the latter are occasionally and indirectly gleaned from my four children, whose ages in the year this is being written – 2006 - are 34, 32, 31 and 19). Second, despite my extensive professional contact with chaplains, I have never exercised their role and thus necessarily lack inside knowledge of it. Third, with regard to reading and study, two particular limitations come quickly to mind: first, I have conducted no extensive study of the work of chaplains; second, their work can just as usefully be 'read' through the 'lens' of several other disciplines than my own areas of specialism, for example, with insights drawn from sociology, psychology, politics and pastoral theology.

Thus I embark on this chapter with some relevant experience and many limitations. I approach it, not in a systematic manner, nor within the parameters of one particular discipline, rigorously pursued, but simply by first, identifying some features of the working environment that university chaplains must take into account, second, by bringing out some of the paradoxes inherent in the personal qualities required by and the balancing acts expected of chaplains, and third, by exploring similarities and differences between the work of chaplains and what we usually imply by the term 'professional.' In section one, I discuss the phenomenon of managerialism, defects in the education system, fragmentation and separation as particular challenges for chaplains to address and finally how chaplains can help the personal development of students by facilitating a focus on the big questions of life that can so easily be neglected. In section two, there is an examination of five different balancing acts that chaplains have to manage: between commitment and criticism, between being strongly rooted yet displaying great flexibility, between the possession of an enduring set of beliefs and values and the capacity to be up-to-date in service of effective communication, between giving and receiving, and finally, in doing justice to the contrasting and sometimes conflicting expectations of different clients. In section three, I consider how closely the work of chaplains matches features normally associated with the work of professionals. Then I bring out the need for a balance between the subjective and objective aspects of chaplaincy. Following this, I apply four notions from the literature on work to chaplaincy: these are notions of 'fit', of 'psychological self-employment', of 'distance' and 'the shadow side'. In conclusion, I very briefly compare my chosen metaphor for the work of university chaplains with some alternatives. The national context I draw from is England, although I believe that many of the issues that are discussed here have wider application.

1. THE UNIVERSITY CONTEXT

Universities, like many other public bodies, have been colonised by economic priorities and perspectives. This has led to work intensification and depersonalisation through increased numbers and reduced time for face-to-face contact. The intrusion of managerialism, associated with such features as the all-powerful metaphor of the 'market', increased scrutiny and accountability, strategies that control research, universities serving government-led social engineering and the promotion of entrepreneurialism, and the emphasis on competencies all have been subject to recent commentary (for example, Barnett, 2003; Evans, 2002; Loughlin, 2002; Pattison, 1997; Protherough & Pick, 2003; Robinson & Katalushi, 2005; Sullivan, 2000; Sullivan, 2003). Roberts refers to the 'systematic application of the means of securing ever greater *efficiency, calculability, predictability and control*, sometimes known academe and how these might be subverted in order for a healthier learning environment to emerge, Rendon argues that the stress on mental knowing and accompanying rationality and objectivity happens at the expense of attending sufficiently to the inner life and knowledge of students and that competition is excessively privileged over cooperation and mutual dependence (Rendon, 2005). She shows the coherence (and relevance for an expanded appreciation of the nature of learning) of various developments at the borderlands between education, psychology, cultural analysis and spirituality. Among these developments she cites Howard Gardner's work on multiple intelligences, Daniel Goleman's advocacy of emotional intelligence and Danah Zohar and Ian Marshall's exploration of spiritual intelligence.

Gardner suggests there are seven principal types of intelligence (although this figure has both grown and diminished as he encounters critical response and as his research continues): these are linguistic, logical-mathematical, spatial, musical, bodily-kinaesthetic, interpersonal and intrapersonal (Gardner, 1993). It is generally accepted that universities over-privilege the first two of these, linguistic and logical-mathematical, and that they neglect the others. Goleman's analysis of emotional intelligence includes self-awareness, motivation, self-regulation, empathy, adeptness in relationships (Goleman, 1995). It shows the connections between cognition and emotion and fosters intelligence about some of the more enduring and important aspects of our lives. Zohar and Marshall's exposition on spiritual intelligence brings to the fore qualities such as flexibility and self-awareness, the capacities to face and use suffering, to transcend pain and to be inspired, a reluctance to harm others, a tendency to ask why and what is questions, the ability to work in ways that are constrained by conventional thought (Zohar & Marshall, 2000). Increasingly there are signs that some businesses are becoming alert to the potential of spiritual intelligence as they seek to deploy more effectively their workforce, although some writers, such as Madeleine Bunting, have complained that, by allowing themselves to be complicit in such managerial ruses, employees respond to 'missionary management' by 'putting their heart and soul' into the job and slip into becoming 'willing slaves' (Bunting, 2004).

Chaplains have a role to play in finding spaces and creating opportunities, interstices in university life, for students to consider their inner selves, to engage more holistically, to ask the existential questions that courses do not address, to see themselves in a wider context than 'module fodder' or as part of 'the intellectual production line in the industrial halls of late postmodern capitalist society' (D'Costa, 2005, p.ix). What are these questions? Among them would be included the following. Who am I? Where and with whom do I belong? How have we got here? Why are we here? What might we become? What is really important and worth striving for? How can I make sense of my experience? Where are we going? How can we cope with life's setbacks and our own shortcomings? What kind of community are we building? How do we sort our priorities? Some of these questions will arise from life outside of study, in experiences of residential life at university, in relationships, in work, in community service, clubs, societies and sports, in leisure and other voluntary activities. However, there should also be opportunities for these questions to be addressed in the curriculum, in assignments, prescribed reading and projects. Whether or not the institution fosters such opportunities, it is likely that chaplains will play a key role in helping students to find gaps in the timetable to pause and to face the questions. If the system as a whole promotes a consumerist mentality towards the accumulation of credits and 'knowledge packages,' this can easily slip into surface engagement by students who are tempted to attend what is required, collect what they are entitled to, enjoy what they can and move on as quickly as possible. No matter how central or peripheral to the formal life of the institution that chaplains find themselves to be located, they will wish, without intrusion into privacy, to facilitate attention by students to their inner development – 'the sphere of values and beliefs, emotional maturity, moral development, spirituality, and self-understanding' (Astin, in Chickering, Dalton & Stamm, 2006, p.vii). As Alexander and Helen Astin point out, 'Self-understanding is fundamental to our capacity to understand others: our spouses, partners, parents, children, friends, co-workers, and neighbours, not to mention people of different races, religions, cultures, and nationalities' (Astin, in Chickering, Dalton & Stamm, p.viii). Unfortunately, the fragmented and incoherent approach to education that arises from the emphasis on competencies, technical skills and free-standing (and self-selected) modules amount to the construction of a curriculum experience that resembles an easily dismantled Legoland rather than a serious initiation into the demands and internal goods of long-standing traditions.

2. BALANCING ACTS

Here I note some of the contrasting facets of, apparent paradoxes within and balancing acts required by the chaplain's role. First, without a deep sense of duty and commitment to the institution and its members, the daily demands it and they present would be experienced as inexorable, confusing, debilitating and alienating. Yet loyalty must be tempered by the capacity and willingness to criticise where this is needed. Chaplains must not be subsumed into the institutional machine, which always threatens to dominate other considerations, to undermine community and to sacrifice individuals. Sensitivity to one's own pain, and its causes, is key to recognising the pain of others, and what brings this about. This, in turn, alerts one to the need to address dysfunctional dimensions of institutional life.

Second, without a deep sense of fixed identity and rootedness with regard to her or himself, the chaplain could offer no stability, nor show consistency of response. When we do not display a degree of predictability, those who approach us do not feel confident about how we will react to them. Yet, perhaps more than with many other roles that are played, the chaplain must display flexibility and responsiveness. Many factors come into play here. University populations are constantly shifting, containing a growing number of part-time, mature and international students, as well as students who continue to live at home. There is a huge diversity among students, in terms of class, race, religious affiliation, nationality, intellectual capacity and experience of life. University regulations (imposed from within and externally) are frequently modified. Students experience the loosening of control over their personal lives and an opportunity to experiment with freedom. Then there is the critical and questioning nature of university life, which erodes or dissolves many previously held certainties. Many students work to pay their way, thereby leaving less time for engaging in other kinds of sporting, leisure, political, social and cultural pursuits. In order to maximise use of rooms and to enhance the timetabler's capacity to meet the needs of diverse academic programmes, there is decreasing space and time for community-building. Reduced personal contact between faculty and students is a consequence of severe pressures brought about by increasing student numbers without a parallel increase in staffing, aggravated by the intense pressure on staff to increase productivity from research for external assessment exercises. Without flexibility and rapid responsiveness, the chaplain will miss many opportunities that arise only fleetingly in the maelstrom that university life often seems to be. In a context of constantly shifting boundaries, changing goalposts and mobile horizons, the chaplain needs a strong sense of inner direction and regularity if s/he is to be able to provide space for others. However, if this inner-directedness and personal regularity slip into rigidity and being slowed down by baggage, it is possible to miss the moment that has to be seized. Although always working within constraints, the chaplain has to travel light enough to be able creatively to subvert and transcend them on occasion.

Third, part of this balance between personal steadiness and capacity to move relates to the intellectual 'equipment' and personal formation of chaplains. They need to be able to draw upon a fully internalised and appropriated set of beliefs, habits and values that will serve them reliably in multiple and diverse contexts, often when what is required is an immediate response, with no time for deep reflection or new thinking. However, without demonstrating the capacity to be current, up-to-date and relevant in their communication modes and metaphors, they will not catch the attention or capture the imagination of those they hope to reach.

Fourth, there is a balance to be struck between giving and receiving. Chaplains find themselves called to be available to many people, often at a moment's notice, freely giving themselves away. Surely to carry this off for any sustained period of time requires a lifeline or personal back-up system, one that offers the nourishment of intimacy, affirmation, belonging, relationship, either from a partner, from friends, from peers or from a community. To avoid burnout and being swallowed up by the incessant demands and yet often inadequate or incompletely satisfying response and feedback, while remaining dedicated and committed, chaplains must be ready to say 'no' as well as 'yes'. To say yes to others often means saying no to oneself. However, if we always say yes to others and no to our own needs, in due course that constant yes becomes a tired and tawdry gift, much less worth offering.

A fifth kind of balancing act that chaplains have to conduct is that between the various 'clients' they serve. These will have different, indeed sometimes, conflicting, expectations. I pick out four types of 'clients' or areas of focus. One part of the role is to address some of the personal needs for pastoral support of students and staff and sometimes of their families. A second dimension is to understand and relate to the central academic tasks of higher education, the transmission, promotion, development and application of knowledge. A university chaplain without a keen interest in the life of the mind is probably in the wrong environment. However, surprising though it may seem to some, intellectual pursuits and the search for truth are not always helped by some of the institutional priorities, structures and systems that operate. Thus, an effective chaplain is discerning about the gaps between rhetoric and reality, between the espoused purposes and the actual effects of organisational ways of working. Third, chaplains represent a faith community that extends far beyond the confines of any particular university. Links with their sponsoring faith community should be maintained, so that there is a two-way flow of insights, support mechanisms and challenges between the university and the faith community. This is regardless of arrangements for remuneration, resourcing, oversight or other kinds of provision or involvement by that faith community. Furthermore, in an age when it is acknowledged that the ecumenical imperative and the promotion of mutual respect and good relations between people of different faiths is integral to the work of any Christian, then commitment and loyalty to a particular tradition must be combined with openness to and willing collaboration with those of other traditions. Finally, chaplains help their university to keep in mind the common good of the local, national and global society in which they are located and to which they should contribute. Thus, chaplains play a part in widening horizons, helping people move away from resting in a consumerist, inward-looking and self-seeking mentality and encouraging awareness of and responsiveness to external needs. Thus one might claim that the chaplain has to be capable of moving easily between these several areas of focus for their attention and energies: there is the cognitive focus of the academic life; there is a pastoral and therapeutic focus in serving students; there is a spiritual focus that mediates between a religious tradition and the university context and there is a moral focus as chaplains assist in turning attention towards the world beyond the campus. Intervening in the interstices between the personal, the academic, the institutional, the religious and the social, chaplains have to combine consistency of values and flexibility of response as they move back and forth between these aspects of their work.

3. PROFESSIONAL AND PERSONAL

To what extent is university chaplaincy similar to and different from other professional work? Professions have intellectual, technical/practical and moral dimensions. Gardner & Shulman identify six characteristic features of professions:

1. a commitment to serve in the interests of clients in particular and the welfare of society in general;

2. a body of theory or special knowledge;

3. a specialized set of skills, practices and performances unique to the profession;

4. integrity under conditions of both technical and ethical uncertainty;

5. an organized approach to learning from experience ... and thus of growing new knowledge from the contexts of practice;

6. a professional community responsible for the oversight and monitoring of quality (Gardner & Shulman, 2005, p.14).

Chaplaincy work displays some of these characteristics, but not all. The first and fourth characteristics are evidently applicable to them, but the same cannot yet be claimed for the others. As for the second and third characteristics, if we ask what prior education, training and preparation chaplains require, we find that there is no clear template of expectations by universities or the church. There is no required body of knowledge that must be brought to the arena of university chaplaincy, even if there are desiderata. The fifth and sixth characteristics belong together, with the sixth being a prerequisite for the fifth. Although there are informal networks that bring chaplains together, there is no single confraternity that comprises a professional body. There are no publicly acknowledged mentors or models for how the tasks of chaplaincy are to be conducted. There are no agreed rules of engagement. Appointments to chaplaincy positions are ad hoc rather than systematic and display various degrees of rigour. If we focus on the career structure for chaplains, again we find no obvious picture. Chaplaincy often features as a valuable interruption, stepping stone or sideways move, but not as an integral feature within a career and with no apparent lines of progression being available. As for standards and accountability, there are no established procedures agreed between church and university for dealing with substandard work by chaplains. Although there is a great deal of learning from experience, this tends to be at the personal level and is not necessarily fed back into either universities or churches.

However, despite my comparison, at first unpromising, of chaplaincy work with the notion of professionalism, there is an important aspect of professionalism that chaplains should hold onto. This relates to the interweaving of the subjective with the objective dimensions of the role. An interesting convergence about the need to preserve a creative tensions these two dimensions can be seen in two publications from 2004, each of which is aimed at an international audience: the first, *Philosophical and Spiritual Perspectives on Decent Work*, is the fruit of deliberations between the International Labour Office and the World Council of Churches, both based in Geneva (Peccoud, 2004); the second, *Compendium of the Social Doctrine of the Church*, produced by the Pontifical Council for Justice & Peace in Rome. Both of these documents stress the need for attention to be paid to the material or objective conditions in which work takes a place, yet always keeping in mind the subjective and spiritual dimensions of the worker. The objective conditions include 'the sum of activities, resources, instruments and technologies used by men and women to produce things' (Pontifical Council, 2004, p.157). They also include considerations such as health and safety, remuneration and the right to form associations and join a union (Peccoud, 2004; Pontifical Council, 2004). The subjective dimension is closely linked by the International Labour Office with ethical concerns: is there space in the workplace for dignity, respect, responsibility, justice, solidarity and care? (Peccoud, 2004, p.46). The Pontifical Council (p.157) describes the subjective dimension of the worker as 'the activity of the human person as a dynamic being [with a] personal vocation.' The subjective 'must take precedence over the objective', according the Pontifical Council (p.158).

One way of distinguishing between the objective and the subjective, in the context of this chapter, is to consider the objective as referring, not only to the conditions under which the chaplain works, and the circumstances, which include cultural, social, institutional, and ecclesial aspects, but also as referring to what has to be done to meet the needs of the various clients mentioned earlier. The subjective can then be taken to refer to the inner life of the chaplain. This inner life will include passions that link purposes and values with emotional investment. As some recent commentators on work in the professions have claimed, 'an integration of passion and professionalism is notoriously difficult to sustain in the course of a working life' (Damon et al, 2005, p.28). The very personal investment required to exercise the role effectively can be destructive as well as a source of creative energy. 'Keeping a sense of mission alive while not letting it get out of hand is possible only for those who really believe in the mission and have enough self-perspective to remain wary of dangers such as arrogance, megalomania, misguided beliefs, and a host of other distorted or mistaken judgements that anyone can have form time to time' (Damon et al, p.29). As Damon and his co-authors suggest, 'Finding the right equilibrium between analytic distance and human connection is a tension that appears in some form in all professions' (Damon et al, p.30). Chaplains will recognise the challenge entailed by maintaining this equilibrium. The same tasks can be experienced, at different times, neutrally, as a duty, negatively, as a burden, or positively, as a joy. What turns the activity from one experience into another will be a combination of both subjective and objective aspects that are complexly and mutually interactive and impossible entirely to separate. As two other recent commentators on work have astutely asserted: 'A profession becomes a vocation when those doing it believe that its challenges matter, and when the work connects them to what they value most' (Nakamura & Csikszentmihalyi, 2005, p.62).

As a way to cast a little more light on the nature of the workplace environment and role of chaplains and especially to bring out more fully how the objective and subjective dimensions are interwoven, I briefly deploy four notions drawn from literature about the world of work. These are, first, the notion of 'fit', second, of 'psychological self-employment', third, of 'distance,' and finally, the 'shadow side' of organisational life. Let me start with the double-sided nature of 'fit.' Professor of Government, Russell Muirhead has recently analysed key aspects of how work can fit us and how we can fit our work. He distinguishes between "social fit" and "personal fit." The first relates to the match between what we can offer and what society needs. The second is more concerned with whether our work meets our needs. 'Work is a good fit when it calls on the aptitudes and talents through which we can best contribute to society. ... When our abilities are aligned with the tasks or jobs society needs performed, work fits. This is "social fit"' (Muirhead, 2004, p.2). Although it can be pleasing that our work meets the needs of others and even more pleasing if we can legitimately believe that we are doing such work well, this does not necessarily guarantee that there is a personal fit. 'We might still find that the work fails to engage our interests, purposes and most distinctive capacities' (Muirhead, p.2). It is one thing to know that our work is doing some good for others; this is, however important, not the same as feeling that this work is doing us some good and expressing who we are in any adequate manner. A personal fit with work 'contributes to our own development [and] engages us in the service of ends we endorse, expresses something of who we are, or develops our powers in ways we experience as good' (Muirhead, pp.2, 49, 170). Although social fit and personal fit are connected, they not easily reconciled. While we can cope for a while if personal fit is partly sacrificed for the sake of social fit, we cannot sustain over the long haul its total neglect, for this will cause the springs of our motivation and creativity to rust over and eventually be eroded. Like other professionals, chaplains need to keep a watchful eye over the match they experience between the demands of flexibility (if there is to be a social fit) and the elusive promises of fulfilment (if there is to be a personal fit). 'The tension between serving social needs and serving our own purposes is at the heart of the problem of meaningful work' (Muirhead, p.49). Social needs and our own purposes should not be seen as operating entirely separately. Both will change over time, according to changing (external) circumstances and growing (internal) maturity. Although we may begin a line of work, such as chaplaincy, with a strong sense of what we hope to achieve in it, we should be open to the ways that the very purposes we sought to put into practice as we began can come to be seen in a very different light as we struggle with the realities, successes and disappointments that come with more experience. That is, purpose can not only be brought *to* our job, but they can also emerge *from* being immersed in it. In this sense, our mission is simultaneously both partly behind us, driving us on, and partly ahead of us, waiting to be discovered, yet attracting us forward.

Next, I consider what might be meant by being psychologically self-employed, since attention to this notion might help us to ensure that social fit does not undermine our ownership of our work. One way to describe professional ownership is, to use a phrase from psychologist Robert Kegan, hiring the 'psychologically self-employed' (Kegan, 1994, p.170). I take this phrase to mean that, despite the fact that someone else devised our job, set the parameters for our role and even calls us to account for how well we meet their priorities, this still leaves us space for creativity; we can put our own stamp on the work. As Kegan, (quoting Roland Barth) puts it, 'the discrepancy that matters is not between "what I am doing" and "what they want me to do," but rather between "what I am doing" and "what I want to be able to do"' (Kegan, 1994, p.170). When this discrepancy is transcended, then professional ownership is possible.

Kegan offers a very useful analysis of key aspects of being a worker, all of which I believe apply to professionals. He says we are expected as workers:

1. To *invent or own our work* (rather than see it as owned and created by the employer).

2. To *be self-initiating, self-correcting, self-evaluating* (rather than

dependent on others to frame the problems, initiate adjustments, or determine whether things are going acceptably well).

3. *To be guided by our own visions* (rather than be without a vision or be captive of the authority's agenda).

4. *To take responsibility for what happens to us at work externally and internally* (rather than see our present internal circumstances and future external possibilities as caused by someone else).

5. *To be accomplished masters of our particular work roles, jobs, or careers* (rather than have an apprenticing or imitating relationship to what we do).

6. *To conceive of the organisation from the 'outside in,' as a whole; to see our relation to the whole; to see the relation of the parts to the whole* (rather than see the rest of the organisation and its parts only from the perspective of our own part, from the 'inside out')" (Kegan, 1994, pp.152-153).

In my view, none of Kegan's first five points here either imply or require an unduly individualistic understanding of or approach to professional ownership; his final point directly contradicts such a narrow interpretation. That is, they complement, rather than undermine, the need for social fit, as described above. I believe that most chaplains would acknowledge that, in the interstices of their workplace and in the midst of the multiple demands of their diverse 'clients', there is still scope for interventions that flow from personal fit in the form of psychological self-employment as outlined by Kegan.

While Kegan's notion of being psychologically self-employed requires a high degree of voluntariness and thus implies the absence of coercion, this does not rule out the exercise of strong influences which we might choose to accept. The third notion, taken from the literature on work, which I find helpful in guiding practice, is that of distance. Being a professional involves, among other things, establishing the right distance between oneself, the service one provides and the recipient. The self can intrude too much, distorting the activity, and imposing on the recipient, leaving them, in this case, the student, with insufficient space for *their* initiative. This is establishing too little distance, or under-distancing. However, the self can remove itself too much, rendering the service mechanical rather than personal. This is over-distancing. Philosopher

Mike Martin puts it thus: "Proper professional distance is a reasonable response in pursuing professional values by avoiding inappropriate personal involvements while maintaining personal engagement and responsibility. In contrast, under-distancing is the undesirable interference of personal values with professional standards. And over-distancing is the undesirable loss of personal involvement, whether in the form of denying one's responsibility for one's actions or in the form of failing to care about clients and community" (Martin, 2000, p.86). In the case of under-distancing, one's own feelings intrude too much on the other person and on the activity; in the case of over-distancing, they are insufficiently engaged. When there is under-distancing, what the professional wants dominates the activity; when over-distancing occurs the professional fails to own their actions or the results of these. There are salutary lessons here for chaplains, who must reflect occasionally about how this notion of distance applies to them.

Fourth, I suggest that chaplains might be rewarded by reflection on the relevance of 'the shadow side' of work. Gerard Egan reminds managers of the need to become fully aware of the 'shadow side' of their organisation: 'the unspoken, unacknowledged, behind-the-scenes stuff that stands in the way of getting things done efficiently, or even getting things done at all (Egan, 1994, p.xi). "The shadow side consists of all the important activities and arrangements that do not get identified, discussed, and managed in decision-making forums that can make a difference" (Egan, 1994, p.4). Among the categories of shadow-side activity Egan includes organisational culture and social systems, individual styles and behaviour, internal politics, and the hidden curriculum that is conveyed (Egan, 1994, p.8). In the shadow side there is the hiding of defects, unwritten rules of conduct, deliberate ignoring of policy, alternative renderings of priorities and the putting up of facades. In the shadows one might find indifference, naivety and cynicism as well as structures of influence that parallel rather than overlap with official structures. Egan identifies the damage caused by leaving the shadow side in place as including psychological, social and financial aspects. It can disrupt relationships, distort priorities, undermine productivity or effectiveness, waste time, blur communication, lead to confusion and dissipate concentration of focus and energy. The shadow side is the place where good practice is ignored or insufficiently built upon and where poor practice is left uncorrected. It can also be a place where the past exerts too strong a hold or where change meets its strongest opponents. Given the huge range of clients they deal with, the multiple constituencies they serve, the numerous encounters they experience, the contrasting perspectives they have to negotiate and the diverse aspects of the life of their universities that they come to see, chaplains will recognise the crucial importance of being discerning about the shadow side of their organisation. The shadow side will offer allies and opponents, welcome opportunities and awkward challenges, gaps between worthy ideals and less attractive actual practices that can be lamented or creatively exploited.

*** *** ***

University chaplaincy, as a place of work, could be said to be dancing on the edge, if we wish to emphasise its often liminal nature in relation to the church or to the university. It could be said to be like dancing over the depths or being suspended over 70000 fathoms, to echo Kierkegaard (Kierkegaard, 1968, p.208), if we wish to emphasise the feeling of risk that accompanies it. Dancing involves a cycle or pattern of holding on and letting go, of moving forward and falling back, of turning around, of entering into the music and being carried by its melody and rhythm. Chaplains should be good dancers and catholic in their musical tastes. In addressing institutional, intellectual, spiritual, personal and social needs in the university, chaplains will come into contact with efforts to promote (and to resist) various types of ownership, proprietary, professional and participative (Sullivan, 2005), finding themselves simultaneously belonging and not belonging to the guardians of the university mission, the other academic and professional staff who contribute to university work, the large numbers of students, ancillary staff, visitors and members of the public they encounter during the course of a typical year, and the wider community of the church they represent. I could have used the metaphor of bridge-building to describe their work, but this might have implied either that they are there to be walked over or that their work merely involves bringing people together without the personal investment and exposure that chaplaincy inevitably demands. An alternative metaphor might have been signing on dotted (that is, not joined up) lines or putting one's signature on moving lines, to acknowledge the dynamic and fluid nature of university life. Again, while doing justice to the personal contribution, this signature metaphor fails to do justice to social fit. My chosen metaphor for chaplaincy work, interstitial interventions, is meant to imply that, despite liminality, work at the margins can be fruitful, that one has to know the shape of the big pieces and be conscious of where the edges are in order to slip into the gaps, that one has to put oneself 'on the line' if the intervention is to be felt by others, and that discernment is required in order to be able to recognise the best places and times to make such interventions. This means that chaplains have to be ready to be vigilant, visible and vulnerable.

REFERENCES:

Barnett, Ronald, *Beyond All Reason*, Buckingham: Open University Press, 2003.

Bunting, Madeleine, *Willing Slaves*, London: HarperCollins, 2004.

Chickering, Arthur, Dalton, Jon & Stamm, Liesa, *Encouraging Authenticity & Spirituality in Higher Education*, San Francisco: Jossey-Bass, 2006.

Damon, William, Colby, Anne, Bronk, Kendall & Erlich, Thomas, 'Passion & mastery in balance: toward good work in professions,' *Daedalus*, summer 2005, pp. 27-35.

D'Costa, Gavin, *Theology in the Public Square*, Oxford: Blackwell, 2005.

Egan, Gerard, *Working the Shadow Side*, San Francisco: Jossey-Bass, 1994.

Evans, G. R., *Academics and the Real World*, Buckingham: Open University Press, 2002.

Gardner, Howard, *The Unschooled Mind*, London: Fontana, 1993.

Gardner, Howard and Shulman, Lee, 'The Professions in America today: crucial but fragile,' *Daedalus*, summer 2005, pp.13-18.

Goleman, Daniel, *Emotional Intelligence*, New York: Bantam Books, 1995.

Kegan, Robert, *In Over Our Heads: The Mental Demands of Modern Life*, Cambridge, Mass: Harvard University Press, 1994.

Kierkegaard, Soren, (translated by David Swenson & Walter Lowrie) *Concluding Unscientific Postscript*, Princeton: Princeton University Press, 1968.

Loughlin, Michael, *Ethics, management and mythology*, Abingdon: Radcliffe Medical Press, 2002.

Martin, Mike, *Meaningful Work*, New York: Oxford University Press, 2000.

Muirhead, Russell, *Just Work*, Cambridge, Mass: Harvard University Press, 2004.

Nakamura, Jeanne & Csikszentmihalyi, Mihaly, 'Engagement in a profession: the case of undergraduate teaching', *Daedalus*, summer 2005, pp.60 – 67.

Parks, Sharon, *Big questions, worthy dreams: mentoring young adults in their search for meaning, purpose, and faith*, San Francisco: Jossey-Bass, 2000.

Pattison, Stephen, *The Faith of the Managers*, London: Cassell, 1997.

Peccoud, Dominique, *Philosophical and spiritual perspectives on Decent Work*, Geneva: International Labour Office, 2004.

Pontifical Council for Justice & Peace, *Compendium of the Social Doctrine of the Church*, Rome: 2004.

Protherough, Robert & Pick, John, *Managing Britannia*, Exeter: Imprint Academic, 2003.

Rendon, Laura, 'Recasting Agreements that Govern Teaching and Learning: An Intellectual and Spiritual Framework for Transformation,' *Religion & Education*, 32(1), Spring 2005, pp.79 – 108.

Roberts, Richard, *Religion, Theology & the Human Sciences,* Cambridge: Cambridge University Press, 2002.

Robinson, Simon, and Katalushi, Clement, *Values in Higher Education,* St Bride's Major, Vale of Glamorgan: Aureus and the University of Leeds, 2005.

Steiner, George, *Lessons of the Masters,* Cambridge, Mass: Harvard University Press, 2003.

Sullivan, John, 'Wrestling with Managerialism', in *Commitment to Diversity*, edited by Mary Eaton, Jane Longmore & Arthur Naylor, London: Cassell, 2000, pp.240 – 259.

Sullivan, John, 'Skills-based models of leadership' in *Religion In Education* volume 4, edited by William Kay, Leslie Francis, & Keith Watson, Leominster: Gracewing, 2003, pp.205 -232.

Sullivan, John, 'The Dynamics of Ownership,' *Journal of Education & Christian Belief*, 9 (1), Spring 2005, pp.21 – 33.

Zohar, Dana & Marshall, Ian, *Spiritual Intelligence*, New York: Bloomsbury, 2000.

Chapter Three

A SPIRITUAL PRESENCE ON THE FRONTIER

KEVIN EGAN

Theologians writing today in the area of pastoral care pay attention to context. Whether one acknowledges it or not, all pastoral care takes place in a particular context such as a school, a parish, a hospital, the workplace or in a higher education setting. One of the most significant contributions of the report *Dancing on the Edge* is that it describes in detail the context in which chaplains and chaplaincy teams work. Ask those whom the chaplain serves to describe the role and you will get a wide range of different and in some cases conflicting answers. Ask the chaplains themselves to explain what are they about and they struggle to find words that will adequately describe their role. Whatever difficulty one experiences in trying to describe the role of chaplain, no one will dispute that the chaplain on the ground needs to have clarity about their role in order to do the work. In this paper I wish to propose a job description for a chaplain. I describe the chaplain as "A Spiritual Presence on the Frontier." Here I have in mind not just the role carried out by the chaplain but his/her symbolic presence in an institution of learning. Several of the contributors to this volume share a similar view that spirituality is at the core of chaplaincy,

How do you understand spirituality?

Recently a colleague and I facilitated a conference for CN3, Chaplains' Network @ Third Level in Ireland. As they conversed in small groups we asked them to address the following questions: How do you understand spirituality? Do your students see themselves as being spiritual or religious? Do you see yourself as working in the area of religion or spirituality? Sometimes it is only after you've asked a group to address a question that you discover how difficult it is to answer. What I discovered is that the conversation which takes place around the question is of more value than the answer itself. It came as no surprise that spirituality is an elusive term to describe let alone define. For this reason experiential descriptions of spirituality work much better than conceptual definitions. This is not to deny that the latter are very necessary. I find it insightful to listen to the words people use to refer to spirituality, words like energy, connection, meaning and lifestyle. I especially appreciate Ronald Rolheiser's description of how spirituality functions in one's life:

> We all have a spirituality whether we want one or not, whether we are religious or not. Spirituality is more about whether or not we can sleep at night than about whether or not we go to church (Rolheiser, 1999, p.7).

The quotation makes direct reference to what disturbs sleep, in other words, anxiety. Spirituality helps one to face the "limit" experiences of life, suffering, death, failure, abandonment, uncertainty - all of which are the sources of much anxiety.

If you ask people to describe spirituality you will find that certain common themes surface. One of them is connection - a sense of being connected to others, connected to mystery, connected to those who came before and those who come after. In this context, spirituality refers to the diverse ways we answer the heart's longing to be connected with the largeness of life. It consists in giving oneself to something bigger than oneself.

At the chaplains conference which I facilitated I showed participants a clip from the movie Rabbit Proof Fence and asked what had it to say about spirituality? The story concerns three girls who run away from an orphanage in Australia in the 1930's. If an Aboriginal woman had a child by a white man, the law prescribed that the children be taken from her and raised by the state. Thousands of children were taken from their mothers and raised in orphanages throughout Australia. At the time it was government policy to train aboriginal children as domestic workers and integrate them into white society. The movie is based on a true story where the three girls evaded their captors and walk 1,500 miles to where their mother lives. Spirituality is a central theme in the movie; the spirit of the children, the spirit of the people who helped them with food etc. There is one scene where the local storekeeper informs their mother that the children have run away from the orphanage. She goes and rests her hand on a great wire fence that runs by the store. This fence runs down through the middle of Australia, dividing the country into east and west. It was put there to confine the rabbits into one part of the country. Just after you see their mother with her hand on the fence you see a shot of the children discovering the fence and holding on to it. They are no longer "lost;" they know the fence can lead them home. I would describe this as a mystical moment in the movie. Children and mother are separated by over a thousand miles yet they are connected and have a sense of hope, that all will be well - to paraphrase Julian of Norwich. The short clip conveys to us that spirituality is about courage, kindness, practical help and connection.

DO YOU SEE YOURSELF AS SPIRITUAL OR RELIGIOUS OR BOTH?

The academic literature on spirituality draws a distinction between spirituality and religion. The distinction goes back to William James who argued that there are two kinds of religion, internal and external, personal and institutional (Tacey, 2004, p.140). According to Sandra Schneiders, religion is in trouble and spirituality is in the ascendancy (2000, p.1). Contrary to what some may think, spirituality is by no means incompatible with religion but it is existential rather than creedal. It is "intensely intimate" and is not imposed by an outside authority (Tacey, 2004, p.8). People readily confuse religion and spirituality and therefore dismiss spirituality. Many young people today will describe themselves as spiritual rather than religious. Some of the young people at the conference I facilitated did not see the two as opposed to one another. As they saw it, one could be both spiritual and religious, though some would describe themselves as more spiritual than religious. Research supports this position The relationship between "being religious" and "being spiritual" is not a zero-sum proposition. In other words, they are not distinct but interdependent concepts. In America most people see themselves as both (Marler & Hadway, 2002, p.297).

The question we should be asking ourselves is what do our students mean when they use these terms and what nuances of meaning should we be listening for? I am impressed when I hear young people making these distinctions because it means that they are not thinking in black and white terms. In using these terms young people are putting a distance between themselves and organized religion. It is almost as if the journey is what is important at this time for them, just like the 'journey' home is what is important for the children in the film. There is a danger that leadership in organized religion might interpret this distance as rejection. I think a more accurate interpretation would be: "we don't understand your language, your symbols or your rituals; rather than we want nothing to do with you." In the past organized religion tried to claim ownership of spirituality with the result that a spirituality which was not attached to organized religion was seen as deficient in some way.

David Tacey in his book *The Spiritual Revolution: The Emergence of Contemporary Spirituality,* quotes an Australian Catholic Priest who asks: "How can the churches get excited about the new spirituality if it is not putting bums on church seats?" (Tacey, 2004, p.20). I could not imagine my friends working in chaplaincy services making this comment. Chaplains are in a unique position to see spirituality as an inclusive term covering all pathways that lead to meaning and purpose (Tacey, 2004, p.38). According to Tacey "we need a new language of the spiritual that does not collapse the spiritual into one or another competing religious traditions" (2004, p.203).

YOUTH SPIRITUALITY

I addressed this topic recently when speaking to a conference of third level chaplains. I searched for an image to describe youth spirituality and gave this quotation from David Tacey:

> Youth spirituality is like an underground stream beneath our ordinary work, and yet this stream is rarely noticed. It keeps flowing, but the life-giving waters are not utilized, tapped or directed into the dry places of culture. Adult society marches ahead with a business-as-usual attitude, while the large volumes of spiritual water surge forward silently, beneath notice, towards some unknown destination (Tacey, 2004, p.51).

My purpose is presenting this quotation was that I wanted to suggest to chaplains that spirituality is alive and well. People are by nature spiritual beings and so their spirituality must be operative someplace in their lives - the image of an "underground stream" captures this. It also suggests to chaplains where to look for spirituality - look for it below the surface in obscure places. "Youth spirituality may not be very churchy, but that doesn't make it non-religious or anti-Christian" (Tacey, 2004, p.79). One of my nephews recently undertook the ritual pilgrimage of adult transition namely, the trip to Australia. I see his spirituality present in his courage to travel, his trust in his friends that they would take care of one another, his generosity to share his funds when he was the one with the steady job, his efforts to stay connected with family and friends at home. If we are serious about encouraging spirituality in young people we need to provide a place where they can tell stories about their experience and explore its depth dimension. Some of the most effective spirituality programmes today are tapping into young peoples' thirst for travel and providing them with experiences where they spend time in a developing country and have an insertion experience. Built into such programmes is the provision of time where the experience can be reflected on and the stories told.

Tom Beaudoin, in his book *Virtual Faith: The Irreverent Spiritual Quest of Generation X (1998)*, identifies four theological themes characteristic of Generation X:

i. an abiding suspicion of religious institutions

ii. the sacred nature of experience

iii. the religious dimension of suffering

iv. ambiguity - a hesitancy to affirm religious orthodoxies and deep uncertainty about self and gender (1998, pp.177,178).

Young people have a strong "post-modern" scepticism about the validity of eternal truths and explanations. They are searching for a "post-modern" spirituality. The challenge is to make contact with the inner life of the student which is where spiritual formation begins.

SPIRITUAL LEADERSHIP

The population served by the college chaplaincy (both students and staff) is characterised by diversity. There are people at many different stages in the life cycle, people of different cultural and racial backgrounds, people with different gender and sexual identities. In terms of spirituality, there are those who could be described as "spiritual dwellers," in the sense that they identify with a particular tradition and feel at home there. Others could be described as "spiritual seekers." They see themselves as spiritual but do not feel at home in any tradition. Then there are others who might be described as "anonymously spiritual." On a conscious level they don't see themselves as spiritual yet their values and the way they live indicate that they are. Many of the chaplains I have spoken with are searching for ways to make contact with this group.

The National Ecumenical Agency in Further Education (NEAFT) with the support of the Learning and Skills Council (LSC) has recently produced an excellent resource handbook for chaplains: *Faith and Further Education: A Handbook (LSC, 2005)*. Drawing on the work of G. W. Sollis, the authors speak of chaplaincy as encompassing three roles: the caring pastoral role, the spiritual guide, and the moral guide (LSC, 2005, p.15). I would like to emphasise the institutional dimension of the spiritual guidance role. Essentially it involves caring for the "soul" of the institution. The following comment from a chaplain aptly illustrates this role. "My principal tells me she wants me to be independent of the college structure. She wants me to tell her how it really is in the college, and not to hold back if things are going wrong" (LSC, 2005, p.16). The spirituality of an institution is expressed partly in its guiding myths and assumptions. The chaplain has a role to play in helping the institution to critique and inform these. What I am referring to here is the prophetic role of the chaplain vis-a-vis the institution. I was exploring recently with a group of chaplains their relationship with the educational institution where they work One of them made the comment that while there is an expectation that they will provide a professional service, there is also an expectation that they will not "ruffle any feathers." The group acknowledged that this expectation influenced how they carried out their role. They were able to identify several "justice issues" in the College that they had neglected to address.

There are new developments taking place in the field of workplace spirituality which explores spiritual not just in personal terms but in organizational terms. Spirituality can best be understood at a variety of levels ranging from individual to organizational. The spirituality of organizations finds its foundation in the spiritual nature of the human person; because we are social beings, spirituality will have a social dimension. Institutions can be said to have a personality, an inner disposition, a "soul" analogous to but separate from the individuals that form them. This is referred to as the spiritual dimension of the organization (Howard & Welbourn, 2004, p.43). The spirituality of an organization resides in the vision, values, policies, practices and culture that shape how it goes about doing its business. When a learning organization becomes self-serving and ignores the purposes for which it was founded, its spirituality becomes diseased. With regard to institutions of learning, one can legitimately ask the question: What is the spiritual purpose of this institution?

The job of a chaplain would be much easier if there existed a consensus among educational leaders that their institution has a spiritual purpose. The institutional role of the chaplaincy service would be much better understood and supported. The fact that this is not the case, does not take from the urgency or validity of the task. I would want to say to chaplains of all faiths that one of your main tasks is to nurture the "soul" of the institution. Only if you attend to this task will the institution develop its potential for promoting human well-being. I will offer some suggestions as to how you might do this when I explore strategies for promoting spiritual well-being.

Why Opt for a Spiritual Role?

I can see distinct advantages in using "spiritual" rather than "religious" language to describe the work of chaplaincy services and the chaplaincy role. I am using the term "spiritual" in the wide sense to encompass a variety of roles. I will begin by enumerating the reasons in favour of the term "spiritual."

- It allows one to address what is acknowledged as a universal human need or dimension of the human person.
- It can serve to build a bridge with a generation alienated from churches and institutionalised religion.
- It allows one to connect with both "dwellers" and "seekers" - those who feel at home in the tradition and those who do not.
- Since spirituality transcends denominational boundaries it does not leave one open to the accusation of proselytising.
- As we have seen, spirituality has a personal and organizational dimension. If one describes the work of the chaplain in terms of nurturing the spirit then the role can be seen to embrace both caring for the spiritual needs of students and staff and the "soul" of the institution.
- The report *Dancing on the Edge* vividly described the "tensions" under which chaplains work. Describing that role in terms of nurturing the spirit does not remove those tensions. However, it does point to a creative way of living with them.
- If one conceives of the role in broad terms then new and exciting opportunities will emerge for providing spiritual leadership.

I will now attempt to lay out the case "against" moving away from the "religious" or denominational role.

- It will involve moving away from a well established and accepted way of working and the giving up of ground that was hard fought for.
- There is a danger of losing what is distinct about one's religious identity and tradition.
- There is a danger of losing denomination support which is crucial to the provision of present day services.
- There is a danger of neglecting the pastoral needs of students and staff who wish to belong to a distinctive Church community.

- The less spirituality is connected with a religious tradition that more vulnerable it becomes to being hijacked by groups and individuals with an agenda that may be far from spiritual.

As I list the reasons "for" and "against" I ask myself what kind of change am I envisioning? To use terminology from the world of business, I am talking more of a change in brand name rather than a change of ownership. Of course a number of students will always maintain their denominational roots and chaplains their denominational links. However, if the service is to respond to a changing population and emerging needs, it needs to go through some sort of identity transition and present itself in a new way.

Over the past few months I have been involved in conversations with third level chaplains and hospital chaplains. The focus of the conversations was around addressing emerging needs in their work. While there are many complex issues to resolve I was deeply impressed by the high level of commitment and energy in both groups. The entry of lay persons and women into the service has changed it greatly. The level of student involvement in chaplaincy teams is high. Students told me how it is very difficult for them to be involved on a parish level at home because the parish system is so closed, whereas at college the chaplaincy service is open and supportive of involvement. Chaplaincy services are changing. The "gap" between the faithful and those who lead them is much less in chaplaincy services than it is in others areas of church life, for example, in parishes.

There is no point in aspiring to give spiritual leadership if one is not living a spiritual life. The nature of chaplaincy work is such that one could not engage in it for any length of time without having spiritual resources. The greatest resource available to chaplains is the quality of their own spiritual life and support system. Last year I conducted an end of year conversation with a chaplaincy team. I opened it with a question inviting the chaplains to talk about an incident connected to their work that touched them in some way. Both they and I were taken back by the depth of our discussion. I felt we were in a sacred place and the telling of the story proved to be a spiritual experience for us who were listening. It became clear to me that despite the difficult nature of the work this group of people live and work out of a spiritual place. Their work impacts on their faith and their faith informs the work. I am in no doubt that such a group of people have the basic requirement to give spiritual leadership.

THE CHAPLAIN AS INTERPRETATIVE GUIDE TO THE LEARNING COMMUNITY

Institutions of higher education hold a special place in the story of human development. They perform a meaning-making function and for this reason their work has a spiritual dimension. The sad thing is that many institutions of learning do not recognize this. For historical reasons they broke their denominational ties and since then have denied that they have any spiritual mission. Yet, the very activity of learning calls for openness to truth which is in essence a spiritual stance. Learning, it has been said, is "experience understood in tranquillity" (Handy, 1997, p.225). The contemplative stance is basic to the learning process. Who better to teach, foster and promote this stance than the college chaplaincy service?

The Quaker writer Parker Palmer in his book *The Courage to Teach* explores the inner landscape of a teacher's life. Teaching, like any truly human activity, emerges from one's inwardness. "As I teach I project the conditions of my soul onto my students, my subject and our way of being together" (Palmer, 1998, p.2). He stresses the communal dimension of teaching. "To teach is to create a space in which the community of truth is practiced" (1998, 90). I see the chaplain as a key member of this learning community. In the words of Charles Gerkin his/her role is to be an "interpretative guide" in that community (1986). Sometimes this role is carried out in a pastoral care context where one helps a student to make sense of what is going on in their life at this point in time. On another occasion the context may be academic, where the chaplain assists colleagues in accessing the religious tradition in order to throw light on some topic under consideration.

THE ROLE OF MENTOR

I am attracted to terms which can be used to describe the chaplaincy role in non-religious language. Sharon Daloz Parks in her book *Big Questions Worthy Dreams: Mentoring Young Adults in Their Search for Meaning, Purpose and Faith* speaks of institutes of higher education as mentoring communities in the formation of adult faith. She sees faith in universal rather than denominational terms. It is present in the every day activity of meaning-making (2000, 26). In her view, human development, meaning-making and educational-professional practice are interrelated. Higher education is distinctive in its capacity to serve as a mentoring environment for the formation of meaning and faith. "Every professor is potentially a spiritual guide and every syllabus a confession of faith"

(2000, 159). The role of spiritual guide is not unique to the chaplain. However, he or she professes to have a specific training and competency in this area.

Sharon Daloz Parks has a background in developmental psychology. It is no surprise to find her stressing not just the role of mentor but the importance of a mentoring community (environment). Her description of the qualities of such a community could equally apply to the college as a whole or to any of the services that make it up such as the chaplaincy service. Her description of the features of a mentoring environment gives one a sense of the functions performed by an educational institution and the chaplaincy service within it:

i. It provides a network of belonging and serves as a community of confirmation and contradiction.
ii. It extends hospitality to the "big questions" - questions of meaning, purpose and faith. (cf. Appendix I of this chapter).
iii. It provides an opportunity for an encounter with otherness - those who are outside of one's tribe.
iv. It provides initiation into habits of mind that make it possible for young adults to hold diversity and complexity and to wrestle with moral ambiguity.
v. It helps to develop and articulate the dream which in its fullest and most spiritual sense is a sense of vocation (Parks, 2000, pp.136-148).

Once a chaplaincy team has some clarity around these functions and tasks, then it can go about planning and putting programmes together to promote these. It is also in a better position to collaborate with others who share a commitment to some of the same tasks.

The theme of vocation is one which can be explored without having to use explicitly religious language. In workshops I frequently explore with participants Frederick Buechner's notion of vocation as "the place where your deep gladness meets the world's deep need" (Buechner, 1993, p.119). The language he uses is very experiential and spirituality begins with experience. He starts with the self and then moves towards the needs of the world. His definition corrects many of the false "religious" understandings of vocation which insists that our lives must be driven by "oughts" (Parker J. Palmer 2000, 15). It is possible to explore spiritual themes without getting bogged down in religious language. It is possible to find a language to talk about the spiritual with people who do not share one's spiritual tradition.

SPIRITUAL LEADERSHIP IN THE LEARNING COMMUNITY

I think there is great potential in Margaret Wheatley's understanding of the role of leadership as providing a place where conversations can take place (2002). She notes that change begins when two people share a concern and engage in a conversation. I would suggest that conversation is the preferred mode for engaging in the work of spiritual development. Conversations about what? Sharon Daloz Parks would say conversations about the big questions. Frederick Buechner might want us to talk about those times when our deep gladness meets the world's deep need. The kind of conversation I am talking about calls for openness and vulnerability. One should not expect to emerge from a real conversation intact. To quote the poet Seamus Heaney, a real conversation will "catch the heart off guard and blow it open." Such conversations may be rare in our institutes of higher education yet they are the very stuff the institution should be about. In this context one could ask: How might the chaplaincy service take leadership in providing opportunities for such conversations?

I intend to answer this question by telling stories about people who have tried to do this in a variety of settings. Naturally, I will start with myself! I teach a course entitled "Spirituality in the Workplace" on a Masters Programme in Management for Voluntary and Community Services. Most of the students have a management role in the organization they work with. At the beginning of the course students struggle to come to terms with the word spirituality and its relevance to management. Some take a slightly "paranoid" stance and see it as a course to bring religion in by the back door. Each year I find the course only gets off the ground after the students have completed their first assignment. The assignment is simple; to have a conversation with a colleague or friend about the spiritual dimension of their work. The doing of the assignment shatters their preconceptions and assumptions. Contrary to expectations they find that the interviewee readily engages in the conversation. They discover a depth to colleagues they never thought was there, and for many the exercise proves to be a spiritual experience in itself. I quote some comments from students who wrote on their response to the exercise:

"The interview refreshed me at the end of a busy week."

"What began as an assignment, and an exercise in information sharing, became an experience that challenged and enriched me."

"I found the process of carrying out the interview a calming and spiritual experience."

This exercise has convinced me that the way to nourish spirituality is to involve people in conversations about what matters to them.

Stephen Pattison writes of his experience in being invited by the NHS to explore spirituality with health workers. Instead of giving lectures he set out to provide a forum where people could tell stories. He found that it is possible to enquire into the spirit of the NHS by way of its symbolic structures embodied in images, myths, rituals, disciplines and narratives. He makes the point that "the stories organizations tells about themselves and their activities, the foundational myths that guide the organization, are enormously important for providing orientation and direction" (Pattison, 2000, p.17). One way of gaining an insight into the spirit of an organization is to try to find a visual image for it. Stephen Pattison describes an image that came to him as he tried to think about the "personality" of a teaching hospital he used to know well. The image that presented itself was of "a wizened old man in a white coat sitting on his own in a room high in a tower and counting money with an avaricious expression on his worried face" (Pattison, 2000, p.15). The image aptly captured the "soul" or spiritual state of the hospital at that point in time. It leads to an understanding of the hospital in which the bottom line is finance.

Inviting people to use images can be a very effective way for exploring the spiritual dimension of an experience. Images invite us to relate to them. An image "discloses and surprises by revealing familiar and unexpected aspects of meaning in our experience" (O'Connell Killen & deBeer, 1994, p.38). I can't but notice that the title of the research paper *Dancing on the Edge* make use of an image to describe the role of chaplain. At the CN3 Conference I referred to earlier, we invited chaplains to come up with an image of how they saw themselves and their work. We also asked them for an image of how they saw the chaplaincy and the institution they worked in. This is a "right brain" exercise. I was impressed by the way participants engaged in it. They were able to name things that otherwise would never have been acknowledged.

After I read the *Dancing on the Edge* report I let my imagination run and came up with the following image for the role of chaplain. I found myself comparing the chaplain to a practitioner of alternative medicine who gets hired by a mainstream Medical Centre. By and large the medical staff are happy to have this person in the Centre. However, the management informs him that the NHS will not give him professional recognition. They advise him not to make his presence too obvious and that they will have to find alternative ways of paying him. Does this image relate in any way to your experience of being chaplain?

Recently I read an article in the *Journal of Pastoral Care and Counselling* which tells the story of how a group of hospital chaplains responded to staff members who were interested in finding joy, "finding soul" in their work again (King, Jarvis & Cornwell, 2005). For over a year they discussed programmatic ways to address this issue and came up with the "Finding Soul at Work" programme. The primary purpose was two-fold: "to deepen our sense of soul at work" and "to contribute to the soul of the institution." The secondary purpose was three-fold: "to build small group community, to learn from one another, and to foster seed-cells to go forth and talk about these issues with other staff informally" (King, Jarvis & Cornwell, 2005, p.265). What the programme did was provide a space where stories could be told. One of the conclusions of the groups was that "soul" could be found in groups like this. One of the goals of this programme was to foster community. Time and time again I find that whatever one does to build up community in an organization also contributes to the growth of spirituality within it.

IN CONCLUSION

I have been making the case for placing spirituality at the centre of the chaplaincy project and promoting it in an inclusive and all embracing manner. I have tried to demonstrate that spirituality needs to be nurtured not just at a personal level but at a community and institutional level. I have gathered together some reports/stories of people who have undertaken this task in a variety of settings. In the course of this I find myself using a wide variety of terms to describe the role of the chaplain: a spiritual presence or guide, a mentor, an interpretative guide in the learning community, a spirit-linking leader. Describing what you do with a focus on spirituality will not solve all your problems. There remain numerous difficulties to be overcome. For example, ambivalence over definitions of spirituality, the tendency to equate spirituality with institutional religion, the danger that some group (denomination, institution) may try to hijack the process for their own ends. To quote David Tacey "we are caught in a difficult moment in history, stuck between secular systems we have outgrown and religious systems we cannot fully embrace" (2004, p.2). If the mystery we call God is active in our world our experience of the sacred is going to be uncertain, creative and full of surprises. Those who sense a call to nurture the spiritual are by no means backing a losing horse. As Karen Armstrong points out, as soon as God is declared dead, God is found to be alive again because the archetypal idea expresses itself in a new way (1993, p.408). It takes spiritually attuned people to be alive and attentive to the emerging spirituality, to see in this present crisis an opportunity for new thinking and new ways of being "religious."

APPENDIX I

What are some the questions young adults ask?

- Who do I really want to become?
- How do I work toward something when I don't even know what it is?
- Am I loveable?
- Who will be there for me?
- Why is suffering so pervasive?
- What are the values and limitations of my culture?
- Do my actions make any real difference in the bigger scheme of things?
- Do I want friendship, partnership, marriage? If so, why? With whom?
- What is my society, or life, or God, asking of me? Anything?
- What is the meaning of money? How much is enough?
- Is there a master plan?
- Am I wasting time I'll regret later?
- What constitutes meaningful work?
- How have I been wounded? Will I ever heal?
- What do I want the future to look like - for me, for other, for my planet?
- What is my religion? Do I need one?
- What are my real talents, preferences, skills, and longings?
- When do I feel most alive?
- Where can I be creative?
- What am I vulnerable to?
- What are my fears?
- How am I complicit in patterns of injustice?
- Will I always be stereotyped?
- What do I really want to learn?
- Do I want to bring children into the world?
- How do I discern what is trustworthy?
- Where do I want to put my stake in the ground and invest in life? (Parks, 2000, pp.137-138).

REFERENCES:

Armstrong, Karen. 1993. A History of God. London: Heinemann.

Beaudoin, Tom. 1998. Virtual Faith: The Irreverent Spiritual Quest of Generation X. San Francisco: Jossey-Bass.

Gerkin, Charles. V. 1985. Widening the Horizons: Pastoral Responses to a Fragmented Society. Philadelphia: Westminster Press.

Handy, Charles. 1997. The Hungry Spirit. London: Hutchinson.

Howard, Sue & David Welbourn. 2004. The Spirit at Work Phenomenon. London: Azure.

King, Stephen D. Jarvis Debra & Cornwell, Marilyn. 2005. "Programmatic Staff Care in an Outpatient Setting" Journal of Pastoral Care and Counselling. Vol 59.No. 2. Fall 2005 p. 263-273.

LSC. 2005. Faiths and Further Education: A Handbook. Coventry: LSC.

Marler, Penny long & C. Kirk Hadaway. 2002. "Being Religious" or "Being Spiritual" in America: A Zero-Sum Proposition." Journal for the Scientific Study of Religion. 41:2. p. 289-300.

McGrail, Peter & Sullivan John. 2005. Dancing on the Edge: A Report into Catholic Chaplaincy in Higher Education. Conference in Catholic Bishops in Catholic Education.

Palmer Parker J. 1998. The Courage to Teach: Exploring the Inner Landscape of a Teacher's Life. San Francisco: Jossey-Bass..

Palmer, Parker J. 2000. Let Your Life Speak: Listening to the Voice of Vocation. San Francisco: Jossey-Bass.

Parks, Sharon Daloz. 2000. Big Questions Worthy Dreams: Mentoring Young Adults in Their Search for Meaning, Purpose and Faith. San Francisco: Jossey-Bass.

Pattison Stephen. (2000) "Organizational Spirituality: An Exploration." Modern Believing. Vol 41. No 2.

Rolheiser, Ronald. 1999. The Holy Longing: The Search for Christian Spirituality. New York: Doubleday.

Schneiders, Sandra. 2000. 'Religion and spirituality: strangers, rivals, or partners?'.In The Santa Clara Lectures (California), 6 (2), p 1.

Tacey, David. 2004. The Spiritual Revolution: The Emergence of Contemporary Spirituality. Hove, East Sussex: Brunner-Routledge

Wheately, Margaret. 2002. Turning to One Another: Simple Conversations to Restore Hope in the Future. San Francisco: Berrett Koehler.

Websites:

http://www.teacherformation.org
http://www.neafe.org
http://www.lsc.gov.uk

Chapter Four

A SEAT AT THE TABLE?
CHAPLAINCY AND STUDENT SERVICES
IN A CHURCH UNIVERSITY

STEVEN SHAKESPEARE

ADVENTURES IN LILLIPUT

I stared at the chair, thinking 'How on earth do I get into that? And how will I get up again?' As a parish priest and school governor at the local church primary school, I was sizing up the seating arrangements for my first governing body meeting. We gathered in a classroom, and it was only then that I realised just how small primary school chairs had to be. In the end, it was a slightly comical sight, as governors in various stages of middle-aged spread squeezed into undersized seats and tried to fit their now gargantuan legs under the table.

The issues we faced as governors were often driven by national factors and politics, be they curriculum questions, league tables or workload agreements. And there were also significant local dimensions to our situation. How were we to be a church school in a deprived, multifaith area? The children came from a host of backgrounds and cultures, including a significant number from Somali Muslim homes. Many spoke little English when they arrived at the school. The problems of broken homes and crime overshadowed quite a few young lives.

I begin here, because for me this was an important experience of being on the interface between church and world. It was a place which was both marginal and central at the same time. Marginal, because our school did not register on league tables despite its enormous impact for good on the achievements of children; and because the interests of the church could not simply assume centre stage. We always had to engage in dialogue with agendas that were not our own, and discourses for whom Christian faith was an unknown or threatening quantity. But it was also an experience of centrality. As I moved to become chair of the governing body, I became aware of the huge privilege we had in helping to shape the ethos of an institution which was to form the lives of young people for years to come.

Squashed into our tiny chairs, the governors were made physically aware of the children and families we served, and of the sometimes uncomfortable nature of the roles and realities we had to negotiate. I believe that discomfort was important. It helped us do a better job, because it grounded us (almost literally!) in the life world of the school.

The experience of chaplaincy in a church-founded university can sometimes be eyed enviously by chaplains in secular higher education contexts. Having worked part time in a large secular university chaplaincy team, I can relate to this. In a church foundation, chaplains seem to enjoy an acceptance and status for which their colleagues in other settings have to work very hard indeed, with no guarantee of success. Church university and college chaplains work from a position of acceptance and strength. They have their seat at the table.

There is some truth in this judgement. But like any simple picture, it hides a more complex reality. This paper will explore the opportunities, dangers and ambiguities which surround chaplaincy in church universities, particularly with regard to its relationship to wider structures of student services.

It is relevant to focus on the partnership with student services, because this is an area where the boundaries become either fluid or contested, depending on your point of view. The priorities of the sector, the institution and the professions represented in student services encounter the self-understanding of chaplains. And chaplains, even when employed by their university, also face a church constituency. They have to tell some kind of story about how their work relates to the missions of the university and of the church. Here, the edge upon which chaplains dance becomes an interface, a meeting of worlds.

BEGINNING WHERE WE ARE

My current context, Liverpool Hope, is a university with an ecumenical (Anglican and Roman Catholic) foundation. It came into being as a result of a merger of three colleges, two Catholic and one Anglican, originally founded by the churches to promote teacher training. Liverpool Hope has always had an emphasis on extending educational opportunities. Two of its founding colleges were established in the mid-nineteenth century to extend such openings to women.

Now a full university, Liverpool Hope has over 7000 students, about a thousand of whom study in a dispersed network of regional sixth form colleges. Its main campuses are in south Liverpool and inner city Everton, the latter being the focus for work in creative and performing arts. Alongside education and arts, it now offers a range of opportunities across the humanities, social sciences, sport and health, business and computing sciences.

Liverpool Hope's mission statement says that it is 'an ecumenical Christian foundation', which strives, amongst other things, to educate 'the whole person in mind, body and spirit' and 'to sustain an academic community, as a sign of hope, enriched by Christian values and worship'. In its statement of values, the university says that one of its aims is 'to take faith seriously, being fully Anglican, fully Catholic, fully ecumenical, fully open to those of all faiths and beliefs'.

The university is thus open about its Christian origins, and committed to bringing its Christian ethos to bear on its current work. Arguably, some HE providers in the UK with a Christian foundation have sought to play this down over recent years, seeking a more comfortable accommodation with a pluralistic, if not secular, society. This has not been the case at Liverpool Hope. Under recent institutional leaders, its distinctiveness as a university rooted in Christian traditions has been acknowledged and celebrated. Without in any way detracting from the critical freedom of academic enquiry, or the inclusiveness of its recruitment and support policies, it has sought to foster public engagement with Christian thought and values among students and staff.

The articulation of a 'mission' by an institution (or its leaders) and the way that mission is interpreted, owned or implemented by staff and students, is of course a very complex business. All sorts of partial, selective and critical readings of the mission occur. Nevertheless, the leadership of the institution seems to offer a healthy opening in which chaplaincy work can be welcomed and affirmed.

That work is embedded within the institution in significant ways. Two full-time chaplains, Catholic and Anglican, are employees of the university, along with a chaplaincy assistant. The chaplains are line-managed by an assistant vice-chancellor in charge of student support and well-being. They take part in the same salary scales and performance review rounds, and are subject to the same policies and procedures as other members of staff. And they are located within Student Services, alongside providers such as counselling and health, accommodation, student funds, careers, support for students with disabilities and others. The co-ordinating chaplain attends fortnightly meetings of the heads of the various student services, and both chaplains meet with the assistant vice-chancellor every two or three weeks.

In some ways, therefore, the chaplaincy is spared some of the anxiety about role, institutional location and accountability articulated by some chaplains in *Dancing on the Edge* and elsewhere. However, the critical question then arises as to whether the chaplaincy's seat at the table isn't just a little too comfortable.

Does the chaplaincy lose its distinctive or prophetic voice? Does its role and identity get squeezed into a box, its contribution only understood in a very narrow way? In short, does life get too easy for well-accommodated chaplains, who lose that sense of speaking on and for the margins, and promoting the transformative gospel of the kingdom?

BEING THERE

Dancing on the Edge remarks on the ambiguity that frequently attends chaplains' relationship to the university they serve. Lack of formal structures can have the negative effect of making the chaplains' role opaque to the institution. Personal relationships play an important role. That's fine when the personalities involved 'click', but it is liable to leave chaplains out on a limb when key personnel change. Equally, a change of chaplain can leave the new post-holder having to start again from scratch.

In this context, the relationship of chaplaincy to student services at Hope provides an important defining context and stakeholder position within the university. It enables several things to happen (Robinson, 2004, p.91).

Firstly, it clarifies the chaplains' structure of accountability, plugging them in to a system of management and review. This sends out important messages. To other staff, it underlines the fact that chaplains are colleagues 'in the same boat', sharing working conditions, budgetary frameworks and the like. To students, it provides an institutional underwriting for the work chaplains do. They are not mavericks, pursuing their own idiosyncratic agenda, but university staff. They can be expected to abide by university codes of conduct and policies, and subjected to the same disciplinary and grievance procedures as other staff. For instance, when a student made a complaint about an aspect of the chaplaincy's work at Hope, it was important that an agreed process was in place, through which the issue could be resolved in a transparent way by the university itself.

Secondly, it compels the chaplaincy to take seriously the overall mission and strategies of the university, and conversely provides an opportunity for chaplains to inform wider debates about student welfare. For example, the chaplains at Hope have been able to raise issues of concern about inappropriate evangelistic activity by various groups on campus. This was prompted by various instances: external groups coming on to the campus to proselytise without any authorisation; Christian groups –'cold-calling' on other students or putting undue pressure upon them to convert; publicity for events which was not honest or open about the evangelistic nature of the activity. Chaplains were able to offer an understanding of these groups and the ability to open dialogue with them, whilst acting as 'gatekeepers' for the university community. The support of the rest of Student Services in producing guidelines on this area was crucial.

On the other hand, chaplains have been expected to play a part in aspects of the student experience, from induction to personal tutoring to graduation. Their presence and input at university occasions like these is the norm. This is especially important in a church foundation, where chaplains also need to resist defining their role solely in relation to committed Christian students. Their vision needs to be expressed as a concern for the whole body of the university, a topic to which we shall return.

Thirdly, the link encourages co-operation between different services. At Hope, this has meant working with colleagues on a special induction day for mature students with families, offering events as part of the international students' programme, sharing information and concerns with the counselling service, or using the careers service's network of publicity to promote vocations events.

Chaplaincy thus benefits from easier working relationships with other aspects of student services. It is not that personal relationships and goodwill cease to matter, but that there is a more transparent context within which mutual confidence and goodwill can be fostered. The 'normality' of chaplains being involved in many different aspects of the work of student services is particularly important in a church university. It helps chaplains to 'earth' their sense of how the values of the kingdom of God relate to the real issues and agendas of students and staff. It helps them to perceive more deeply what it means to see the university as already within God's purposes, not as strange and hostile territory, into which they have to 'inject' a sense of God's presence. Conversely, it means that when the university talks about student welfare, its own mission commitment to taking questions of faith seriously is not marginalised or ignored. Chaplains can help to keep alive the rumour of the university's founding vision and ethos, and be provided with the space and resourcing to make an effective contribution

If this model offers strong advantages to chaplains – especially in a church university – we must nevertheless face a lingering question. Does it institutionalise chaplaincy to such a degree that its cutting edge is blunted?

ONE-EYED CHAPLAINCY?

Any institutional arrangement for chaplains will have negative aspects. After all, human institutions share in human imperfection and fallenness – and chaplains can be co-opted into structures which hinder the expression of their calling.

No institutional location is neutral. Being part of student services certainly offers chaplains a significant opportunity of engaging with university life. However, it can also involve chaplains in collusion with the way religion and faith can be compartmentalised and processed by secular discourses – discourses which are present and active in church universities as they are in all parts of contemporary culture.

The disadvantages of this position might include the following dimensions:

1. BUYING INTO A NARROW VIEW OF STUDENT WELFARE

It is possible to envisage the chaplains getting so sucked into an essentially secular 'social work' model of student care, that the distinctiveness of what they have to offer is lost. An example from my previous part time involvement in the chaplaincy of a large secular university can help to tease this out. The full time chaplain was (unusually) employed by the university and was part of student services. Partly due to this, and partly because of the personal expertise of the chaplain, the chaplaincy was given the task of providing 24 hour emergency response cover, to cases of student pastoral distress. The chaplaincy was expected to act as a kind of safety net for student crises. However, this model not only imposed unsustainable and sometimes inappropriate demands on the chaplaincy team, it also led to the loss of emphasis upon substantial faith concerns. (The practice was eventually reviewed and changed, with crisis response being located elsewhere in student services).

Without wishing in any way to disparage practical, pastoral care as an expression of Christian ministry, this example shows how particular models of care can result in a reductive approach on the part of the chaplaincy. If chaplains bear witness to the holistic sense of God's presence in the university, they need to explore ways of integrating pastoral care with prophetic witness, worship, and a Christian engagement with the life of the university and the business of teaching and learning. Far from being a narrow or sectarian view of chaplaincy, it is this kind of dialogical approach to ministry and mission which allows Christian faith and the concerns of the university to enrich one another.

This point is especially important to chaplaincy in a church university, where the dialogue between faith and reason is embedded in the heart of the university's mission. Chaplains have a role in keeping that conversation alive and in the public realm, resisting the privatisation (and commodification) of religious belief and practice.

It is therefore vital that church university chaplains seek multiple ways of engaging with the life of the university, and do not confine themselves to partnership with student services (though this remains a core commitment). For example, in Liverpool Hope, chaplains have worked with colleagues in widening participation on making connections with young people from faith schools. They have offered input to the curriculum, in lecturing, seminars and panel discussions. They lead worship as one part of the centrally organised 'foundation hour' programme, which sets aside an hour each week for people to gather and reflect in different ways on the university's mission. They sit on a 'Mission and Values' group which advises the Vice-Chancellor on maintaining and deepening the university's Christian ethos, and which brings together representatives of academic deaneries, the students' union, governors and others.

Other church universities will offer different, sometimes greater, opportunities for chaplains. The point is that chaplaincy ministry (though often working with very small numbers of people at any one time) has to see the bigger picture. This should not be mistaken for hubris. For one thing, it is a recognition that chaplains have to work in partnership, and that the university's mission is not the preserve of Christian 'professionals' but needs to be owned across a broad constituency.

2. ALLOWING THE INSTRUMENTAL ENDS OF THE UNIVERSITY TO OVERRIDE THE INTRINSIC VALUES OF THE GOSPEL

Higher education is big business – and a political football. It can become target-and finance-driven. The danger for chaplains is identifying so strongly with their institution that they lose critical perspective on this, or on more local issues.

In fact, it is too simplistic to contrast the values of a secular commercialised world with some supposedly pure and pristine account of the gospel. The gospel is made known in incarnate form, it engages with a broken world from within. I am not suggesting that chaplains should occupy themselves with a purely spiritual dimension of reality. For Christians, there is no such thing. The kingdom takes root and grows in the muck and mess of real life.

However, Christians are called to bear witness to realities – of divine love, and the sacred worth of people, of just and forgiving community – which cannot be turned into the means to other ends. They are worthwhile in themselves, make present a transcendent reality which is not within the power of our plans, projects and targets.

Chaplains have an opportunity to articulate this within a church university, whose ethos should rule out narrowly functional accounts of teaching, reason and knowledge. Again, however, they do not do this alone. Points of connection can be found, for example, with academics who are actively seeking to resist the reduction of education to a commodity. For our purposes, this underlines the point that chaplains need to have a perspective which is facilitated by, but not limited to, that of student services.

3. NEGLECTING WIDER CHAPLAINCY RESPONSIBILITIES

Face to face work with students is central to chaplaincy work, but this goes beyond pastoral care alone. It is about relating the gospel to the questions and concerns of young people, and of mature students who have often had to make huge changes and sacrifices to pursue their education. From informal conversation and hospitality, to more organised experiments in discussion, prayer and action for justice and peace, chaplaincy has a role in accompanying people at various stages of their spiritual search. Chaplains have a key role in making space for life-changing conversations and encounters to take place.

For instance, the chaplaincy has recently worked to set up a Make Poverty History student action group, concerned to campaign on issues of global justice. Part of the process has been helping this group to learn how to run itself, and take over leadership from the chaplaincy. In this way, the chaplaincy facilitates a new dimension of student engagement, but tries to let it find its own form and voice. This is a move away from relationships of dependency, but also from overly individualistic pastoral models.

Moreover, a significant element of the chaplains' role is to extend this ministry to staff, and in a sense, to the institution as a whole. Engaging staff – through individual guidance, involvement in chaplaincy group activities, training, shared projects – is vital. And it can have a knock-on effect. After all, it is the whole body of staff which will determine how the university's mission looks and feels on the ground.

Ministry to the institution has already been touched on. Sometimes the work done helping to shape a university ethos finds a more visible expression, as in the recent case at Hope when a senior and long-term member of the staff died suddenly. The day after we heard, the chaplaincy held a simple service to register people's shock and grief. Over two hundred staff gathered at very short notice from all parts of the university. In the midst of tragedy and sadness, it was a great privilege for the university chaplains to hold the staff's collective grief in God's presence. The event was partly made possible because of our Christian foundation. The connections which existed with senior managers and the provision of a big chapel space were assets we could call on to bring the university community together.

That wider ministry also involves forging connections with broader church structures. Recent conversations in the Church of England have highlighted the potential for mutual benefit which exists between the church and church universities and colleges (Archbishops' Council of the Church of England, 2006). Chaplains' connections to diocesan and other structures, as well as simply being useful networking in itself, can play a part in forging those more substantial links.

That can mean challenging local church's perceptions of both higher education and chaplaincy work, which can be seen as only about gathering a student worshipping community. Chaplains can alert the church to a deeper engagement with student lives, and the world of teaching and research. Active collaboration can grow out of respect and understanding – but only if chaplains resist the temptation to distance themselves from local churches, and show understanding of the issues which face them.

Finally, as in all universities, chaplains can play a key role in facilitating information, guidance and dialogue around interfaith issues. At Liverpool Hope, we do not have any officially recognised representatives for other faith traditions (though a process does exist for doing this). However, we do call on staff members and others with expertise should we need guidance, and we provide information on places of worship and student societies for a range of faiths. An area of work which needs developing is active promotion of interfaith dialogue and co-operation, especially given current global tensions.

Two points needs to be made about the need to keep alive a wider vision of chaplaincy's role. Firstly, what has been said about the situation in church universities applies in many ways to chaplaincy in other settings. No chaplain will want to mutely accept a reductionist account of their role. The difference lies in the potential openings provided by a church university's mission and ethos and the positive expectation placed upon the chaplaincy service. The challenge lies in discerning those opportunities which further the values of the kingdom, can result in wider partnerships and conversations, and are manageable within the limited resources of the chaplaincy - and taking hold of them with both hands.

Secondly, this is not about chaplaincy *versus* student services, or any other part of the university. Often, other services and individuals play a key role in calling the university back to a fresh expression of its ethos (such as committed environmentalists challenging it to take its stewardship of creation more seriously, for instance). Chaplains will need to be alert for these voices, and allow themselves to be pushed out of their complacency on some issues. And, as ever, they will always need to be ready to refer students to other services which have the appropriate expertise they need.

Behind all these questions of institutional location and identity lies something more fundamental and yet elusive: storytelling. The chaplains have to inhabit different languages, different narratives: the story we are told about the role and purpose of higher education in the UK; our particular institution's history, which tells people what its roots and relationships are, and what it hopes to become; the stories that local and national churches are telling about themselves, whether they are about decline and marginalisation, or empowerment and new opportunities. All of these weave in and out of one another. And, for chaplains, the question arises of how we inhabit the Christian story itself in and through all of these other narratives.

Another participant in the colloquium that led to the creation of this book spoke of the chaplain's role in terms of simultaneous translation, a complex and multi-layered praxis in which three languages may be involved. It is a compelling image. It alerts us to the difficulty, the risk, the particularity and yet the ultimate possibility of communication across seemingly insuperable barriers. Translation is always interpretation, because no language maps point for point on to any other. Its semantics, grammar and network of allusions are always different. And yet translation remains possible, because no language is self-contained. Language by its very nature is fluid and open enough to disturb notions of a fixed, unchanging, enclosed identity (Derrida, 1998).

Language cannot be reduced to an abstract system. It lives through use, practice, communication, encounter, repetition and refreshment in ever-changing contexts. Most powerfully, it works through being organised into narratives which tell us who we are and where we are. Chaplains need to be good story tellers, with an ear for different dialects, ambiguities, metaphors and plot twists. And they need to be translators, skilled at working across a variety of languages and stories. They lose this ability if they allow all of this complexity to be absorbed into a narrowly secularist narrative, or if they tell a particular type of unworldly or domineering religious story which allows no room for other voices.

Of course, the Christian story 'itself' does not exist in some realm cut off from the particular languages of the secular and the religious, with their structures and institutions. Its power is that it is a story *about* translation, about embodied communication. The Word becomes flesh at a specific place and time, and the Spirit is shed to make this Word accessible to people *in their own tongue* (Acts 2.8). Christianity does not divorce flesh and word from spirit and speech. And so, in conclusion, I offer just one suggested metaphor which might help chaplains to locate themselves in that place of communication opened up by the God enfleshed in Christ.

THE BODY'S PLACE

Earlier, we spoke of the chaplaincy having a concern for the 'whole body' of the university. This is of course a metaphor with significant Christian overtones. Without wishing to collapse church and university together, we might be led to ask: in what sense can and does a higher education institution express what it means to be the body of Christ? And how can chaplains understand their calling as part of this body?

The first thing that needs to be underlined is that the body is interdependent (see 1 Corinthians 12). It consists of a rainbow of dialects, experiences, and gifts, none of which is complete unto itself. All need the others to be what they are. Whereas any university would also hopefully accept the need to be a *diversity*, the Christian understanding of the communal body can add a dimension of depth to this ongoing conversation.

The body does not impose uniformity, demanding that all speak with the same voice. At the same time it acknowledges that we are 'members one of another' (Romans 12.5) – fundamentally interrelated in ways that call for learning to be open, dynamic, holistic and ethically aware. Learning is inevitably a matter of power and vulnerability, whose nature Christians see transformed in the saving body of Christ. Can power be deployed in service and empowerment? Can vulnerability become an opening for dialogue and mutuality? Here, the chaplaincy's witness to a wisdom made known in God's foolishness can challenge the bluntness of market values imposed in education. Its witness to strength made perfect in weakness can hold the powerful to account (1 Corinthians 1.25). A theology of the whole body resists co-option by either secular or religious fundamentalism, and maintains a stance both prophetic *and* collaborative ('would that *all* the Lord's people were prophets', as Moses says, Numbers 11.29).

The interdependent body is neither monochrome nor monolingual. There is no place for narrow tribalism, even when it is dressed in Christian colours. But the body is also vulnerable to being policed and regulated by forces which are essentially reductive, dissecting and commodifying what should be a living whole. As part of the body, chaplaincy can be part of resisting all that demeans and degrades the body's gifts, and celebrating the transcendent depth through which the divine is made known in the material, cultural, learning world.

Perhaps this metaphor can help us to avoid some of the shortcomings of the language of 'dancing on the edge', which could suggest that chaplains' options are either absorption into the centre or a kind of pure liminality. The problem comes if we invest too heavily in the idea of being on the margins. Marginal voices, marginal people are not asking to be left on the edge, to be romanticised by religious discourses trying to assert their own agendas. Nor do they necessarily want simply to become part of the existing system. They seek to upset the status quo, redrawing boundaries and hierarchies to reflect a very different reality.

At Liverpool Hope, we are beginning to learn what it might mean to have so many students from 'marginal' backgrounds – including a large number of mature students, often rendered invisible by assumptions about the average student profile. They are challenging us to re-think our structures, our teaching practices, our support services. They are not going to leave the university the same as it was before they arrived.

The image of the university as the interdependent body is an attempt to take seriously this need to acknowledge unexpected gifts, to learn a critical and evolving solidarity. It can move us beyond the straitjacket of speaking of centres and edges. As we have seen, in a church university setting, the chaplains would be betraying their calling (and deserting the body) not to take advantage of the opportunities to speak to the heart of the institution. The question is: can we do this with a true sense of solidarity with all the parts of the body? Can we develop a practice of chaplaincy which is truly holistic and inclusive? The relationship to student services gives us a link to the wider corpus, whose significance should never be underestimated. But the chaplaincy above all should never confuse one part of the body with the whole.

We began by thinking about seating arrangements. Should chaplains have a seat at the table? If so, we suggested that it should not get too comfortable. The sense of value, importance and power derived from being part of the structure of things can be seductive. However, simply to reject that seat for a pious dream of free-floating ministry is equally as self-serving. Chaplains need to take the risk of belonging where it is offered, and from there work out how to serve the whole body. That will require the ability to listen to challenging voices, and engage in uncomfortable reflections, so that our domesticated theology and practice is opened to the liberating impulse of the Spirit. This means taking seriously the experiences and perspectives of *all* those who have *already* been invited to the table by God, whether that is acknowledged by the powers that be or not. Chaplains never sit alone.

The tables where we sit can bear many weights: conflicting agendas, personal struggles, the tensions between power and service, between what is good and what is affordable, between commercialism and education. The Eucharistic table is not set apart from these difficult realities, but is the place where community is made as the stuff of the world is offered, broken and shared. Can we re-imagine every table as connected to the one to which Christ invites us to receive him as the weakness and foolishness of God, made flesh in an imperfect world? Through the voices that are allowed to speak, and the voices that are excluded, we could learn to hear Christ's words, wholly welcoming, utterly transforming: This is *my* body.

REFERENCES:

Archbishops' Council of the Church of England (2006) *Mutual Expectations. The Church of England and Church Colleges/Universities. A Report of the Church of England Board of Education.*

Derrida, Jacques (1998) *Monolingualism of the Other. The Prosthesis of Origin*, Stanford: Stanford University Press.

Robinson, Simon (2004) *Ministry Among Students*, London: Canterbury Press.

Chapter Five

CHAPLAINCY AND UNIVERSITY STUDENT SERVICES

SHEILA AYNSLEY-SMITH

The publication of the report, *Dancing on the Edge* provided a timely overview of chaplaincy, its varied interpretations and representations within the higher education community, and one with which I found many resonances. This chapter presents a personal perspective, and does not represent institutional policy or strategy on chaplaincy.

In the context of my own professional role as Head of Student Services at Manchester Metropolitan University, I will explore the relationship between university chaplains and the constituent elements of a modern university in a changing environment. I will then discuss ways in which chaplains contribute to institutional priorities and values and will raise questions of management, accountability and quality assurance, before touching briefly on possible ways forward, particularly in the light of the report's recommendations.

BACKGROUND AND CONTEXT

Manchester Metropolitan University (MMU) is a large, post 92 university which currently has some 34,000 students, the majority of whom are studying full time. Like many former polytechnics, it has grown significantly through a series of mergers; it currently occupies 7 major campuses of which 5 are in Manchester and 2 in Cheshire, at Crewe and Alsager.

The university is structured around 7 faculties with strongly devolved management and administration; identity and culture are largely defined through faculties, although some are, in themselves, diverse. Unusually, the structure and local cultures of the university still reflect some of the traditions of the constituent colleges which , since the formation of Manchester Polytechnic, have contributed to the development of the current institution.

Student Services at MMU comprise a fairly traditional range of support services, including Careers, Counselling, Chaplaincy, Learning Development and Disability, Student Volunteering and Sport; there is close liaison with Student Finance, the Students' Union Advice Centre and Student Accommodation. I am also have responsible for liaison on childcare and student health. There are two main Student Services Centres; one at the central Manchester All Saints campus and one providing a rota for both the Cheshire campuses. The university recently appointed Faculty Student Support Officers who provide generic advice, guidance and study skills support within their own faculties, thus recognising the dispersed nature of the university and the value of localised and customized support (Marr and Aynsley Smith 2006).

CURRENT CHAPLAINCY ARRANGEMENTS

The concept of chaplaincy at MMU is well embedded, although it has never been explicitly defined or challenged as part of the institutional infrastructure. In this sense, it is not (at least to date) significantly different from some of the other support services available to students and staff, in that they are not established by constitutional writ or administrative requirement; their absence, however, would diminish the quality and potential reputation of the organisation. "Ownership", and therefore channels of communication are through Student Services and particularly myself as Head, although for most chaplaincy users, questions of contract and paymaster are irrelevant. As articulated in the report (page 55) chaplaincy at MMU has largely evolved through "through the development of personal relationships".

Chaplaincy and faith provision are at the discretion of respective faiths and churches and there is therefore considerable variation in matters such as involvement or even consultation in the appointment process. At Manchester, we benefit from full time provision through the Catholic chaplaincy which is located on the central Manchester campus, the support of the ecumenical chaplaincy which serves Manchester University, MMU and the Royal Northern College of Music, a Methodist lay preacher who is appointed to serve ten hours per week at the university and the Jewish chaplain who has extensive responsibility across the North West of England. A small budget is allocated through Student Services to support chaplaincy activities and the university makes a contribution to of the ecumenical centre for administration and the salary of its international students' chaplain.

At the Cheshire campuses, local churches (Catholic, Anglican and Evangelical) have included university responsibilities in the remit of relevant priest/vicar/pastor(s), who, depending on other commitments, spend some time on campus. Unlike the chaplains at Manchester, none has a full time brief for higher education. However, relative ease of accommodation at Cheshire means that we are able to make limited, timetabled space available within Student Services for chaplains. The growth of Student Services at Manchester, combined with restricted room availability led, a number of years ago, to the abandonment of a dedicated chaplains' room, although bookable space is available for members of the team who find this useful. The centrality of the Catholic chaplaincy on the main Manchester site, combined with the geographical spread of the university across its five Manchester campuses, diminish arguments for dedicated physical space, which is always at a premium. The Methodist chaplain is well established at the Didsbury (five miles South of the central site) campus, where a room is shared between the different Student Services over the week and where he is well known as part of the Faculty community.

I shall address later the way in which we establish and define the chaplaincy team at Manchester. It is axiomatic that a sense of belonging and cohesion derives from physical proximity and indeed visibility. Therefore at Cheshire, where the chaplains have rooms in smaller buildings and share facilities including the kitchen, there is a sense of personal involvement. At Manchester, chaplains join Student Services in their termly staff development days and they use their personal and professional skills to ensure informed referral.

Some years ago I became conscious that the image conveyed by our chaplaincy did not reflect the cultural and faith dimensions of the university's population. In particular, there is a significant population of Muslim students, many of whom live at home and are deeply committed to of their local communities. I set about making contact with local faith groups, using a range of networks. This initiative was generated through myself and the chaplaincy team but was not driven by any expressed demand from students or staff. Raising the issue with the Students' Union prompted concerns about the availability of prayer facilities but did not elicit demand for pastoral, multifaith provision. This initiative has now been pursued by the ecumenical centre which has established an active multi-faith reference group, which organises well attended social and faith sharing events.

Over time, the individuals appointed to serve the university as chaplains have changed, thus bringing inevitable shifts in focus. More recently, we have started to look at the concept of faith advisers; I have accepted that this is not something which I can achieve on my own, given other pressures on my time and energy. The impact of recent equalities legislation has encouraged the university more generally to address issues of cultural diversity and thus provide both institutional support and a forum for developing a potential structure of multi faith advisers.

THE CHANGING UNIVERSITY CONTEXT

Much has been written about the dynamic higher education landscape and chapter 1 of the report effectively identifies some of the key characteristics of the changing patterns of student life. Notwithstanding some demographic differences at the Cheshire campuses, MMU exhibits many of the characteristics of a large, metropolitan institution. Currently, 64% of our students are from the north west of England, with 42% from the Greater Manchester area; 47% are aged over 21, 59% are female, 11.3% of first year students are of Asian ethnicity, 3.5% are black, 5.4% are Chinese (data from self ascription). A total of 4% (1464) are from outside the European Union and 820 from the European Union. The university has fewer international students than many other institutions of the same size, although there are plans for major growth in this area. The demography of home students reflects national trends in that the proportion of students of Asian origin is higher than that of the local community whilst participation by black Afro Caribbeans is lower. In terms of widening participation, the university achieves its benchmarks for students' socio- economic backgrounds and retention(HEFCE 2005). The recent emphasis on student satisfaction, through the national survey, the TQI website and high profile national newspaper league tables have shown that there is considerable work to be done in ensuring student satisfaction. Over the last decade, the challenges for higher education institutions have grown significantly. Students are entering higher education from increasingly diverse backgrounds, with a range of entry qualifications and expectations. Students are now perceived by many in the institutions and by themselves as clients; they therefore expect a responsive and client focussed service in an environment which is struggling to cope with increased student numbers and diversity in all contexts including academic, social and cultural. The inevitability of student debt affects their behaviour and expectations and leads to a high proportion of full time students working to support their studies. Within the context of a mass system of higher education, both students and staff are struggling to succeed and also to find time for the personal contact which is so vital to success.

The diversity of the student population inevitably brings a significant range of learning and support needs. We have currently over 2400 students who are known to have a disability and therefore require adjustments to support their learning. Partially included in these numbers is a growing number of students who are experiencing mental health difficulties, both long and short term, giving ever greater focus to the need for student support. As indicated on page 21 of the report, chaplains, like other members of the university "are increasingly to reinvent their work, re-establish relationships and be proactive in seeking fresh ways to engage within a disengaged culture". This description applies equally to the learning and teaching process which is influenced by centrist imperatives to deliver a curriculum which both matches the changing student population and maintains academic standards.

CHAPLAINCY AND STUDENT SERVICES

Very little has been written on Student Services generally. In 2002, Universities UK in collaboration with SCOP (Standing College of Principals) initiated a research project on the contribution of Student Services to student retention, culminating in the report "Student Services – Effective Approaches to Retaining Students in Higher Education" (2002). The report recognised that Student Services have a central role to play "particularly in student progression and completion" and identified ten case studies which serve as positive examples of good practice. The project did not seek to define Student Services, but exemplified projects and initiatives which enhance the student experience. In identifying issues which are significant in managing diversity, reference was made to "culturally relevant support: to take into account religious, racial and cultural needs and circumstances" (page 9) but did not specifically identify the role of chaplains.

A more recent survey undertaken by AMOSSHE (the Association of Managers of Student Services in Higher Education) looked at the organisation, scale and scope of service provision in AMOSSHE member institutions in the academic year 2002/3. From the limited number of respondents (37%), 48% had full responsibility for spiritual and faith support and a further 26% had significant involvement. These reports lend further weight to the implicit inclusion of chaplaincy or faith support within Student Services but in a way which is less regulated than other constituent services.

Nationally, most Student Support services include core provision for counselling, disability, student finance, while 57% include careers. All of these professional areas have their own associations which determine codes of practice, provide advice and training and benchmarking. This, despite the existence of organisations such as the Conference of Catholic Chaplains in Higher Education, and the ecumenical Churches' Higher Education Liaison Group, further exemplifies the way in which chaplains are potentially operating independently and without a clear frame of reference, either from their peer group or the higher education institution in which they are appointed to serve.

CHAPLAINCY AT MMU

I shall focus on relationships at the Manchester campuses, since

- Chaplains are specifically appointed by their churches to serve HE
- Relative proximity has facilitated team cohesion.

The way in which chaplains have operated as a team has varied over the years, reflecting different personnel and location factors. Some years ago, I adopted the practice of convening termly meetings with the chaplains. This coincided with two developments:

- The loss of a physical base for chaplains at the central All Saints campus
- The decision by the Bishop to co-locate chaplaincy with the St Augustine's parish on the All Saints campus.

We have continued to meet regularly and have discussed and variously progressed initiatives such as:

- The development of multi faith provision
- The organisation of a conference on spirituality *
- The mounting of a joint chaplaincies' production of the musical 'Joseph and the Amazing Technicolor Dreamcoat' *

* both in February 05

We often take the opportunity to reflect on the nature and role of chaplaincy, As well as routinely sharing information and organising tasks such as contribution to student induction programmes, attendance at Student Services management meetings and support for students in halls of residence. At one point, we extended invitations to these meetings to a wider constituency, including the Orthodox Jewish chaplain and a local Imam. Although they did not attend, the constitution of this group was becoming loosely defined and in March 2005 those chaplains specifically appointed to support MMU and myself held an Away Day to review the role and remit of chaplaincy at MMU and to consider how the faith base might be broadened through such arrangements as the appointment of faith advisers. We agreed that one of the team would be designated as Chaplaincy Coordinator to serve for two years on a rotating basis and this role has until recently been undertaken by the Anglican chaplain appointed with a specific remit for MMU.

Whilst the group which met last year undertook much valuable work, the stability of the team is subject, not only to the normal changes in personnel, but also to the vagaries of the different faiths as they review their resources and commitments. One is constantly aware that faith representatives are part of inter-connecting circles and that support to higher education may only be one part of their role.

I would like to highlight three specific areas of support provided by the chaplaincy. Firstly, we make clear in all of our presentations and literature that chaplains are available to all members of the university – students, staff and their families. Many staff use the Catholic church on campus for weddings and funerals; where chaplains are able to have a physical base, they provide an impartial sounding board ("within but not of the University"). They are available to support staff, students and families in the event of a student death; last year the joint chaplaincies' musical provided an appropriate focus for raising funds for Make Poverty History and a number of events were arranged following the South Asian Tsunami. This enables the University to respond to events and crises in an appropriate way which does not compromise its secularity.

Secondly, as indicated, chaplains are a constituent component of Student Services and are promoted as part of the support provision for our students. They provide a unique function in organising social functions, as well as faith events and when it is necessary to draw on all our resources, e.g. for student induction at the start of the year, the chaplains are always willing to contribute to that effort. Although personal relations are usually excellent, some tensions have emerged, partly around language; for instance, do chaplains counsel and mediate? Are they bound by appropriate codes of practice? There are also variations in the way in which I describe the chaplaincy team; they are always included in the diet of provision available to students, but in any university document which might relate to internally resourced provision, they are differently described. The latter instances tend to be in the minority.

Thirdly, the chaplaincy team has provided invaluable support to myself as Head of Student Services. This can be a lonely role, particularly in a situation where I have no deputy or immediate support other than a most valuable secretary. Outwith the line management relationship, chaplains can and have provided personal support and solace; the informal nature of our team meetings can be refreshingly full of levity. They have, individually, provided objective commentary on institutional matters, often giving a fresh perspective. Email availability also enhances communication and responsiveness.

MANAGEMENT AND ACCOUNTABILITY

My role in the appointment process varies according to faith arrangements and conventions; I have been involved in the appointment of the majority of our current team and have endeavoured to provide a form of induction. The chaplains themselves have provided a network for new appointees in orientating them and introducing them to colleagues. Resourcefulness is an inevitable element of the chaplain's role. However, the chaplains do not report to me and they are not accountable to me for their work; other than via the team meetings and annual reports (see below) nor can I ask them specifically to undertake a task. I therefore cannot dissent from the phrase "operating within an ambiguous set of parameters"(*Dancing on the Edge*, Part 2). If there were any concerns or complaints about chaplains, it is likely that they would be directed to me in the first instance; however, without formal institutional recognition (and indemnity), there remains a vulnerability around the role.

Reflecting the voluntary nature of the relationship with the university, the chaplains are not contractually subject to institutional systems or processes. Whilst we try to include them in Student Services' procedures, the nature of the relationship inevitably leads to a certain degree of inconsistency and ambiguity. These are exemplified in two key areas: strategic planning and quality assurance.

Within Student Services at MMU, we have a well established system of annual reporting, which has variously been titled Annual Operating Statement, Planning Statement, Strategic Plan, reflecting the latest terminology from within the institution and the Funding Council for England (HEFCE). Over the last two years, we have refined this process by drawing up a strategic plan structured around the key strategies and policies of the university's strategic plan 2003-2010. I have continued the practice of writing a fairly detailed overview identifying key achievements and priorities in the preceding year which is discussed by formal University committees. In recent years, there was no separate report from the chaplains and any references which I made in my report drew on my own experience and interactions with the team. However, the appointment of a chaplain within the ecumenical centre with specific responsibility for MMU and our internal designation of a coordinating chaplain has provided a clearer focus. She has been both diligent and creative in responding to requests for information and has drawn together a chaplaincy strategic plan and has rolled it forward in accordance with our procedures. For this purpose, chaplaincy is presented as a core service.

Similarly, we developed a service level framework for Student Services which sets out, for service users, be they students or staff, our role, remit and method of operation and identifies the services which users may expect. Chaplaincy provision is included in this statement, which makes clear that the chaplains are funded by their faiths. We are also working on improving our web pages; this is a job which universally depends on dedicated commitment and interest. Again, the chaplaincy/faith pages have been updated by our energetic and committed coordinating chaplain.

The issue of the assurance of the quality of provision introduces many other dimensions. Many of our services are subject to external standards; Counselling is subject to the code of practice of the BACP (British Association for Counselling and Psychotherapy) and the Careers Service has achieved the Matrix Standard which is a quality standard for information, advice and guidance services approved by the Guidance Accreditation Board. All our services and projects elicit feedback from users and we maintain detailed statistics on usage. The diverse nature of chaplaincy functions, allied, I suspect, to the professional environment in which they are working, means that we do not routinely have hard data on the clients seen/supported by our chaplains and information on their activities tends to be anecdotal. This situation may be tenable under current contractual arrangements; were we to present a case for more institutional support and resource, we would need much harder data. In the world of key performance indicators and targets, evaluation of service delivery which relies on overview and anecdote is potentially vulnerable. This is not to say that our chaplains do not gather feedback from service users and certainly the Catholic chaplaincy holds a twice- termly forum and an annual open session in order to gain feedback from participants in its activities. Through our chaplaincy team meetings, this is an area in which we have resolved to share good practice.

The Matrix quality standards achieved by the Careers Service, referred to in the previous paragraph, is an accreditation process which a number of other HE Student Services have achieved across the board. As yet, I am not aware of any service which has included chaplaincy in this process, other than where the chaplains are directly funded by the university.

In October 2004, Student Services achieved accreditation under the Investors in People award; this recognises the support given to the professional development of its staff. Again, we were not able to include the chaplains, as they are not subject to our internal processes. We do, however, include chaplains routinely in staff development events and have contributed financially to their attendances at conferences and to professional training and courses.

LOOKING TO THE FUTURE

It is tempting to stay with the "Ain't Broke" philosophy and to continue to focus on the quest for a multi faith approach to chaplaincy at MMU. However, I believe that the report's descriptors, including "loosely coupled" and "ambiguous" will not be fit for purpose in our target dominated and increasingly litigious environment. It is important that there are safeguards both for the chaplains' contribution and in order to define more clearly the university's responsibilities in relation to chaplains.

The report's proposals (page 86, recommendation 3) for national guidelines on formal agreements are valid and should form a sound basis for future debate amongst all denominations. At MMU, my hopes for the foreseeable future are to maintain faith provision, to develop it in such a way as to reflect the cultural and faith balance of our community and to continue the work which we have started on defining the role and remit of our chaplains in order to ensure that we provide high quality, modern and inclusive support in all aspects of our students' lives. Despite –and perhaps on account of– organisational complexities and ambiguities, chaplaincy remains for me a valuable and dynamic dimension of the university's provision.

REFERENCES:

Grant, A.(2005) The organisation, scale and scope of student service provision in Amosshe member institutions. *Journal of Student Services in Higher Education (Amosshe)*, 1, pp12-20 http://www.hefce.ac.uk/news/hefce/2005/perfind.asp

Marr,L and Aynsley Smith, S. *'Putting the student first: developing accessible and integrated support'* in Thomas,L, Barfield,S and Hixenbough,P (eds) *Perspectives in Personal Tutoring* in Higher Education, York, HE Academy (forthcoming)

McGrail, P. and Sullivan, J. (2005) *'Dancing on the Edge: a Report into Catholic Chaplaincy in Higher Education'*, Liverpool Hope University UniversitiesUK (2002) *Student Services – Effective Approaches to Retaining Students in HE*, London: UK

Chapter Six

STUDENT COMPOSITION, CHAPLAINCY CLIENTELE, AND CHANNELS OF COMMUNICATION

SIMON ROBINSON

ESKIMO KNELL

> Following the success of a computer game based upon a scenario set in the frozen north the computer software development company was asked by the client to develop a second game. This time the client wanted increased shock value, and the inclusion of the death of children. An added incentive would be that the agreement of the game developer to this concept would lead to the rapid release of monies still owed to them for the first game.
>
> The manager of the software firm and his engineering staff were uneasy about this request - though initially a little unsure why they felt this unease. As a result of discussions with his staff, the manager decided that it was important to clarify the situation. He wrote to his client's legal department and asked if they would confirm in writing that the company wished him to develop a second game and that it was their intention that this should involve increased horror and the death of children. No such confirmation was received - and the money owed to the software development company was rapidly released.

I have used this case with a number of student groups, leading to many different responses. Most interesting were those of the first year undergraduates. Without revealing the response of the software manager, students were asked to work in groups on how they would respond to the client's request. One group suggested that it would be possible to accede to the client's request, provided that the story was a moral one such that any violence could be resolved in the ending- in other words providing it was clear that the 'baddies' lost. Another was not too sure about showing the death of children- hence they suggested that it not be shown, just heard from off screen. Another group felt there was something wrong with client's request, and that they should not respond to it in case it harmed the company's reputation. Yet another group said that they saw no problem with accepting the client brief and that they would make the children Eskimos. When asked why, they replied, 'because this would fit in with the location of the game and because no one would really care about Eskimo children'.

I begin with this story to illustrate the gulf that is there for between much of modern student culture and the Christian church. One might look upon the final student response with horror. The very idea of such distancing smacks of racism and worse. Little better are the ethics of self interest held by the previous group. However, I suggest that a more careful response would see these as demonstrating that many traditional students entering university are in fact late adolescent. Because such students are also largely middle and upper middle class, they have not faced major issues in their own lives about how one might handle plurality and complexity. Hence, faced by an 'ethical dilemma' their concern reflects a level of moral and spiritual maturity which falls about level three of the Fowler or Kohlberg stages of spiritual or moral maturity. In other words moral meaning is less about engaging moral issues, and the human experience at the centre of them, and more about finding a right answer, or one that responds to pressure of peers or of stakeholders.

Of course, the picture of the modern student is much more complex, and in this chapter I will first spell out the wide-ranging nature of modern students. Nonetheless, there is a gulf for most students between them and the Church. I will then consider what kind of students tend to make use of chaplaincy. In the final part I will make some observations on how chaplaincy might begin to bridge the gulf between church and student culture. In this I will suggest a view of chaplaincy which respects denominational integrity but goes beyond boundaries.

THE MODERN STUDENT

There is no typical student. In the past two decades steady widening participation has seen a student profile which includes:

- Traditional students
- Increasing numbers of international students
- Increasing numbers of non traditional students.
- Postgraduate students.

TRADITIONAL STUDENTS

It is easy to assume that widening participation has changed the student profile considerably. In areas such as disability this is very much the case. Some 3% of students have some form of disability. In some universities the proportion is as high a 6%. Such changes are fuelled by law.

However, in terms of class, the majority of students still seem to be in the traditional mould. The 2003 Student Living Report (Unite 2003) notes that despite the attempt to widen participation there has been little success in terms of encouraging those from the C2, D and E socio-economic background. The report (with surveys conducted by Mori) shows that 83% of students come from A, B, C1 background. The 17% from C2, D, E background are one percentage point down from the previous wave of students.

The most recent Unite Report (2006) suggests that the vast majority of students are white and from the UK, and that the main reason for them coming to university is occupational utility. The financial pressures on traditional students and their parents have clearly worsened, not least with the introduction of fees. Nonetheless, those without a job have remained the same as four years ago (58%). The main difference is that there is an increase in those who are in employment needing the money for essentials- 57% in 2002, 71% in 2005).

The profile of the majority of these traditional students is of late adolescence, with a majority not clear about the next steps after university. Nonetheless, this is balanced by the increase in vocational degrees and professional qualifications, not least in areas such as healthcare.

INTERNATIONAL STUDENTS

International students are increasingly a significant percent of the student population. By 2000 over 313,000 international students entered Britain, with almost 100,000 on postgraduate courses. This compares to just over 200,000 in 1990. The top five countries which supplied international students outside the EU were the USA, China, Malaysia, Hong Kong and Japan. The top five countries from the EU were Greece, Germany, France, Eire and Spain. The top three areas of study were Business and Administration, Engineering and Social and Political Sciences.

The rise in the number of international students is due to some key factors:

- The high reputation of British Higher Education.
- The opening up of communist and former communist states to the west, especially China.
- The increased mutuality and exchange in the EU. The ERASMUS programme, enabling study abroad, for instance, was set up in 1987.
- The importance of the English language to global communication, and thus for jobs. In 1998 it was estimated that over 750,000 international students took short English language courses in Britain.
- Higher Education in Britain has become increasingly globalised, developing links with international universities and sometimes setting up departments in other countries.

Such an increase has also been a source of finance for the universities, especially with full cost fees charged to students from outside Europe. In 1999 the government encouraged this marketing, setting a target of 25% of the global market. This has led to great competition for recruitment of international students. Practice here has been variable, with some universities promising a great deal of support and offering little once the student has arrived. Cheek by jowl with this utilitarian approach is the increased awareness of the need to care, with most universities appointing international student advisors. Moreover, many universities are viewing international students as a key part in the internationalizing of HE, providing global perspectives in the curriculum and in relation to the local community.

NON-TRADITIONAL STUDENTS

There has been a gradual increase in non- traditional students. They are mature, will often have responsibilities with families, may be part time and have a job, and may come from lower socio economic groupings. Some of the more recent universities now have a majority of such students. Indeed, one university has 75%, leaving the more traditional students feeling more marginalized.

For the non-traditional student the experience of HE can be a major challenge. Key problems experienced by mature students include:

- The experience of HE as a major life-changing experience, fuelled by emotional and financial investment.

- Using HE as a way out of certain things- an unsatisfactory marriage, poverty and so on. This can be all the more problematic for students who graduate well but who do not then get the employment they had hoped for.
- Cultural and learning shock, as the first two cases showed. Access courses are designed to help people into the HE experience, but even these can be problematic as they are usually student centred, whilst many university courses are centred in the discipline.
- The fear of failure can loom large for people who everyone assumes are adult and therefore should not have any intellectual problems. The investment in time and energy is such that failure can generate shame for the mature student.
- Personal problems which are already deep-seated. The converse of this is that many will come who are emotionally mature and thus able to handle possible difficulties.
- Financial sacrifice can reinforce a sense of guilt in the student. Sacrifice of time and attention lead to a member of the family feeling left out and left behind. In the second case the sons were unhappy to lose their mother to HE, and also to necessary part-time employment.
- The challenges of freedom and a very different culture and values can cause the mature student to question previous values and previous belief systems.

Because of the investment in life up to this point a sense of change can be very traumatic. It does not have to be the immediate challenge to a marriage, for instance, but may be a gradual build up of a woman's sense of rights and freedom, something can have real knock on effects in the marriage and lead to resentment from the partner.

POSTGRADUATE STUDENTS

The life of the traditional postgraduate student can be very problematic:
- Some simply use postgraduate studies to put off the evil hour of having to work through the tasks of late adolescence.
- Some use the postgraduate experience to take their relationship to the parental life-scripts further. For some this involves a desire to please the parents and achieve ultimate success. For others there can be

unconscious questioning of that dynamic. A key problem for most PhDs is isolation. Some, especially in the sciences, will find that they work in laboratories alongside other researchers, forming a small community. In other areas the researcher will tend to work for long periods by herself and later subject her work to other researchers or supervisors.
- Identity. The postgraduate is neither student nor fully accepted teacher, though he is in the world of both. In some departments he is not welcome in the junior common room, and only welcome in the senior common room when there are no senior staff around.
- Purpose. At some point many postgraduates begin to question the whole point of the exercise. For many this begins when their expectations are no longer matched by reality. They may be doing very sound work, but work that will not get them the top job they wanted or the life style they had hoped for. Once again, vocation and life scripts begin to be tested.
- Problems with supervisors. The postgraduate student is entirely reliant upon the supervisor. For some, she may not be the right person, and a poor dynamic can quickly develop. Students often feel that if they have got a bad supervisor they can't survive. This is a common problem for international students.

Postgraduate experience is, however, changing massively. Increasingly postgraduate work is about occupational utility. The market for MBAs seems limitless. This includes a high number of international students, with universities increasingly basing business school outposts abroad. In turn this leads to an increasing number of postgraduate students who hardly ever visit the 'home' campus. In turn, the push for new 'customers' has led universities to develop forms of postgraduate work through Continuing Professional Development in business and the professions.

STUDENT IDENTITY

Underlying the differences in the student profile are some common aspects of student identity:
- The student experience is very much about transition, be it from late adolescence to adulthood, from one life-style to another, from one occupation to another, from MPhil to PhD.
- The massification and commodification of HE raise core issues about identity. Recent research (Gibson-Sweet, 2006) suggests that students

see themselves as customers rather than 'students' or even members of the university. The view of student as customer raises questions about academic identity and about how far students see themselves as part of the academic community, including accessing academic freedom (Barnett, 2000). Membership, and thus belonging, tends to be only experienced at departmental, school or club level.

- Increasing stress on distance learning has led to many students' main experience of HE as being through WebCT, or part time/ evening work. There is less and less evidence of a learning community with clear boundaries.
- Modern student culture can be seen as the epitome of the post-modern experience (Robinson and Benwell, 1999). There is no overall cultural narrative that informs the experience or identity of the student, but great diversity. The Student Union exemplifies this radical pluralism, with a strong rights based support of all student groups.
- The increasing numbers of students who have had to take part time employment also leads to less time available for study, and reinforces the identity of the student as customer.

CHAPLAINCY CLIENTS

CHRISTIAN INTERNATIONAL STUDENTS

If the *Guardian* is to be believed (Robinson and Benwell, 1999) then chaplaincy to Higher Education is fast declining and the only real 'customers' are international students. Many international students, it is argued, come to university with the expectation that chaplaincy will provide care and support. They come with traditional church expectations, and often directed by their home pastors to the chaplaincy.

Such an argument ignores the many aspects of wider chaplaincy work and assumes a church model of chaplaincy. Nonetheless, many international students do gravitate to the chaplaincy. For some international students, especially those who can expect international continuity, such as the Roman Catholics, it is natural to use chaplaincy as their base. For the most part, however, international students are a very mixed and complex group, with many different expectations and needs.

UK STUDENTS

There is often the assumption that UK Christian students will come to university and happily become part of the chaplaincy. Parish priests will refer students to chaplains, often without the permission of the student. But, of course, in many cases the chaplain is the last person the Christian student wants to see. This is her chance to move away from the traditional church. Connected to this Christianity on campus is something much bigger and diverse than chaplaincy.

Members of the Student Union are happy to include many different Christian groups in their ranks, and very happy to be involved in working with interfaith and inter Christian groups. One university has a Christian Medical Fellowship, Christian Union, Catholic Society, SPEAK (Christian justice group), Student Christian Movement, Anglican/ Methodist Society, Chinese Christian Society, and an Orthodox Christian Society. This has led to an increased sense of a plurality at the heart of the Christian community, and an awareness of different view-points within different societies. One Christian Union of over 150 members includes 5 Roman Catholics. They like the Biblical emphasis, and still go to Mass. The Christian Union (CU) is also increasingly aware of the debates within their ranks on 'post evangelicalism', and increasingly open to the ethical debates on issues which up to ten years ago were perceived in hard line ways. Again it is not a matter of the CU retreating from a Biblical position, but rather recognition that even Biblical based faith has many complexities.

This crossing of hitherto firm boundaries is also reflected in student approaches to denominations. The vast majority of students, Christian and non Christian, have little or no understanding of Christian denominationalism. University has always been a place for Christian students to explore different approaches to the faith. One group of Christian students goes to a middle of the road Methodist next door to their Halls on Sunday morning and then to an evangelical Anglican church in the evening. There are groups who migrate en mass to the popular evangelical churches of the year, be they Baptist, Reformed Baptist, Anglican or Independent. With the increase in different student groups this takes on even more interesting mixes. One CU president uses a High Anglican Church for her local congregation and members of an Anglican/Methodist Society go to a monthly Orthodox Chaplaincy service.

At the same time there are Christian students who do not want to be part of any student groups and who prefer to go to low key or middle of the road churches and best of all do not want to be noticed as students.

Alongside the plurality of Christian life is also a shift in emphasis from the intellectual or doctrinal to the affective and participative approaches to faith. The Christian Union's, often very cerebral, concentration on the doctrinal meaning of scripture, has been replaced by more holistic practical and social concerns. The precise definition of the statement of faith is less important than the desire to pursue mission through friendship. As one UCCF (Universities and Colleges Christian Fellowship, the national body of the Christian Union) leader put it recently at a conference, this also reflects 'a culture increasingly dominated by symbol and image, with less prominence given to the written word'.

What does all this say about student religious culture? It points to a polyvocal Christian culture which as Meeks notes, writing of the 2nd century, is nothing new (1993). At the same time there are real changes, loosening of old boundaries and focusing more on practice and collaboration, and membership of different communities. Student experience is in any case a time of transition and this can tend to involve faith development.

Faith developments may lead students to all kinds of different groups, often beyond the church. Jamieson (2002) notes those younger Christians especially who purposely move away from formal church to marginal or liminal groups. The first of these largely define themselves in relation to what they have left, deconstructing the former views and beliefs. Liminal groups will tend to look forward, often developing their own patterns of worship. Many Christian student groups have taken on marginal and liminal characteristics, regardless of any national group aims. Some SCM groups, for instance have been made up of a majority of students who do not have links to local churches and who find their spiritual identity in the groups. Students may also move into very different group experiences, such as an internet community. A good example of this is the Ship of Fools (ship-of-fools.com). This is advertised as a magazine of Christian unrest and has its own interactive community. It includes a wide range of Christians.

The point is that any or all of these might be involved in chaplaincy in different ways. Some, such as the CU, can, in certain universities, become associated with chaplaincy. Others will work with chaplaincy.

Non Christian Students

Non-Christian students of a wide variety use the university chaplaincy. These include:

- Students with pastoral problems. For many students this might be the end of a long trail, having not got what they were looking for in the counseling service or department. Some associate the chaplain with their experience of secondary school. Others see the inclusive and unconditional care offered by chaplaincy.
- Ultimate life crises. Increasingly universities are seeing the chaplain as a core part of their response to student death, with counsellors referring students to them when students have suffered bereavement of fellow students or members of their family
- Fellow travelers. The wider the network of the chaplaincy, the more groups of global justice and social concern, such as Amnesty International, choose to use the chaplaincy premises and to relate to the chaplaincy in different ways.

It is possible then to see:

- a core group who uses chaplaincy as their spiritual and social centre.
- other groups who are happily part of the chaplaincy and possibly several other Christian centres.
- others who might be happy to use the chaplaincy premises for their activities (Christian or not).
- others who are happy to work closely with the chaplaincy, not least for major mission or justice events.
- Others who are happy to be associated with chaplaincy in broad terms.
- Others who are not part of the chaplaincy or any related network but who use chaplaincy and the chaplains as part of their psychological support.

Like students in general, such Christian and non-Christian students may well be going through transitions, psychological and spiritual, and be looking for a particular place to belong to, where they can find care. Like members of the wider church students have widely different reasons for being associated with the chaplaincy.

CHANNELS OF COMMUNICATION

Given the huge numbers of students, the many different expectations and the different needs and different student pathways to chaplaincy, there are several questions about communication. The first must be, what is the chaplaincy trying to communicate- denominational identity, Christian identity, inclusive community, inclusive pastoral role, the diversity of the polyvocal church?

Depending on the answer, different channels of communication emerge. Denominational identity, for instance, can perhaps be best communicated through the networks of the denominations. This means being part of a strong national denominational network such that new students would be referred to the chaplain. Similarly it means using local churches to show students that chaplaincy is primarily about the denominations and how to access them. Stressing denominational identity on campus might, however, have the effect of non –Christian students seeing the Christian Church as fragmented. This leaves one asking questions about how we might have both a sense of denominational identity and also inclusive and cooperative community.

The inclusive pastoral role can easily be communicated through the student support networks. This can signal that chaplaincy involves nonjudgmental, unconditional care. For some Christians this raises the danger of the chaplain avoiding any attempt at moral guidance, and of losing the distinct role of pastor or priest.

Other channels of communication include effective IT. Clearly any organization has to have an effective web page. The danger of this means of communication is that it can focus on populist approaches to 'attract' students. Is the aim of communication to attract or to engage, or both?

As different channels are considered it is clear that all hold dangers, including:
- Focusing on the student as religious consumer.
- Focusing on concerns which are largely about our institutional anxieties. The church committee that wants to see a healthy group of Christian students to keep the church going. Numbers are a sign of success in this respect.

Moreover, the different 'identities' that make up the chaplaincy suggest some values that need to be held in tension, not least between the pastor and the pulpit- unconditional care and moral guidance (Robinson 2001).

So, what are we trying to communicate? I would argue that we should be aiming to communicate the presence of God on campus, and that this by definition is greater than any particular Christian denomination. In turn I suggest that this might involve four broad elements:

- Communicating God's presence. Presence bespeaks physicality and immediacy. It also carries a sense of significance, or making a difference.
- Enabling God's story. Story is about articulation, reflection and discourse, such that the significant meaning can emerge.
- Sharing responsibility. God calls us to take mutual responsibility, and this means partnership.
- Enabling reconciliation. God brings people together, sometimes the most unlikely, and at different levels this involves forgiveness.

This kind of active and significant presence can be communicated in many different ways. Indeed, given the sense of active partnership and diversity it is important that all those ways are used.

PRESENCE

There used to be debates about whether chaplaincies needed centres. However, it is hard to see how a presence of care and acceptance can be communicated without a physical place where worship, celebration, meals and so on can be shared. The centre itself then becomes a channel of communication enabling students to experience community and belonging, but also to be aware of how this particular denominational community relates in significant ways to the wider church presence in the community, and to then other denominations on campus. This in turn provides other opportunities for students to explore or serve. Such presence can also be communicated through the student support networks of the institution. Should the centre be ecumenical and what might that mean? Two or more different centres need not work against a sense of shared presence, so long as it was clear that they were part of the same service, and had a sense of shared responsibility.

A great deal of the communication of presence depends upon what the building and the lay out of the building 'says'. One chaplaincy team invited a practice development expert in to help them reflect on their work, and she noted four things from entering to building to reaching the work room that in some way 'excluded' visitors, or said something more about institutional needs.

From that basis she then explored the student pathways to the chaplaincy, through the extensive student support services, the chaplaincy web site, the local church networks (and how they perceived chaplaincy), the Student Union, to the Student newspaper.

Communicating God's presence in all this is a function of significant, practice-centred relationships and networks of relationships. For this to be effective those who relate to the chaplaincy need to know what difference the chaplaincy makes to them, to be able to assess the value of the chaplaincy in their terms.

Whilst God's presence is embodied in community it is not confined to that. The presence of the chaplain on formal university committees communicates further the concern not just for the student but for the environment in which the student works. Indeed, such presence can be a part of embodying what Rowan Williams (2005) refers to as 'faith in the university'. Such faith involves 'believing, in spite of all the discouragements, that the university has something irreplaceable to offer to human society: by its deliberate pursuing, entertaining and criticizing of questions of widely different kinds, by not allowing the variety to be limited by considerations of short term profit and results, it reminds a society of the fundamental relation between human beings and their environment' (32).

Presence then can embody not just faith in God, but also faith in the university, and such a university is a place where faith, generic or religious, can flourish. Communication has to embody all of this, and the following three areas are in some sense just different ways of working out and making real such a presence.

DISCOURSE

At the heart of a university is the experience of learning. Some students manage to get through university without meeting significant learning, by which I mean learning that enables reflection on how one learns, on underlying values and how they relate to value and belief systems, and on how practice relates to values. Such learning involves character development, transcends the particular concerns of disciplines (Barnett, 1990) and is increasingly explicitly being developed in relation to employability (York and Knight, 2004) and professional development (Carter, 1982).

At the heart of the Christian presence is just such a support for learning which both connects to values, beliefs and practice and which seeks to develop a caring environment within which people and groups can respect and challenge each other's views.

Communicating God's dialogic presence means involvement both in the curriculum and beyond. Chaplains have long been part of the traditional curriculum. However, what this tends to communicate to the student is not so much the chaplain, as the scholar- the expert in a discipline. Increasingly the curriculum is a place where the chaplain as chaplain, and not primarily as scholar, can contribute to the ongoing debate about values, beliefs, learning and professional practice.

THE PROFESSIONAL CURRICULUM

In recent years a number of important developments have influenced teaching and learning in disciplines related to the professions and in the wider developing curriculum:

- There is an increased stress on transferable skills, a holistic view of learning, and the development of reflective practice. This has even extended beyond skills to attention to attitude, qualities, and even virtues (Robinson and Dixon, 1997; Carter, 1985; Megone and Robinson, 2002) and includes awareness and concern for the global community (Collins, 2003).
- The continued stress on learner-centred learning (Rogers, 1983). This stresses the importance of self-directed learning, through which the student develops autonomy.
- The continued stress, especially in the professions such as Engineering, Healthcare and Medicine, on team teaching and the involvement of tutors who can bring a different perspective to the course. Courses for engineers have frequently brought in members of the industry, the community and of other disciplines to provide contrasting and critical perspectives on practice, purpose and accountability. Above all it enables the development of holistic thinking and awareness beyond the narrow confines of discipline or profession.

In the light of such concerns many schools and faculties welcome the involvement of chaplains as part of a wider dialogue.

THE DEVELOPING CURRICULUM

There is now a whole side of the curriculum which is focused on the development of skills, the development of the person and employability. This began through the exploratory work of Enterprise in Higher Education, in which Government money was made available to develop imaginative courses (Robinson, 1996).

This has led to the development of accredited and elective central skills modules, aiming to focus on vocational skills as part of the curriculum. Once more then the driver for such courses is work application, and this opens up courses run by agencies as diverse as careers office and student counselling. One such course is run by Student Action, a student community volunteer society, in coordination with the department of Continuing Education. It includes the theories and issues underlying the process of volunteering, the skills necessary for voluntary work, the stages of volunteer development and the effect of voluntary work on the community.

The chaplaincy fits easily into such a market place of electives. One example of what can be done is the Lifeskills and Spirituality course at the University of Leeds. This is summarized in box 1

BOX 1 LIFESKILLS AND SPIRITUALITY

The course, runs over two semesters, and capable of being divided into two short modules involves:

DEFINING SPIRITUALITY

This invites wide-ranging reflection on the meaning of spirituality, arriving at working definition which is tested throughout the course.

Spirituality is then distinguished from religion, psychology and ethics, and the students are invited to reflect (confidentially) on their own spirituality through working out a life map or values history.

SPIRITUALITY AND HEALTH

The relationship of spirituality to health and well-being is explored. This leads to an examination of the part spirituality can play in the healing process, and an identification of the key skills involved. The focus is on empathy as a spiritual skill and the underlying attitude of unconditional care, especially in terms of agape.

This is developed in relating to hope, faith, purpose and reconciliation and forgiveness, culminating in the idea of shalom.

All this is applied to death, dying and bereavement.

CONFLICT RESOLUTION

The dynamics of forgiveness and reconciliation are developed in relation to the skills of conflict resolution, including contexts such as the family.

WORK

The nature of work in terms of purpose, vocation, hope and faith is examined. How this ties in with professional decision-making and management is then examined, along with and the underlying skills. This includes work culture and whistle blowing.

COMMUNITY

Different kinds of community, how they learn and develop identity and meaning, are examined. The different meanings of these communities are tested and the underlying skills of community development in a postmodern age articulated.

GLOBAL ISSUES

Spirituality and how awareness of global issues, especially, poverty and the care of the environment, is developed and connected to everyday life, including issues about multi national and state responsibility.

THE DIVINE

Because a significant part of the course is seminars where the different spiritual narratives of the students are shared the Divine is not absent up to this point. However, thoughts about the transcendent other are drawn together at the end, not least issues about how we can know such an 'other', or even talk about him.

Once again this module is student-centred, enabling reflection on the 'other' (be that self, other person, group, environment or the divine), on how we respond to the other, and on how we generate significant life meaning for ourselves and others through those relationships. Precisely because such reflection does not shirk the conflicts in idea and feelings that might arise, it enables dialogue which works through to criteria for challenging different spiritualities, not least as to whether they are healthy or not.

The course is assessed by a reflective learning journal (examining how the student connects the ideas to their own spiritual journey). The reflective journal and seminar work are key to building up inter-textual dialogue. The journal invites reflection on:

- The seminars, noting what was discussed and critically analyzing this.
- The skills and qualities practiced.
- How the issues raised connect with their home discipline.
- How the issues connect with their own spirituality and any vocation.
- Any issues that made the student feel uneasy.

The chaplaincy team is responsible for most of the course, but external teachers can be brought for different sections, or members of departments. Particularly fruitful is the possibility of working with chaplains from other sectors, such as healthcare, industry and prisons. Also useful is to have an industrial consultant who can reflect on how the course ties in to work issues.

CURRICULUM NETWORKING

Increasingly departments are being asked to reflect on the global perspective of their courses. The Toyne Report, for instance, recommended that,

> "Responsible Global Citizenship should be recognized as a desired learning outcome; 'Enabling responsible citizenship' should be recognized as a core business of learning institutions and a legitimate purpose of lifetime learning" (Khan, 1996). Whilst core modules can be organized on this theme this also has a clear relevance to most vocational courses. The overview of this is something that chaplaincy is ideally placed to facilitate and accompany. Leeds Metropolitan University, through the pioneering work of Gwen Collins, has developed a Global Perspectives Network, with academic, administrative and support staff from all departments. It aims 'to stimulate debate, to share ideas and materials across Faculties, and to contribute to the formulation of university policy' (Collins, 2003).

Such a network then directly affects the curriculum, but also can affect the policy of the university. At its centre is a global spirituality which sets out 'global perspectives', including how they can be embedded in the curriculum, how the student will benefit from such perspectives and what academics might aim for.

CROSS UNIVERSITY AND NETWORK DEBATES

Chaplains are among the few key people who can enable cross-university debate. This can enable real interdisciplinary debate or debate on key campus issues. It can also be a safe space for debate which the wider church is not comfortable in hosting.

FRINGE CURRICULUM

In addition to the traditional and developing curriculum there are a number of different ways in which chaplains can be involved in the non formal or fringe curriculum.

Personal development modules and seminars. The Student Union or Student Support Services quite often offer short courses in personal development of different kinds, such as developing the skills of befriending. This is primarily a network for students who might want to develop some aspects of themselves. Chaplaincy can be usefully a part of such a network, with short courses available to all students, such as one on different kinds of spiritual and devotional techniques, or vocation.

Chaplaincy outreach programmes. These are designed to pick up controversial issues on campus and develop reflection and debate. This may mean the chaplaincy setting up speakers they may not always agree with. Such one off sessions can be set up in collaboration with departments.

Participating in regular public lectures and seminars. At one level this involves monitoring the occasional lectures and seminars in the University and ensuring that there is a chaplain at the ones which are most likely to enable fruitful dialogue.

Working through involvement in the core experience of the student, the learning relationship, the chaplain can communicate God's presence and concern for dialogue in very real ways:
- Establishing a framework for dialogue about spirituality which can be shared by Christians and non Christians alike. At one level this gives

up the claims of the Christian Church to being the centre of any and all spirituality. By doing so it enables others to claim this area of belief systems in a way that makes sense to them and which enables better conversation between Christians and others.
- Focusing on student development that transcends disciplines (cf. Barnett, 1990).
- Enabling connections between the different disciplines and the church.
- Enabling a connection between spirituality, religion and occupational utility

Central to all these ways of communicating are reflection, the articulation of narrative and meaning, and dialogue. Sometimes the chaplain is there to hold the ring, create the space and empower the group or person to reflect and take responsibility for meaning. Sometimes, the chaplain communicates a more explicitly theological truth. Sometimes both go on at once in conversation that can enable mutual challenge in the context of practice.

RESPONSIBILITY NEGOTIATION

At one chaplaincy conference an enthusiastic chaplain leapt to his feet and cried out that he had found the core role of chaplaincy- the role of prophet. My then colleague's enthusiasm was understandable. Most chaplaincy conferences used to be about a desperate attempt to find a distinctive identity- and here it seemed, at last was a job that no one else on campus could do. The chaplain in question even looked the part, with a long beard.

Then it began to dawn that, actually, any university campus is filled with prophets, who share a concern for justice, including:
- The Students Union- with its frequent campaigns
- The Christian Student Groups
- The other Religious groups
- Secular student groups, such as People and Planet and Amnesty
- The AUT
- Some members of staff, not least those who blow the whistle

What is important is for chaplaincy to find ways of sharing this role, involving at different points the negotiation of responsibility. Sometimes that might mean reinforcing, the role of others, in which case the communication comes through the same means as the partners in prophecy. At other time it means chaplaincy being the centre of prophecy, enabled through debate or close working with management. One example of this is setting up debate about how the Student Union might respond in assisting students who want an abortion. A public debate around the issue, including the Union, enabled the justice concerns of the Union to be put alongside different perspectives, practices and views of justice and care. Another example is of setting up a debate around the theme of academic freedom and what that might mean to academics and to students.

Negotiation extends from prophecy to pastoral care. The very process of working through responsibility for pastoral care and counselling with the counselling services, for instance, enables:

- clear boundaries to be drawn
- appreciation of the limitations and importance of what each has to offer
- dialogue about the core ideas of care on campus, and the underlying values. In all this the spiritual dimension becomes increasingly understood and recognized

The communication that occurs in such practice is significant and enables the role of the chaplaincy to be communicated through counselling and other student support services.

Responsibility is further negotiated through work with local churches. If communication is viewed in a linear way it would be possible to have leaflets about local churches in the chaplaincy, and leaflets about chaplaincy in the churches, telling people what is on offer. If, in addition, however, the very same churches and the chaplaincy work together throughout freshers' week to provide free hamburgers for the students then the real, practical connection between the wider church and chaplaincy and how they relate become apparent, enabling real conversation.

Another practical way of communicating is through negotiation of care with the local churches. If the core need of international students, for instance, is to have a community of identity and care, then an international centre/club could provide the home for that. Such a home would be most effective if chaplaincy and local churches shared responsibility for it, maximizing support and resources and increasing networks.

A final example of this is in the increased concern in universities for citizenship and service learning. The church as part of the local community can become part of this whole activity and can benefit greatly from student volunteer work. The chaplaincy can broker that kind of activity and also be involved in the delivery of the service learning.

There are, then, many different networks through which chaplaincies can communicate their shared concerns, care and views of justice, through negotiating responsibility for practice that makes a difference. The very act of negotiation communicates commitment and meaning.

RECONCILIATION AND CREATION

The final element of the character of presence is shalom- peace and justice alongside re-creation. Once again we can see this as core to any theology of chaplaincy, and those insights have to be shared, in worship, dialogue and practice. However, such concepts and their related practice are not exclusive to theology. They emerge most strikingly in a community of practice, and, as we know from experience, any such community has to learn to forgive continuously.

Chaplaincy might enable this process in different ways.
- Embody learning and forgiveness in ecumenical relationships
- Work with the management. Being in the university but not of it means that chaplains can provide unique perspectives for management, helping to generate a workplace that embodies spirituality.
- Bringing together the most unlikely of people. Work across the university can enable the most unlikely of people to talk and effect reconciliation.

CONCLUSIONS

Chaplaincy belongs to the university but is not owned by it. It is important be a part of the university, feel a member, otherwise students will not see and feel the relevance and concern. It is important to be apart from the university; otherwise the distinctive perspective of the chaplaincy could be lost. But a religion that is based upon a God who is both one and many, a God whose identity is discovered in relationships, and embodied through partnerships, should not find holding all these things together that difficult. The message for chaplaincy is that communication is a function of relationships, and effective communication is a function of relationships that make a difference, to the student as person, the student as member of the university, the student as religious, the student as preparing for professional life, the student as citizen, and the student as a child of this planet and of God.

In one sense then the thrust of this chapter is: get the relationships right and the communication will follow, and be appropriate and meaningful. Getting those relationships right means meeting the student in those areas of concern and development.

Implied in this also is a challenge to the churches:
Come out from behind the boundaries we have placed within our communities, between our communities and between our communities and the world. Most of these are designed to defend us from challenge, learning and significant practice- i.e. practice that makes a difference.

Recognize that God works across and beyond boundaries and that most recognize him not in church, but in the moments when they move through transitions- crossing personal, professional and public boundaries that cause them to question meaning and identity, and thus develop.

Give chaplaincy its proper place in the mission strategy of the church- relating to the heart of the university, not dancing at the edge. With 50% of 18-30 year olds to be involved in HE by 2010, that is where real time and commitment should be going- both establishing meaningful relationships and proclaiming God's story. And that can only be done with all the Churches working effectively together.

REFERENCES:

Barnett, R. 'Supercomplexity and the Curriculum', *Studies in Higher Education* 25 (3), 2000, 255-265.

Barnett, R. *The Idea of Higher Education*. Milton Keynes, Open University Press, 2000.

Carter, R. 'A taxonomy of objectives for professional education', *Studies in Higher Education*, 10 (2), 1985, 135-149.

Collins, G. *Going Global at Leeds Metropolitan University*, a discussion document from the Global Perspectives Network, January, 2003.

Connor, S. *The Post Modern Culture*, Oxford, Blackwell, 1989.

Gibson- Sweet, M. Student Identity, in *The Experience of Higher Education*, Troubadour, publication date 2007.

Jamieson, A., *A Churchless Faith*. London, SPCK, 2002.

Khan, S. *Environmental Responsibility: A Review of the Toyne Report*, DfEE, Welsh Office, Dept. of the Environment, 13.

Meeks, W. *The Origins of Christian Morality*. New Haven, Yale University Press, 1993.

Megone, C. and Robinson, S. (eds.) *Case Histories in Business Ethics*. London, Routledge, 2002.

Robinson, S. 'To Boldly Go: A tale of spiritual enterprise in Higher Education', *Crucible,* January- March, 1996, 12-19.

Robinson, S. and Dixon, R. 'The Professional Engineer: Virtues and Learning', *Science and Engineering Ethics*, Vol. 3, number 3, July 1997, 339-348.

Robinson, S. and Benwell, M. 'Christian chaplaincy in the Post Modern University', *Modern Believing*, 41 (1), 1999.

Rogers, C. *Freedom to Learn for the 80s*. Columbus, Merrill, 1983.

Williams, R. Faith in the University, in Katalushi, C. and Robinson, S. (eds.) *Values in Higher Education*, Leeds, University of Leeds Press and Aureus, 2005.

Yorke, M. and Knight, P. *Embedding employability in the curriculum*. York, Learning and Teaching Support Network, 2004.

Reports.

Student Living Report 2003, UNITE, _http//www.unite-group.co.uk

Student Living Report 2006, UNITE

Chapter Seven

CHAPLAINCY:
THE VIEW FROM THE OTHER SIDE

GEMMA SIMMONDS

In 1998 I witnessed two significant events in the life of the University of Cambridge and its Catholic chaplaincy. The first was the funeral in Brompton Oratory of Mgr. Alfred Gilbey. The second was the day commemorating the 50th anniversary of the awarding of degrees to women. Both occasions attracted large crowds, the first to participate in the Tridentine funeral rite for the former chaplain to the Catholics of the university, the second to witness a multitude of elderly women processing to the Senate House in order at last to attend the ceremony conferring their degrees from which they had been barred until 1948. It was of particular significance to me that I witnessed both events as one of the chaplains at Fisher House, where Gilbey lived for over 30 years, and from which he effectively barred women until his departure in 1965, believing that university was no place for a woman.

I was the third member of my order, the Congregation of Jesus (formerly Institute of the Blessed Virgin Mary) to hold the post of assistant chaplain, after Sisters Amadeus Bulger and Helen Southcott. This paper is a reflection on my years as chaplain in Cambridge and the two years that followed as chaplain in Heythrop College, University of London. It includes further reflection on my experience as a graduate student of the University of Cambridge after I had left both jobs. I make a number of observations that may be common to the situation of other women chaplains or women to whom university chaplains minister, but I am aware that most of what I say is from a personal perspective. I am grateful for help received in my reflections from former students of Cambridge and London Universities: Siobhan Cox (née Catney), Al Davidian, Rachel Dunkley Jones, Matthew and Jo Fernandez Graham, Fiona McFarlane, Gerard McGrath, Anne Murphy, Br. Erik Varden OCSO and Fr. Joe Wheat. Their observations reinforce how difficult it is to confine my remarks with any confidence to exclusive questions of gender, while also confirming my suspicion that gender still drives many of the issues I discuss.

The situation of the Catholic chaplaincy in Cambridge is, like many other Cambridge institutions, *sui generis*. The place itself is a fascinating building, part ancient historical gem, part ghastly 1970s utility. Perhaps this says something about the ecclesiology that I found prevalent within the chaplaincy. Fisher House is owned by the lay Catholic fellows of the university, and rejoices in its autonomy both from the university at large and from the Catholic hierarchy itself. Until Mgr. Gilbey's death, after which a substantial legacy made a certain difference, the chaplaincy was run on meagre funds and its activities were largely subsidised by the fact that the chaplain and his assistants (chosen independently by the senior chaplain) worked for a minimal stipend rather than anything that could be called a living wage (cf. Chapter One, 4:2.2.1). During my time at Fisher House the Anglican chaplain of one of the wealthier colleges had a yearly entertainment budget that was more than four times my annual salary.

It is not possible to offer factual evidence in describing the origin of an ethos, and again I repeat that what follows is a matter of my own observation and perception. Libby Purves, in her memoir *Holy Smoke*, forgives the misogyny associated with the Gilbey era but is relentless in her condemnation of its snobbery (Purves: 112-121). There were still vestiges of both in my undergraduate days in the late 70s, but by the time I returned in the 90s it was the misogyny that seemed to have lingered, all the more pernicious for being largely unconscious. Like *A Tale of Two Cities,* my three years in the Cambridge chaplaincy were both the best and the worst of times. From the pastoral and spiritual perspective, they were some of the richest years of my apostolic life, and the students were a delight: bright, enquiring, challenging and loving, they were full of faith seeking understanding as well as of the usual student *angst*, wound up several degrees by the intensity of the Oxbridge terms and the huge pressure, both internal and external, that is brought to bear on students in a university with such a relentless culture of high achievement. From the perspective of my own experience as a female chaplain, dealing with what it is to be a woman ministering in the church in such a role, it was often an experience of pain and contradiction, confronting me with dilemmas I had previously managed to avoid in a female-run environment where questions of authority did not clash with those of gender.

Cambridge itself has a certain history of hostility to Catholicism that goes back to the Reformation. This is perhaps the origin of a somewhat embattled attitude among some students and senior members who seemed to feel that the Faith of Our Fathers was still in need of defending against enemies within and without the circles of true orthodoxy (cf. Chapter One, 1:3.4). It was not an atmosphere that encouraged the pushing out of ecclesiological boundaries. At the same time, Cambridge had at that time a particularly belligerent section of the Student Union, unfriendly to the established church and convinced that Catholics are not Christians at all. Their insistence that their Catholic fellow-students would go to Hell if they did not convert and become 'true' Christians was unhelpful to those experiencing their first wobbling steps of autonomous faith life, independent of home and parents (Simmonds, 1997a). It also meant that great emphasis was put on equipping students to give an intellectually credible account of their faith.

In many ways the Catholic chaplains occupied an enviable position. The chaplaincy operated as a ready-made community centre in the centre of town. We had our own chapel, where Mass was celebrated every day, attended mostly by students, retired academics and townsfolk. On Sundays a full sung Latin Mass was celebrated in the chapel that attracted a fiercely loyal attendance among students and fellows alike. It was followed by a sung English Mass in the hall, transformed overnight by the sacristy team from a utility hired out to raise funds for the chaplaincy. With a folk tradition of dubious musical value but great warmth of response attached to it, that Mass also attracted a loyalty that often went with a greater enthusiasm for and familiarity with post-conciliar attitudes, social engagement and openness to experimentation. The number of Catholic fellows who attended this Mass was small. The third Mass, without music, was known by the chaplains as the 'Mass of the Dead' and catered in the evening for those whose Saturday night or Sunday morning activities prevented their being able to attend a morning service.

My fellow chaplains were both Dominicans and the students were privileged to hear superb sermons from them as a regular feature. There was also an emphasis on the teaching of sound doctrine to students whose faith was often strongly challenged by those with whom and by whom they were taught. While developing expertise in their own fields of study, many students felt at a disadvantage in a faith context where the poverty of catechesis and religious education on offer in much of 80s Britain had sometimes left them floundering. The strong sense of community within the chaplaincy could act as an attraction or a repellent to students, but many found there a base from which to build a confident, adult faith (Simmonds: 1997a, pp.141-5). That confidence was reflected in the role of the chaplains, and often envied by our Anglican colleagues (cf. Chapter One, 3:2.2). Almost every college in Cambridge has its own chapel, all Anglican with the exception of the Catholic foundation at St. Edmund's College. Each college chapel had its chaplain and sometimes a dean. Some chaplains served well-endowed chapels and were strongly supported by the college fellowship, while others struggled against hostile or indifferent colleagues and college councils eager to turn chapels into concert halls or libraries. The fragility of their position drove some chaplains into justifying their position by presenting themselves as academics who happened to fulfil an ecclesial function, while others went principally down the student services and counselling route.

I personally found considerable support and friendship among the Deans and Chaplains group, which met on a regular basis. The fact of my being a woman, and thus being perceived as a layperson, appeared to make a difference to this. The Catholic chaplaincy in Cambridge did not have a strong reputation for ecumenical expansiveness, but my not being a priest turned to my advantage, since it somehow took me out of an 'official', ecclesiastical realm into one where possibilities for collaboration seemed much broader, and I presented less of a threat. In the goldfish bowl of Cambridge it was also easier for me to attend Anglican services without this suggesting unintended implications on either side, and even the Eucharist, a delicate area round which to tread at the best of times, seemed to be an easier issue to negotiate for me than for the other two chaplains (cf. Chapter One, 2:4.1). I became chaplain in 1995, at a time when there was a considerable increase in Cambridge in the number of ordained female Anglican chaplains. Apart from the strong friendships I developed with most of them, I also found myself serving as the Catholic representative on the organizing body of the Cambridge Deans' and Chaplains' triennial mission to the University.

In my first year I had organized a Week of Guided Prayer at Fisher House. Its success took us all by surprise, and it became the foundation of four Christian Life Communities founded for undergraduate and postgraduate students from Fisher House. CLC is a lay-led organization of Ignatian origin, whose members meet regularly to reflect on their lived experience in the light of faith and prayer, and to commit themselves to the furthering of God's kingdom through their daily lives. Members of those original CLC groups have themselves gone on to found other groups, both Catholic and ecumenical, in Britain and Ireland. This idea spread to the Deans' and Chaplains' mission, and again enjoyed a runaway success among both students and senior members of differing faith traditions (Simmonds: 1997a, pp.147-148).

My own background in Ignatian spirituality allowed for an area of ecumenical activity that was less focused on doctrine and thus less potentially confrontational. It was not an activity particularly understood or supported by some within the Catholic community, who seemed to see it as theologically inept, the sort of touchy-feely, flower-power Catholicism perceived as the provenance of doctrinally uneducated religious women, and regarded with the same sort of dismissiveness as was ecumenism. My status as a woman made ecumenical activity in general and work in spiritual direction in particular easer among some students and many of my non-Catholic colleagues. The same status and activity engendered hostility or indifference in some Catholic quarters.

Of the three chaplains, I was the only one with a background in counselling. Both my colleagues did excellent one-to-one work with individual students, and I am sure that we all had strengths and weaknesses in this area that were balanced out by one another. There are differences, however, in the way that many students will perceive a woman chaplain when dealing with some areas of personal trouble. My experience suggested that talking to a woman over sexual matters, or personal relationships, was often seen by both students and senior members as easier than addressing the same matter with a man, although a reversal of this would operate among those who felt the desire to take such a matter into a priestly, sacramental context. The same split between the theological and the counselling aspects of chaplaincy seem to operate here. For some students, struggling with the ethical and moral aspects of sexuality was a matter for discussion with a priest, whereas the practical aspects seemed to sit more easily with me as a woman chaplain. In researching this article, I asked a number of undergraduate students of that era how they perceived a female chaplain. I asked them to try their best to separate their experience of me personally from their perception of my role as a female chaplain. Their answers largely reflect and consolidate some of my own perceptions listed above, but they also challenge the basic premises in important ways,

> 'I found the sessions you organised on relationships with [One Plus One] invaluable. I can't imagine a male chaplain thinking up

> that one [...] Incidentally, that was the only NFP [Natural Family Planning] training we ever received (this particular session was, in fact, included at the suggestion of a married student couple) and has stood us in good stead over the last seven years. It was mentioned very briefly in the marriage preparation course but not enough to give a practical working knowledge of it. I think that is where women chaplains differ from men - the teachings and insights offered tend to relate more to the practical side of living the faith in your daily life, be it as a student or in preparation for the big wide world. The main thing I learnt from the men was a deep appreciation for the theology behind the beliefs and traditions, which was good but largely intellectual. Whilst I can't use any of those theological arguments on [my children] at the moment to motivate them to be good, I can adapt some of the meditative prayer methods [...] or the praying through drawings, etc, which we did on CLC retreat to give them some feel of the wonder of God's creation'. [JFG]

The same principle worked here, however, as in the ecumenical context. The very strength of my female, lay status could operate to the advantage or disadvantage of my ministry. If some saw this side of my ministry as a strength, others seemed to see it as yet more proof that women chaplains represented the soft underbelly of inane, liberal Catholicism.

A similar ambivalence operated with regard to what I was able to model as a woman ministering within the Catholic church. When I arrived, there had been a period with no formal arrangement for a female chaplain since the departure of my predecessor some years before. Some female students had begun an informal society within the chaplaincy as a sort of 'women's space', where women's issues and feminist ideas could be discussed. The group was tolerated, amid indifference or explicit mockery of varying degrees of friendliness, by the male students, but there was a note of anxiety not only among them but among some female members of the group. They introduced me to it with words of caution, apparently afraid that I might rock a delicate balance by being over-strident in my feminism. At an early point I confirmed these fears by arranging a visit by a visiting scholar to the university who had considerable fame overseas as a feminist theological writer. Exuberantly and sometimes belligerently challenging, her visit dismayed most of her audience both on intellectual and 'political' grounds. This was too in-your-face, and the women's group quietly died its own death, the point of meeting the women students' needs having apparently been met both symbolically and actually by my presence on the chaplains' team.

Questions of gender difference seem to depend, to some extent, on how these differences were perceived in other areas of students' lives,

> 'the main difference between women and men chaplains I found was quite similar to the differences between women and men in general. For instance if we were organising something at the chaplaincy [...you] could be counted on to foresee the nitty gritty details which needed to be dealt with whilst the men would probably have done it on a wing and a prayer expecting the girls to pick up those kinds of things. [...] From the spiritual point I did notice that quite of few of the girls and some of the lads were hesitant to confide in the male chaplains but quite happy to approach the woman chaplain. That may be down to personal characters partly but there is a sense of the mother figure which students identify with and relate to - in a kind of surrogate mother away from home type of thing'. [JFG]

One woman spent her first year as an eighteen-year old student without a female chaplain until I appeared in her second year,

> 'I was very young, of course, and more shy, but I think I found it harder to approach a man. I'm not sure if it was just that you had the more outgoing personality or if you were a woman, or if it was me being that bit older and more confident, but I found it easier to sit and talk to Sister than to Father'. [SC]

This issue of young women feeling confident enough to approach a priest is repeated in several student testimonies,

> 'Perhaps firstly it conveyed a sense of being in a place that wasn't just run by men [...] places that are entirely run by men have a tendency to be scary places, and having a female there made it less so. It also meant that there was someone there who felt approachable, and someone who I thought might understand things that I would never have expected a man to understand. Yes, stereotypes are exaggerations, but women are generally so much better with feelings! Perhaps there is also something in having a female role model. As a woman priests can seem very distant figures, far removed from our everyday lives and experiences,

somehow a woman bridges that gap. Maybe it's different being a man and going to church - being able to relate to all the male figure heads, but from a woman's perspective seeing how women fit in to the picture was important'. [FMcF].

The defence of the faith v. spiritual direction split was often (mistakenly, on both counts) perceived by students as a Dominican/Ignatian one. It may, however, have reflected certain conscious and unconscious differences both in the chaplains' respective traditions of religious life and in our personal approaches to ministry. Certainly among ourselves and in public we polished a running Dominican v.Ignatian gag to perfection over our years together, and students appreciated the variety offered by contrasting approaches,

'It was good to have that variety, to see your different responses to things. An entirely Dominican or Ignatian approach would have been very limiting, whereas a combination of the two was highly complementary' [SC].

But what, if anything, was specific to gender in all this is harder to pin down. It is worth, I think, allowing the students' voices to be heard for themselves. Among two male respondents, one sees the gender difference as adding an important balance,

'Having both male and female chaplains meant that we could receive different kinds of support from each and feel able to show certain sides of ourselves to one that we would have been uncomfortable showing to another [...]I think that is invaluable. [MFG]

The other sees

'aptitude depending so much more on charism than gender' [EV]

The women are equally unwilling to be dogmatic on the matter of gender, but point to issues both about my own role and their perception of it that clearly do point to it:

'From my perspective, it is difficult to separate out the particular approach/skills/ attitude towards what the job was about from the questions of gender and authority. What I mean is that it's not inconceivable, of course, that a priest might have the ability to accompany people in spiritual direction and listen to people's experience at the affective level and stay with them there. But neither was it accidental that (in this case) those skills were only allowed in as a kind of adjunct, in the person of a woman - and a religious. The Catholic establishment valued very different skills in its (priest chaplains) - so that meant that there was a marked split between some of what you were offering and how you saw your role, and the very cerebral mission of presenting the public face of Catholicism in a rather embattled and lofty way, defending the faith and trying to give students the intellectual confidence to do the same. I don't think that split is necessarily or only gendered, but of course it's utterly about power and about the risks of allowing oneself and others to be vulnerable and wounded rather than putting all the emphasis on fighting the battle and shoring up the defences'. [RD]

This correlation between female gender and the perceived ability to listen in a certain way is also pinpointed (but also questioned) by a student who was not part of the Catholic community *per* se and who has since experienced student chaplaincy in America.

'While I wasn't part of the Catholic community in Cambridge, I was so grateful to have your compassionate ear during those rather dark days when I was very much struggling to come to terms with my faith and identity. I don't know if I would have interacted diff-erently with a male spiritual counsellor at the time. I was certainly needing and looking for the receptivity traditionally associated with the female principle, but I don't know whether it occurred to me that such a trait wouldn't be found in someone male in the same position. I do know that in the past I have feared the judgement of both males and females who wielded any kind of spiritual authority over me. But the fear was not (I don't believe) more intense in accordance with gender.

I can definitely say that you were open and present to my spiritual and emotional needs in a [different] way [from] the pleasantly removed male college chaplains I encount-ered in Cambridge before you. [...] Predictably, I did not feel such an invitation to intimacy with male chaplains I encountered, but again, this could just have been the limitations of those particular chaplains. [...]

I am comfortable assuming that receptivity and mindfulness are probably more available from female chaplains, than their male counterparts. Collegiate environments like Cambridge - and

> Columbia - seem to attract as many intellectual - and social- 'good old boys' among those supposedly in positions of ministry as any other professor or fellow. Often where one might expect wisdom and understanding, one finds the implacable curio-sity and clinical regard (but seldom compassion) of a scientist, of a theologian, of an acad-emic'. [AD]

Students also had things to say that were specific to my being not only female but a female religious, since this also placed nuances on my presence as a female chaplain.

> 'As a religious you were caught in the all-too familiar bind of being 'sister' (authorised/safe/respectable...) and being a threat because you didn't act in the deferential manner of second-fiddle to the clergy. What seems to be wanted is women who adopt the (old-fashioned) nun routine, i.e. don't actually challenge anything. So it's not only about whether the person in that role is female or male that matters, but how far they conform and how far they're willing to challenge the formidably-defended hierarchy of intellect, abstraction and prestige with the willingness to allow personal experience, pain, confusion, uncertainty and contradiction into the picture. Of course I'm overstating my case here, and clearly the clergy witness and minister to all those things in private, one-to-one situations. But it's about how much vulnerability is allowed or admitted in public, in sermons, in public prayer, in opportunities for people to develop their spirituality'.[RD].

I would want to reiterate that penultimate sentence, since both my male colleagues had excellent and highly effective ministries with individual students and senior academics on a one-to-one basis in ways that I could not come near. Certain aspects of my life in Cambridge were the best experience of collaborative ministry I have ever had, and this often happened at the level of formal teaching and exploration of doctrine as well as more private, informal 'spiritual' (as opposed, in an explicit sense, to intellectual) ministries. This was more a matter of perception, often projected onto us by others, but it fed at a deep level into areas of our own self-definition as well as public perceptions of what each of us was there for.

Another female student reinforced this as in some senses a struggle for power, not in a personal sense, between individuals, but in the sense of how the perceived roles of each chaplain came to symbolize wider issues in the church.

'Having been at a convent school where one part of the Catholic establishment (female religious) was seen as being subordinate in unhelpful and inappropriate ways to the other (the clerical hierarchy), and reinforcing that subordination in the bright, questioning female pupils that we were, what I perceived of your role in a 'political' as well as a personal sense was crucial to my own development into a committed, adult Catholic woman. It was important to me to see (and hear) a Catholic woman in a public role challenging structures and pushing out theological boundaries as well as being willing to "be real". It was hugely important to me to hear you in public – both formally and just standing up at the end of Sunday Mass and saying things, even if it was just giving out notices, alongside the priests. You stood with us in the congregation or in the choir, but your voice had every bit as much authority as theirs and there was no question about your equality with them and their acceptance of that. That was really important, as well as hearing and seeing you being assertive, feisty, whatever – and cracking jokes – it was good that you didn't take yourself or the priests too seriously!' [AM].

This departure from a 'conventional nun' role was important elsewhere too.

'From a very personal perspective, I can say that had there not been a woman there, or had there been only a nun running a rosary group, I very much doubt that I would have continued to be involved in the chaplaincy. The value for me of one-to-one spiritual direction from someone who listened and supported me through a time when I was struggling to survive was incalculable. I cannot imagine that I would have been able to find my own voice or to explore my own faith and prayer in a way that felt authentic had there not been someone there helping that process along, bridging the gap, reassuring me that there was a place for me as a young woman within a church structure that often felt deeply alienating.' [RD].

This matter of having a public voice had its ironic side. The proliferation of individual college chapels means that Cambridge has some twenty or so services of Evensong per Sunday evening, so we did the rounds of college chapels preaching at the invitation of our Anglican colleagues. This was where I was able to find a public voice in my official capacity as a chaplain, but there was no possibility of my doing so in either of the two Catholic chapels of the university, since Mass was the only service regularly on offer. The senior chaplain had reason to be absent on a sporadic basis when only the two of us were on duty, so that Mass in this heavily sacrament-oriented community could not be provided. He took the courageous step of inviting me to lead Eucharistic liturgies without a priest and I would preach in that context. The senior academics and more conservative of the regular student Mass-goers mostly stayed away. Despite carefully printed orders of service that included the Vatican's own justification of such services in circumstances of necessity, some complaints were received that I was attempting to usurp a priestly role. It is to my colleague's credit that he ignored them, but that seemed to be as far as it felt possible to push out boundaries that female Catholic colleagues in other university chaplaincies were regularly stretching.

The limits to my situation were clear to one female student who was herself in a leadership role and with whom I collaborated closely in practical terms at a time when the senior chaplain was absent,

> 'I became aware, from a distance, of what you couldn't do – of where invisible lines were drawn. I had been at a convent school and I never saw the nuns there in that light, but I became aware that you had a struggle. When [the senior chaplain] was away on sick leave I saw how reliant you had to be on priests to say Mass – it seemed like a big focus, suddenly'. [SC]

This was and is not a question of a personal power struggle between individuals. It is a question of how the public role of a significant female authority figure within a chaplaincy community is perceived by female and male members of that community and how this impacts in both the private and the public spheres. I had a particularly close bond with one of my colleagues, who demonstrated and articulated an endearingly refreshing and open approach to his own priesthood and his collaboration with a woman colleague as friend and equal. This played as important a part in challenging perceptions and presuppositions as did any attitude or behaviour of my own.

The final question revolved around the title of chaplain. An article in the *Tablet* at the end of my second year described me as 'Assistant Catholic chaplain in the University of Cambridge'. An irate reader wrote in to protest that no woman or lay person had the right to claim such a title. While discomfort with this title is reflected in other institutions (Chapter One, 2:3.2) for other reasons, here it was about the perception of an implied claim to equality with priests. In another publication I answered this challenge with a light-hearted look at the origins of the word 'chaplain', meaning 'cloakroom attendant' (Simmonds: 1997b). The article also questioned attitudes to women's ministry as they were reflected by differences in terms and conditions of employment between England, the US and Europe. Some of my own frustration with the restrictions of my position seeped into the article. This gave offence in a manner I had not intended, but which pointed to my having touched a raw area in ecclesiological sensibilities.

Returning to London, I found myself in the position both of sole chaplain and in charge of Student Services in Heythrop College, University of London, where I had previously been a graduate student. The contrast there helped me to clarify how much of my Cambridge experience had been determined by my gender. I have spoken above, as has RD, of the ambiguity around my perceived position as the public face of spirituality and spiritual direction in a context that at times had little respect for or understanding of the terms. Here it was different, since I was in Jesuit territory, and everyone understood without question that side of a chaplain's ministry, whether male or female. The question of chaplaincy as 'defender or the faith' disappeared too in a college entirely dedicated to the study of theology and philosophy and with a staff and student body, male and female, from multiple faith (or lack of faith) backgrounds. I developed an interesting dynamic with the small but articulate number of Muslim women studying in the college, being the first port of call in their struggle to establish a Muslim prayer room on the premises.

My public profile was chiefly that of the Student Services provider, so that again perceptions of my role changed, especially among those students who never darkened the doors of the chapel, or saw me chiefly in my role as principal (and often only) fan and cheerleader of the college football team. But there was also a serious public role for me as co-ordinator of all college chapel activities from the public liturgies at the beginning and end of the academic year and Masses, both the quiet daily Eucharist and the once-weekly sung college Eucharist. Here my preaching was not considered problematic, and as my priestly colleagues on the academic staff took it in turns to preside at weekly and college Masses, the students were accustomed to the overlap between the preaching voice and that of someone who otherwise features simply as a lecturer in their own academic discipline. For a variety of reasons, however, my female colleagues chose not to occupy the liturgical space in any way, so once again I became the only female voice heard in that particular arena.

Within a context where spirituality features as an academic discipline alongside philosophy, theology and psychology, a less sharp divide between 'proper' theology and the spiritual/psychological disciplines is normal, and less likely to lead to the assigning of inappropriate gender roles. In a student body with a high proportion of older, part-time students, many of whom were engaged in some form of ministry themselves, whether priestly or lay, the figure of the 'public religious sister' or the woman in ministry had far less significance. And yet it still appeared to be important, from anecdotal evidence from students, to have a woman in charge of Student Services, where a good deal of my work involved providing safe containment and referral to outside agencies and health professionals [GM]. Such was the increase in the therapeutic aspects of my workload that I finished by enrolling in a diploma course in psychodynamic theory at the nearby Westminster Pastoral Foundation.

One student of whom I saw a good deal of the time both in my liturgical & my spiritual roles picks up on the gender significances, nonetheless,

> 'as university life tends to be male dominated [among the]lecturers etc - it is important for that to be balanced out by the presence of a female chaplain. Female chaplains also tend to be more adept at listening, to have greater empathetic skills, be more focussed on the pastoral care of students and less focussed on the purely liturgical side of chaplaincy as male priest chaplains can be. It is also true - maybe for undergrad-uates more than postgraduates - that a female chaplain can ease the process of leaving home and mother in particular' [JW].

It is interesting that this particular student has himself gone on to priestly ordination and to a variety of chaplaincy roles.

Working in a context where it was unquestioned that women would be in ministry and would be authoritative theological voices changed the dynamic of chaplaincy for me enormously, though it is not clear where exactly that change was coming from and whose perceptions we were dealing with. I found myself missing the challenge of the theological work that I had done in Cambridge, however, and after two years I returned there, though this time as a doctoral student myself.

My decision not to participate actively in the chaplaincy while there as a student chiefly stemmed from a reluctance to blur any boundaries or tread in what had since become others' space. I also went to live at the opposite end of a university whose collegiate system easily turns it into a network of little individual strongholds and had the great good fortune to become part of the small community in St. Edmund's College, which boasts the only Catholic chapel in Oxbridge. It was interesting to find, however, that my years at Heythrop had left me with energies that could not easily find an outlet in the chaplaincy I had left only two years previously. Senior in age but not in status in a highly status-conscious academic context, the pastoral and theological experience I and two other female religious fellow students had accumulated could find little expression within a community even less inclined to recognize and exploit such experiences in its female graduate students than it is in its female chaplains. Alongside other graduates within the Cambridge Divinity Faculty who had pastoral experience, I also found myself chafing at a theological approach that had little time for contextualization. We ended up confining our pastoral energies to our own colleges and to the Cambridge Theological Federation, which comprises a series of individual training colleges for ministry and theology in the various church traditions.

The questions asked by McGrail and Sullivan in Appendix 1 of their report are the same as those I had while university chaplain and have now, on looking back. Things have changed even in the five years since I ceased working in university chaplaincy, and now, at national level, more than half of Catholic university chaplains are women. There has been much change within the system, but I do not see that much has changed in the external framework within which these women operate.

How my gender affected me, my colleagues, the students and the academics to whom I ministered is a matter not entirely clear. That it *did* affect us all in some way I have no doubt. Some of this seems to stem from students' confidence, or lack of it, in social interactions with men, or with members of what is perceived as a priestly caste. Some stems from a certain stereotyped expectation that a woman will be a good listener. There was also a certain theological dualism that perceived a gender-related split between 'serious' theology and its practical, pastoral application.

As a chaplain my gender perhaps gave me a freedom to give public expression to vulnerabilities and struggles that it is sometimes perceived as being unhelpful or inappropriate for a priest to express (Simmonds: 1997a, 148). The change to student status, while having considerable pastoral experience, made it possible to become assertive in theological enquiry in a way that would have been problematic as chaplain. Beneath all these questions lie others around the dynamics of power and its public, symbolic exercise by women in the church. Ten years after I first began in university chaplaincy, the questions remain.

REFERENCES

McGrail, Peter and Sullivan, John, 2005, *Dancing On the Edge: a Report into Catholic Chaplaincy in Higher Education*, Liverpool Hope University.

Purves, Libby, 1999, *Holy Smoke: Religion and Roots, a Personal Memoir*, London, Hodder and Stoughton.

Simmonds, Gemma, 1997a, 'Diverging Paths? Study and Spirituality' in *The Way*, 37, April.

Simmonds, Gemma, 1997b, 'What's In a Name?', *Priests and People*, July.

Chapter Eight

CHAPLAINCY WITH A PARISH LINK

ROBERTA CANNING

INTRODUCTION

My intention in this paper is to reflect upon my experience as Lay Catholic Chaplain to the University at Bangor and particularly to the Catholic students who are part of the Eucharistic community of the local parish. I propose to give a brief account of how the link between parish and chaplaincy developed and to discuss the impact of the relationship on both and how and why it works. I will argue that the instruction from the Vatican that no lay person should be described as a chaplain ignores the role a lay person can play as chaplain to a university and that linking lay chaplaincy to an appropriate parish and parish priest can be very fruitful for chaplains and parish, is an instance of collaborative ministry, and offers a distinctive example to young people of the lay Christian vocation. However I will also argue that what works in one institution at one time is not necessarily transferable to another institution, or indeed, to another time in this institution, and comment on the limitations on chaplaincy to the whole university community when links depend on personal relationships.

ORIGINS

THE PARISH

The close association between the University Catholic Chaplaincy and the parish started when I was appointed in November 2002. I am going to trace the story of the chaplaincy from its foundation, and describe how the link started and then reflect on how the link has developed during my time as chaplain. Since the chaplaincy was not founded in a vacuum, I'll first sketch the history of the parish and the university and say something about the city of Bangor. The parish in Bangor was founded in 1827 when Father Edward Carbery was sent to minister to the Catholics of Bangor and Caernarfon. They were few and poor. In 1834, Father Carbery began the building of a small, rather unobtrusive church - called St Mary's - in the upper High Street, near some of the poorest houses in the town. Coaches and trains brought Irish migrants and so the parish grew. A parish school was founded and was all the formal education most Bangor born and bred Catholics had till it became possible to get permission for children who were awarded scholarships to attend the grammar schools in the nineteen thirties. In the late nineteen fifties, Catholic children were expected to stay at the parish school till they left school, unless they passed to the grammar schools or their parents managed to send them to the independent convent day school or were able to send them away to school.

THE UNIVERSITY

University of Wales, Bangor was founded as the University College of North Wales in 1884. The main part of the college was built in Upper Bangor, on the hill above the Anglican Cathedral. It was founded as a completely secular institution because of the tensions between Anglicans and Nonconformists in the period before Welsh Disestablishment. There was no department of Theology until the creation of the federal University of Wales a decade later. However powerful Anglican and Nonconformist presences were soon created; for instance the Congregationalists moved from Bala to found Coleg Bala-Bangor, the Baptist College was moved to Bangor from Llangollen, and the Anglican Church Hostel was founded and St Mary's an Anglican teacher training college moved from Caernarfon. The culture was Protestant. I've been told that on one occasion in the nineteen forties a professor of the philosophy of religion at one of the Nonconformist colleges resigned after his wife's conversion to Catholicism checked his promising career. Academic staff and students had little in common with the priests or parishioners of the Catholic parish.

THE CHAPLAINCY

By the nineteen fifties, there were Catholic staff and students at the university and there was a feeling that Catholic students needed their own chaplaincy and place for Sunday Mass near the university and the chaplaincy was established close to the Main Arts Building of the College in October 1962, when Fr Michael Richards a priest of Opus Dei was appointed as chaplain. In 1973 the Catholic Chaplaincy was moved to Pendyffryn, a large Edwardian House with a lovely garden - about five minutes walk from Main Arts. A chapel, which could seat more than fifty people, was created from a drawing room and the billiard room. Mass was celebrated twice on Sunday. There was a large, pleasant common room, which could be used for meetings and social events, and a first floor library. There was also a large room (called the Rock

Room) built on to the rear of the building, which could be used for meetings and parties. There were four rooms let to students.

THE RELATIONSHIP BETWEEN PARISH AND CHAPLAINCY BEFORE 1996

At this time, parish and chaplaincy were separate, though married staff with children tended to belong to both. The priest chaplains acted as chaplains at the district hospital and celebrated Sunday Mass six miles away in the Bethesda church which is part of the parish. Once a month the parish priest would go out to Bethesda and the chaplain would say the 8.30am Mass in Bangor. This arrangement changed in 1989, when the newly appointed parish priest became hospital chaplain and the university chaplain took on pastoral care of the community centred on the Bethesda church. This arrangement lasted till 1996. The chaplaincy flourished and produced a number of vocations to the priesthood and the religious life. Almost all students attended Mass at the Chaplaincy and relatively few parishioners knew the chaplain. There is only the one Catholic Church in Bangor and the average Mass attendance in 2004 was around 320. Bangor has had a non-student population of around 14,000 for the last 30 years. However, 30 years ago there were only about 3,000 students; there are now around 9,000, so the university and the students are very significant in the economy and society of Bangor. The size of the city has made it a pleasant and comparatively inexpensive place to study for most students.

THE SHIFTING RELATIONSHIP

There was a major shift in the pattern of student Mass attendance from the autumn of 1996; the popular priest chaplain took leave from the diocese to study for an MA and was replaced by a lay chaplain, who arranged for a Franciscan priest to come to offer Mass on Sunday evening. The declining numbers of students attending Mass meant that only one Mass was thought necessary. The arrangement might have worked had it not been for another change. For many years the parish priest had said two Masses on a Saturday (one in the hospital and one in the church) and three on Sunday in order to accommodate the congregation. In September 1996, the Catholic Church in the High Street closed and the parish bought a large Victorian church from the Church in Wales. Our Lady and St James takes its name from the old Catholic Church and the Anglican Church. It is situated in the heart of the university district and within a short space of time, most students were attending Mass there. A personal anecdote illustrates the change. At the beginning of the Jubilee Debt Campaign, I spoke about it at the chaplaincy Sunday Mass. There were very few students there. I then walked round to Our Lady and St James to meet my daughter who had attended the parish Mass - and realised that there were far more students there. Some students never found the chaplaincy; others preferred to worship in a parish. The chapel had consisted of two rooms linked by three arches. The first lay chaplain divided them again and moved the library down to the room which had been the rear part of the chapel, freeing the old library to be let. There were now six rooms to be let to students. The lay chaplain left in 1998 and was replaced by a priest. Some students attended the chaplaincy and there was a Catholic Society (Cathosoc) but most of the students continued to attend Mass in the parish and so did not meet the chaplain or the CathSoc students who were trying to make things happen at the chaplaincy. One reason was simply that the new parish church is much more visible than the chaplaincy. It is between the station and the halls of residence and between the supermarket and the halls. The chaplaincy is quite well situated between the main teaching buildings and the halls of residence, but is not as noticeable as the parish church.

THE CHANGING STUDENT POPULATION

There may be other reasons why students preferred to go to Mass in the parish. Passing on the faith has become more difficult for schools and for conscientious parents, and so fewer Catholic students are regularly attending Mass on Sunday. My estimate is that at most 100 attend Mass regularly and the likelihood is that there are at least 750 baptised Catholics. Of those who do go to Mass, many just want to practise - to go to Mass on Sunday - and to get on with studying, earning money and enjoying student life. This may be easier if they go to Mass in a parish setting, because they think that no-one will make demands on their time. The changes in university life discussed in *Dancing on the Edge* mean they have little time for anything else. While some are aware that they need to develop a faith that "penetrates the intellect and the heart" and wish they could find time for this " many teachers and students consider their faith a strictly private affair, or do not perceive the impact their university life has on their Christian existence" (Congregation for Catholic Education, 1994, pp.7,11). As one student said to her friends in CathSoc "for me, religion should be a private matter". Many chaplaincies say their congregations are largely made up of international students, but a parish church may seem more normal to international students. Those from Africa and Asia are often mature students who bring their families over with them or who have left them behind, miss them dreadfully, live for the weekly phone call and work to get money to send back. The familiar pattern of a parish church can seem very attractive.

This is illustrated by two of my earliest student contacts. One, a young Catholic woman from Belfast, the daughter of Catholic parents, had grown up in an ecumenical community. As a first degree student she had attended the Christian Union and gone to Iona with the Anglican Chaplaincy and had a little contact with the Catholic Chaplaincy. When she decided she wanted to be a practising Catholic, she started attending Mass in the parish church and returned to it when she came back as a postgraduate just before I was appointed. The other had come from Swaziland to do a PhD accompanied by sons of twelve and eight. They found the parish church and had an immediate feeling of belonging. She asked for her boys to be baptised and developed a warm friendship with the baptismal catechist. The boys became altar servers, she was confirmed and became a minister of the Eucharist. She had been in Bangor for three years when I was appointed lay chaplain. She says she received much spiritually from her six years as part of the parish community in Bangor, but the parish was equally enriched.

I hope what I have said so far illustrates two important points I want to make about this case study. This chaplaincy is linked to the parish because that is where the majority of the Catholic students who wished to attend Mass chose to worship. They either did not know that there was a chaplaincy, or decided they were more comfortable in a parish community. When the previous chaplain left in October 2002, the bishop may not have had a priest available, but there was little point in putting one into the chaplaincy. Priest chaplains build their chaplaincy around the Sunday Eucharist. You cannot do that if the students are elsewhere. Secondly, the parish was already nurturing students through the Eucharist and through the support given to mature students and international students who brought their families.

A RECOGNISED RELATIONSHIP BETWEEN CHAPLAINCY AND PARISH

I was appointed by the diocese of Wrexham to be lay chaplain to the University of Wales, Bangor in November 2002. This marked a recognition that the parish was where the students who attend Mass were to be found.

My role description states that I am responsible for pastoral and spiritual care of the students. It is my responsibility to offer them opportunities to grow in knowledge and understanding of their faith and to develop lives of prayer, mission and service. The parish priest is not the chaplain and has no oversight over the chaplaincy, although the students form part of his congregation with all that involves. I had been a Confirmation catechist and run the parish youth group since 1990. The parish priest has commented that the arrangement worked because I was a longstanding member of the parish. When the appointment was announced parishioners were positive - if a little surprised. They viewed the chaplaincy not as a Catholic centre which offered support to the student community, but as a building which was rather run down and looked grubby and uninviting. The building has been transformed with a programme of renovation. I can certainly identify with the comments of chaplains in *Dancing on the Edge* about the amount of time taken in maintaining buildings; however the parishioners have followed progress with interest and given me a lot of encouragement and support. We already had Confirmation preparation and youth group meetings in the Rock Room and agreed that the parish would use the Rock Room for other meetings since the parish has no meeting room of its own. As they come and go to meetings, the parishioners' awareness of the Chaplaincy and the students' sense of being "among friends" has grown. As one postgraduate said when she went home to Lesotho, "I have loved being part of this Church."

WHY AND HOW THE LINK WORKS

Our Lady and St James is the only Catholic Church in Bangor and this is an important practical reason why the parish/chaplaincy link works so well here. In a larger town with several Catholic churches it would be much harder to be a chaplaincy rooted in the parish Eucharist. There is a Saturday evening Mass across the Menai Straits in Menai Bridge, where a number of Ocean Science students live, but the two Masses in the Bangor church are the only realistic option for most students spending Sunday in Bangor and so I make a lot of contacts before and after Mass and the students see and support each other there. They also find welcome and encouragement from other parishioners. Being at the parish Masses and being available there is an important part of my job. There is a morning Mass at 10.30, with coffee in the Church afterwards, and an evening Mass at 6.30; the combined attendance averages about 300 and so the community is small enough to notice students and newcomers. My impression is that once I was appointed chaplain, parishioners started to chat to the students more freely, to ask newcomers where they are from, and to befriend them. There is a parish welcome minister at each Sunday Mass and this is one way in which the parish creates the atmosphere which makes the students feel welcome and they and the parish priest direct newcomers to me and to CathSoc members. There are many students whom I meet at Church and who chat with me, but rarely, if ever come to the Chaplaincy - yet they do indicate that they value knowing me and appreciate the chaplaincy as a potential source of support.

There is a chaplaincy section in the newsletter in which I announce regular chaplaincy activities, social events and talks at the Chaplaincy and those put on at the university by the chaplains' group. CathSoc members try to be at most Masses to encourage others to come to events. We have offered Sunday brunch, pancake parties and barbecues so that we can draw people back to the chaplaincy after the morning Mass and parties and talks after the evening Mass. The parish priest celebrates a weekday parish Mass in the chapel once a month - otherwise we all worship in the parish church. The Eucharistic community is not divided and we are all strengthened. For the local parishioners, the student presence means the witness of lively young people taking themselves to Mass and the students say that they do not want to be separated off from the wider community. Many chaplains prepare students for Baptism, Confirmation and reception into the Catholic Church. In Bangor this happens in the parish. The benefit of this is that they will be living their faith in parishes, not chaplaincies. Students, through the Rite of Christian Initiation of Adults (RCIA), have joined our faith sharing and Evening Prayer and become part of our community and our students have attended their Baptism or reception in the parish church.

Our parish community includes Catholics from many different countries. There are those who were born or brought up here, many of them descendants of the Irish migrants of the nineteenth century. There are some university staff, though the academics who make up the management advisory group live in other parishes. In every generation the parish has been enriched by Irish migration and now there are a sizeable number of Irish students here as well. There are a number of Indian and Filipino doctors and nurses, many with their families, who are here to work in the local hospital. There is an increasing Polish community and Catholics from other European countries and further afield, brought here by work or marriage. Some have been part of the parish for many years. This means that international students can fit in very easily and be introduced to established members of the community.

CHAPLAINCY LIFE

When I was appointed, my role was defined as providing pastoral care to students at the university, especially Catholic students, giving social, spiritual, intellectual and friendly support, alongside the sacramental ministry of the parish priest. I came to understand that an important part of this is welcome, hospitality and befriending. I have to be available to listen, not as a counsellor, but as a reliable older person who cares, who knows the institution, but is not part of it. I have to be there to encourage those who are lonely and homesick because family is far away. Hospitality is at the heart of the chaplaincy. For those who need it, the chaplaincy has to be a home from home, a place where they know they are welcome. Most of the students who live in the house are good at supporting this and making coffee for callers when I am not here. One student said "Everything we do includes food". This is true - tea and toast after Morning Prayer, coffee and cake after Evening Prayer and gospel reflection, Sharing the Faith over a meal every Monday evening, as well as the purely social - the parties, the barbecues, the pancake parties, Murder Mystery Night. Every year we welcome international students from all continents: however every year the CathSoc core, some of whom live in the Chaplaincy, has come from largely from Britain and Ireland and it is they who provide a community of welcome for those from Europe and the rest of the world. In the year we will have forty to fifty students coming to the chaplaincy at one time or another, though a smaller number on a weekly basis - and at a guess more than eighty will go to Mass in the parish church, again some more regularly than others

COMMUNITY PRAYER

I had been told that the previous lay chaplain had grounded her ministry around the Sunday Eucharist celebrated by the visiting priest and Communion services during the week. Now that the students go to Mass in the parish officially, Communion services would be inappropriate and it was not how I understood my role. We have become more aware that dividing the Eucharistic community is theologically and pastorally undesirable. My task has been to build a student community at the Chaplaincy which prays together using the riches of our heritage and especially the Liturgy of the Hours and gospel reflection. We started with Evening Prayer once a week at seven o'clock before reflecting on the gospel for the coming Sunday. Sometimes the conversation would go on till ten - regardless of whether I stayed. We moved on to Morning Prayer on Tuesdays: this has been particularly helpful for students who live in the chaplaincy and indeed, this year some of them have met for Morning Prayer most mornings even though I was only there twice a week. This year, Jesuit trained prayer guides have led weeks of Guided Prayer (open to parishioners as well as students) with those willing to commit to regular prayer and meditation and talked about Lectio Divina, imaginative gospel contemplation and the Ignatian Examen to groups of students and parishioners. Not surprisingly more students attended the talks than made the weeks of guided prayer. There is no sense of constraint that the group at the talks have been mixed.

ECUMENICAL CHAPLAINCY ON THE CAMPUS

In Bangor, parish based chaplaincy works very well as a way of supporting Catholic students who go to Mass. It is however hard to reach the many Catholic students who never come to Mass in the church and I am sure that my chaplaincy could be more effective if combined with a visible ecumenical presence on the campus, although it is interesting that the Catholic Chaplaincy was the main base for ministry of Catholic Chaplains in most of the institutions described in *Dancing on the Edge* (Chapter One, 3:3.2). The university remains a secular institution, recognising representatives from many denominations as chaplains and listing them in the Student Services Handbook, but we meet as a chaplains' group with Student Services only about once a year and there are no service agreements or structures within which we can work. One problem in this university is that we have no chaplaincy room and so no visible base for ecumenical activity, although wanting to work together as much as we can. We can book lecture rooms for no charge and every year we arrange for visiting speakers to talk on a variety of justice and peace, ethical and philosophical issues and reach beyond the borders of our own church-attending communities. A talk on whether Christianity and Islam are irreconcilable was attended by a hundred students, staff and people from the city. My Anglican colleague takes groups to Palestine every year and they do a powerful presentation of the conditions there on their return. He also takes ecumenical groups to Iona and Taizé. A hundred people attended a Make Poverty History meeting that I organised with the Students' Union. Nonetheless, it is frustrating to be very limited in developing an ecumenical ministry to the whole institution. It was more effective fifteen years ago, when the Anglican, Methodist and Catholic chaplains not only worked closely together but were recognised as counselling tutors by the university and were able to welcome students in the lunch period to a prominent room near the Students' Union. The latter arrangement died when the lunch hour vanished. Only the Anglican chaplain (who has been chaplain since the late 1980s) remains as a counselling tutor. It can also be difficult to get students to attend the events and activities organised by other churches and to develop a more ecumenical mind set and I have no doubt this would be easier if we had a common gathering place on the campus.

LIMITATIONS AND DIFFICULTIES

Chaplaincies and universities are all different and chaplains - clergy, religious and lay have different skills and visions and constraints on them. There are different ways of linking a chaplaincy and a parish. I think I have shown that one reason the link is working well is that the Catholic Chaplaincy at Bangor is based in the only parish church available for most of our students and in a separate building where six students live. The parish priest is very clear that the chaplaincy is my responsibility, but his style obviously suits the students. There is no "Chaplaincy Mass" on a Sunday. Most international students and most active CathSoc people attend the morning Mass, most home students go in the evening. A priest chaplain in a separate chaplaincy can base his chaplaincy around the Sunday Eucharist, draw students into preparation of the liturgy and direct his homily to them. This could make it easier to nurture the students' intellectual understanding of their faith, given that so many are not willing or able to attend the rest of the programme at the Chaplaincy or in the University. It can be frustrating to stand at the back of the church giving out the CathSoc newsletter or invitations to parties or talks, knowing that some will not think of coming. Earlier I quoted the comment in *The Presence of the Church* that too many university students and staff see their faith as a private affair unrelated to their work and study. I think many chaplains would sympathise with this statement as we wish we could reach more students with our programmes. However, I have come to understand that our students need a sense of freedom if they are to make their faith their own. A chaplaincy based in a parish community where they are welcomed when they come to church, and do not think they will be pursued if they do not come to the chaplaincy events, can combine the space they feel they need and continuing pastoral support. In some ways therefore, it may be better adapted to students in our culture. If they are to form an adult faith, we have to let them become adults who are making their own faith journey. In this respect, the chaplain is like a parent who may find the new distance their maturing children put between them painful for a time, but who discovers the joy of a richer relationship with their adult child. A chaplaincy should be a home from home - but not a nursery. The parish with its mix of generations suits this well. It is in the nature of university chaplaincy that some contacts are brief and the chaplain cannot know what fruit there will be.

AT THIS TIME AND PLACE

Bangor is very distinctive. The city is small and most students live in walking distance of the University departments. When the parish church was small and relatively far away, the separate chaplaincy offered Catholic students a rich and varied experience, but there were degrees of involvement and for some it was simply where they went to Mass. For the last ten years, it has been the parish church which is the most visible presence of the Catholic Church in the university and so it became where the students chose to worship. The parish is the only feasible Mass centre for most of the students and offers an experience which feels familiar. So at this time and place a lay chaplaincy based in a parish and a separate residential chaplaincy can work well. It would not have done so before the parish church moved and our pattern would not necessarily be transferable to a larger city, though something similar could work. In England and Wales, there are a number of university chaplaincies linked to parishes. In some, the priest chaplain is also the parish priest. At the time *Dancing on the Edge* was written, Institution 7 had a priest chaplain and a chaplaincy based in an inner city parish, which also had a parish priest. In another city an assistant priest in the largest parish is the priest chaplain to the large new university down the road.

CAN A LAY PERSON BE A CHAPLAIN?

There are clear directives from the Vatican that this is not possible. In the *Instruction on Certain Questions Regarding the Collaboration of the Non-Ordained Faithful in the Sacred Ministry of Priests* (hereafter *Instruction*) we are told that "emergency and chronic necessity" (*Instruction*, 8), have led to the lay faithful performing many tasks normally reserved to the ordained ministry, which is undesirable , since " the ministerial priesthood differs in essence from the common priesthood of the faithful because it confers a sacred power for the service of the faithful." (*Instruction*,12) Although the baptised continue the ministry of Christ within the Church and the world, "it is unlawful for the non-ordained faithful to assume titles such as 'pastor' or 'chaplain'. (*Instruction*, 20) However, I was appointed to be a lay chaplain and there is nothing in my role description which a lay person with appropriate formation cannot do or which could lead to confusion as to my status.[1] I am very obviously a lay person with a family and entrusted by the Church with a ministry which I love. As lay chaplain in the parish, I am a visible sign of the concern of the Catholic Church - hierarchy and community - for students from home and abroad. I have a ministry on behalf of the body of Christ, which is recognised by the body. When I was appointed, I was very familiar with university age young people and it is also true that much of the practical side of running a residential chaplaincy matches my experience very well. I would argue that lay people can be effective chaplains, especially when the chaplaincy is linked to a suitable parish. Then the vision expressed in *The Presence of the Church* (Congregation for Catholic Education, 1994, p.17) is made real:

At parish level it would be desirable for the Christian communities ... to pay greater attention to students and teachers, and to the apostolate of university Chaplaincies. The parish is of its nature a community within which fruitful relationships can be established for a more effective service of the Gospel. It plays a considerable role through its capacity to welcome people.

As in all collaborative ministry, the arrangement can only work if there is clear definition of roles and responsibilities and a good working relationship between parish priest and lay minister. It may be that at the date of my appointment, it may even have been easier to offer hospitality as a married lay person, because of all the adverse publicity about abuse.

NOT NECESSARILY SECOND BEST

I would argue that the decision to appoint a lay person or a religious as chaplain is not necessarily dependent on whether a priest is available; it should depend on a careful assessment of the particular circumstances and the skills and experience needed for the post. Priests and religious are usually cheaper than lay people and there could be a tendency to think that a salaried lay chaplain is a last resort, to be made redundant if a suitable priest or religious comes on the scene. This scenario has not happened in relation to my appointment, but it has happened in other dioceses in relation to non-university appointments. If lay people work for the Church they need to know that their contracts mean more than that the arrangement can be terminated by three months notice. As a matter of justice they need the security they could expect in any other professional appointment - and we must also expect appropriate supervision. Appraisal can be a tremendous help in reflection on ministry. It is not a threat.

VOCATIONS

My postbag shows how much university chaplaincies are seen as seedbeds for vocations to the priesthood and religious life. The opportunity to get to know a priest chaplain can be a very real influence and clearly this is something a lay person does not offer. I respond sympathetically to enquiries, listen to people talking, publicise the myriad invitations to "Come and See". It was in my first year here that I realised that I was providing a different example, because I am a married Catholic with a grown up family: I am a lay person who works full time (in practice) for the Church and does voluntary work for the Church as well. Most of our students will not have a religious vocation, but they are all called to live out their Baptism, to carry Christ in our hearts and witness to Him in our lives. I have come to see that all chaplains have first to try to foster that vocation by example, whatever their own state. In our parish based chaplaincy, the students can witness a devoted priest, all sorts of lay commitment, Catholic family life, the courage and patience of the elderly and others in the face of age, illness and bereavement, justice and peace activity and the Christian ministries of welcome and hospitality.

THE PRIMACY OF HOSPITALITY

It was a priest chaplain who said to me "In the end our work comes down to hospitality". The hospitality and welcome in our Sunday Eucharists and the other rites of the Church is lived out in the parish and our chaplaincy life. Roublev's icon of the Trinity, sometimes called Hospitality, is an inspiration for me, for a chaplain is like Abraham, welcoming the stranger and sitting him down to eat. They have to welcome each as one made in the image and likeness of God and to accompany them on their journey for a while. For the chaplaincy and parish communities, Paul's advice echoes this: "Continue to love each other like brothers, and remember always to welcome strangers, for by doing this, some people have entertained angels" (Hebrews 13.1-2). If the Chaplaincy is a sign to the students, and to the wider world of the university, of the Catholic Church's care and concern for students and staff, the parish Eucharist and the parish community is a powerful part of making both sign and hospitality real.

REFERENCES

Bassett, Lynn. 2006. 'Lay Chaplaincy – a Question of Identity,' *Pastoral Review*, Vol.2, No.4, July-August.

Congregation for Catholic Education, Pontifical Council for the Laity, Pontifical Council for Culture, Vatican City, 1994.

The Presence of the Church in the University and the University Culture. Catholic Church, Congregations for the Clergy, Doctrine of the Faith and Divine Worship, and Pontifical Council for the Laity, *Instruction on Certain Questions Regarding the Collaboration of the Non-Ordained Faithful in the Sacred Ministry of Priests* (Oxford and London: Catholic Truth Society, 1998)

ENDNOTE:

[1] Lynn Bassett discusses the impact on her self-understanding as a hospital chaplain caused by the *Instruction*. She goes on to quote the qualifications of British and American canon lawyers, "In current usage, the word 'chaplain' is used to refer to all those engaged in pastoral activity" (Bassett, 2006, p.24).

Chapter Nine

BEYOND THE CAMPUS: CHAPLAINS FOSTERING OUTREACH ACTIVITY AND COMMUNITY SERVICE

GERARD DEVLIN

'The particular way in which the Spirit is given to each person is for a good purpose.' (1 Cor 12:7)

PART ONE – SETTING THE SCENE

St. Mary's was founded in 1850 with a particular mission of training teachers to meet the educational needs of a rapidly growing Catholic immigrant population. It has continued to grow over the years and presently we have 3,600 students who are involved in a wide range of programmes; teacher training, undergraduate, Masters, research, postgraduate and foundation level. We have a diverse community with students from various nationalities, different faiths and none which is vastly different from the College community which, up until the early 1970's, was predominantly Roman Catholic. The face of the College campus has changed rapidly and today Chaplains are at the intersection of past, present and future, in a context of tradition, modernity, religion, secularism and pluralism.

On reading the report *Dancing on the Edge* I was struck by how diverse the practice of Chaplaincy in Universities and Colleges is today. Many Chaplains work alone or in Chaplaincy teams, on a single campus or on two or three sites; some may be full-time, others part-time; some employed by the University/ College others employed by the Diocese and the local Bishop. In the Church College where I work the Chaplain was previously appointed by the founding religious community and would sometimes move from that role into lecturing, then come back again to the position of Chaplain. This unstable practice changed when I was appointed by the governing body in September 1996.

In the ten years that I have been involved as College Chaplain it is fair to say that the role has changed with increasing demands on Chaplains and also on the Institution. In the past there was not the heightened expectation for young adults to enter into higher education yet today the aspiration of the government is to have 50% of young people in University education. In the past within the

Catholic church we have seen University/College Chaplaincy as a ministry to a marginal and privileged youth sector, whereas in fact it is fair to say that it is where the vast majority of 17-22 year olds are. This is a time when young people are concretising the values that guide them through life and it is important that the Chaplaincy works alongside the students to help and encourage them on their present journey. In the Church College where I am Chaplain, the Chaplaincy is central to the life of the Institution providing ongoing pastoral care and support for students and staff regardless of religious affiliation, with a particular focus on the spiritual growth of the Christian community. Developing the potential of students takes place in the context of a caring community which encourages students to develop their skills and talents creatively in service to each other, to the wider needs of society and the Church.

ST. MARY'S AS A CHURCH COLLEGE

The typical role of Chaplains today in their pluralist and secularised context is interventionalist, servicing at the interstices of student and staff needs. At St. Mary's however, the Chaplain continues to preserve a highly integrated role in the organisation and operation of College life and I am in the unique position of having open access to all in the Institution, making links between academic departments and other College services. I also have an additional key community role of developing relationships with many outside agencies in a process of 'new networking'. Unlike some Institutions mentioned in the Report *Dancing on the Edge* of March 2005, the Chaplaincy in St. Mary's enjoys a high profile role in what is a Church College and is involved in the decision making process of the Institution, a practice also commended by the Church of England (Dearing, 2001, p.71). The Chaplaincy, then, is integral to the Mission of the College and not an appendage assigned to the periphery.

Chaplaincy is about a concern or the whole corporate life of the institution. It includes obvious and expected work such as pastoral concern for all members of the Institution and is widely seen as central to the institutional promotion of College vision, structures and activities (Dearing, 2001, p.71). As Chaplain I am invited to senior management development days each year, I submit a report to the governors four times each academic year and I am also invited to meet with senior staff on a regular basis. This intimate sharing in the initiating and promotional work of the senior staff and governing body is rather exceptional in University life where Chaplains today tend to have an uncertain or ambiguous relationship with the Institution (Chapter One, Part Two).

The integrated role of Chaplain extends also to active inclusion in the Academic Board and attendance at school meetings. I am a member of the student services committee which reports directly to the Governing Body, and I am a member of the Equal Opportunities Committee. In the words of the report I am an 'honest broker' but also a person with vision, drive and enthusiasm to move the institution forward and maintain its Catholic and Christian ethos (Chapter One, 2:3.1).

At the beginning of a new academic year we provide new and existing students with Chaplaincy booklets which outline the many groups and activities. We have information leaflets regarding outreach programmes and application forms are included to be completed and returned before the ministry training commences. We have the help of the domestic staff to ensure that booklets are placed in all student accommodation and they display posters in a prominent position. We also have Chaplaincy noticeboards designated for our use at strategic locations in the institution. A College website is monitored and regularly updated by a member of the IT staff. The Chaplains are invited to make their own presentations at Induction days for new students and staff alongside the College Principal and other members of the senior management team. We have recently been involved in the making of a DVD which will be shown on open days and sent to schools and FE Colleges throughout the country. Again this highlights the importance attached to St. Mary's Chaplaincy in presence and practice quite distinctive from other examples given in the report (Chapter One, 2:3.2).

As Chaplain I report directly to the Principal, who is my line manager and meets with me on a regular basis, taking personal responsibility for my appraisal each year. The College management structure shows clearly my link to the Principal (*See Appendix*). The enduring centrality of Chaplaincy in a Church College like St. Mary's appears in College governance, structure, and organisational contacts with both academic and supporting staff and in the general programme of welfare and care for all aspects of College life (Dearing, 2001, p.71). It is a privileged position which requires energy and enthusiasm to ensure that Chaplaincy remains central to the corporate plan and mission of the College.

My own approach to Chaplaincy is designed to fit the unusual combination of tradition and modern educational drive and efficiency which is distinctive of St. Mary's. As a community its members include students, academics, service staff, parents, guardians, alumni, members of the worshipping community and representatives from outreach organisations. Our relationship to the Diocese and the religious order who served the College faithfully for over 100 years has shaped institutional identity. The College may be described as a community of choice; staff and students choosing to belong and, as with any community, hopefully they will help to foster the development and continued growth of our College community and share common values on the campus and beyond.

MISSION

The prime task of the Chaplain is to encourage and serve the students who are an integral part of the community for "young people are, and ought to be, encouraged to be active on behalf of the Church, as leading characters in evangelisation and participants in the renewal of society" (Pope John Paul II, 1988, # 46). As Chaplains we must recognise the talents, nurture the creativity, encourage initiative and empower the energy of the students to ensure that they work closely with others building up our own community and reaching out with openness to the wider community with the hope that we can all make a difference in the short and long term.

OUTREACH

At the beginning of each new academic year we encourage students to use their gifts and talents in service to others. Members of voluntary organisations join with the Chaplaincy team at the Clubs and Societies evening during freshers week to talk with students and encourage their involvement throughout the academic year. The identity of the College as 'Catholic' demands fidelity to the mandate given to us in scripture that we demonstrate our love of God through our love of our neighbour (Mark: 12: 28-34).

It has often been said that Catholic social teaching is our "best kept secret" and, sadly, it is not present as a grounding reason for the existence of voluntary service in the community and outreach programmes. Many of our students come from a privileged background and, as Chaplains, we are trying to challenge the students to re-evaluate their lifestyles and their allocation of resources from the perspective of others who do not share our comfortable lifestyle. Opportunities that enable students to identify with others who may need our help can prove extremely valuable in dispelling stereotypes and misconceptions associated with poverty, drug addiction, HIV/Aids and other marginalising conditions.

The gospel imperative to love our neighbour as our self is easier to comprehend when the self is seen in the eyes of the vulnerable other. It is important that we encourage students to follow the example of the gospel and live out the good news in our everyday lives. On Holy Thursday Jesus showed how perfect his love was; *'If I then, the Lord and Master, have washed your feet, you should wash other's feet. I have given you an example that you may copy what I have done to you'* (John 13:1-15). This is what I would like to do myself as Chaplain and my aim is to encourage others to do the same. In developing outreach programmes we must create opportunities which will allow our students to serve. The students often return with positive stories from their experiences and they are providing others with a reason to hope as well.

Students are consistently reminded that we all have a 'preferential option for the poor' which is used as the motivation to ground their work with voluntary organisations. These outreach programmes connect the College to our local community, to a central London programme and also to some national and international links.

Reaching Out

The conception of contemporary Chaplaincy is based on the view that service is intrinsic to the learning process, for the witness value of personal involvement by students and staff in serving the needs of others should never be underestimated. Students are good at generating awareness of what needs to be done, the witness potential of service does engage the entire community and results in fundraising and greater involvement. The students are partners with those being served and it is important to provide interaction. Students are required to commit to a specific placement and some choose to gain credits towards their final degree through such activity.

As a College we aim to nurture a fruitful relationship with our partner voluntary organisations, to ensure there is trust, support and collaboration at personal and communal levels. A good example of the College and Soho Family Centre working in partnership shows volunteers from both places combining their talents, time and energy in renovating and painting a new improved facility. Our students have also gained a new perspective on service as they hear a person living with HIV/Aids tell of volunteer work with those dying of Aids in local hospitals as they visit the CARA Centre in central London.

Our aim is to ensure that we work in partnership with voluntary agencies who share the responsibility of making a difference. Once contact is made, ignorance can no longer be an excuse for inaction and indifference. When contact has been established the student and the College community relate closely with the voluntary organisation and we answer with a personal response to the challenge put before us in the Gospel of Matthew *'For I was hungry and you gave me food; was thirsty and you gave me a drink; I was a stranger and you made me welcome; naked and you clothed me; sick and you visited me; in prison and you came to see me..... in so far as you did it to one of the least of these brothers or sisters of mine, you did it to me'* (Matthew 25: 31-4).

ST. MARY'S AS A EUCHARISTIC COMMUNITY

As a Catholic community the celebration of the Eucharist is vitally important, since our sharing together 'fuels' a committed living which promises that love, justice and a reaching out to others is possible. At our core as a Catholic College is a community that takes and blesses, breaks bread and eats, pours the cup and drinks. A community which breaks open the Word of God and goes forth to live out the values of the Gospel in our everyday lives on the campus and beyond. It gives students the opportunity to take part in liturgical ministries and minister to their peers. As a Eucharistic minister they can also take Holy Communion to members of the College and local community. The College Chapel and the Chaplaincy Centre is at the centre of our College campus and at the centre of what we are about as a Christian community. Many of the students currently involved in ministry enjoy service, find it rewarding and see it as an expression of their own identity. As the students take part in the various ministries and develop new skills there is a growing awareness that service is a necessary part of baptismal commitment in the Church. The Church is by nature a communion in which all the baptised are called to participate and share responsibility, with the staff and students we aim to work together in ministry to build a shared vision of church, working closely to build up the Lord's kingdom.

CHURCH COLLEGE AS COMMUNION

Communion is used to describe the way individual people relate to one another. Baptism and Eucharist are the foundation, sign and nourishment of the Church as Communion (1 Corinthians 10:16). When we respond to God's call to share responsibility and collaborate in building up the kingdom of God, we experience what it means to be in Communion. Communion stresses the vertical relationship with God as well as the horizontal sharing with other Christians.

The Ecclesiology of Communion promoted in the Second Vatican Council demonstrates the vision of what we are called to be as Church (Extraordinary Synod of Bishops, Rome, 1985). The Church is a dynamic reality in which all are responsible as active participants in the mission of Christ. The people of God is a community of active people who use their charisms in diverse forms of ministry to promote co-operation, collaboration and communion as they build up the kingdom.

The recent pastoral plan produced by the Diocese of Portsmouth speaks of the need to build up a strong sense of community in a world which is fragmented and has lost its sense of communion. 'Our vision - our hope – is of ourselves as the gathered community of the disciples of the Lord, united in baptism and bonded together by Christ in the Eucharist. Our Mission is to live out the communion in the power of the spirit that we proclaim the Gospel by words and become the good news by our way of life' (Hollis, 2005).

The Eucharist celebrates the equal dignity of all as members of the people of God, promotes reconciliation and sustains each of us in the call to ministry. It also promotes greater collaboration of staff, students and members of our worshipping community in the building up of the Kingdom. In the report, *Dancing on the Edge* it was generally felt that there was a low percentage of Catholic students attending Chaplaincy Eucharists. This point was echoed recently by Dr. Diarmuid Martin, Archbishop of Dublin, when he said that *'The most dramatic surprise was the drift of young people away from active Church life. I can now go to parishes on a Sunday where I find no person in the congregation between the ages of 16 and 36. None at all"* (Intercom, 2006, p8). This is not my experience as we have a large attendance at the Sunday Eucharist and a large number of the young people are from Ireland. We have a good attendance at the weekday Mass and one day each week on a Tuesday, lectures are suspended between 12noon–1.00pm to give staff and students the opportunity to attend our weekly community Mass and liturgy. Celebrating the Eucharist together as a community empowers all in the call to ministry and ministry is enhanced by the individual's union with Christ. Every Christian has the same spiritual aids common to all, among which the active participation in the Eucharist *(Apostolicam Actuositatem, No4)*. In a Catholic

College I feel that the Eucharist is the fountain from which all ministry flows and the living spring that sustains all engaged in ministry for the Sacrament of our neighbour cannot be separated from the sacrament of the Altar. The daily bread that we break in the Eucharist has to be transformed by us in our mission into the bread of the kingdom, the bread of fraternal benevolence and beauty (Olivier, 1995, pp.4-5).

I am also aware that we have students from other faiths and none, many of whom choose to participate in the Eucharistic Celebrations as Ushers, Readers and as part of the Music ministry. Our aim is to involve as many students as possible in ministry and outreach programmes and, as an inclusive community, we try to ensure that all students feel welcome and that their contribution is valued at all times.

We now have a rich diversity on campus in terms of ethnicity, nationality, age and patterns of study, we are a multi-cultural community and over the past few years we have seen an increase in students from the Sikh, Hindu and Muslim traditions. We have constructed a multi faith prayer room with washing facilities below the main College Chapel and it is fairly well used. My observation would be that, sadly, not many students from these traditions choose to take part in the outreach programmes which are presently running successfully but we will continue to work hard to ensure that they know what is on offer and, hopefully, they will volunteer to take part in the not too distant future.

PART TWO – MOVING FORWARD

As a Church College Chaplaincy our aim is to produce young people with ideas and dreams, with a vision of what they want to achieve in life, who have a strong sense of service, of care and compassion for those in need and, above all, a love of life, a zest for living life to the full. Our aim is to build up our own community who will go forward to rediscover and redefine our sense of service. St. Mary's does have a strong sense of community as was highlighted in a Quality Assurance Subject Review Report (October 2000) which stated: 'An admirably strong feeling of community exists for both students and staff within the College, at the heart of which lies a Chaplaincy whose far reaching spiritual and pastoral care extends to those of all faiths and none. The reviewers regard the feeling of community and the ethos of the College as an exceptionally positive feature of the provision'. This sense of community is centred in the Eucharist and sustained by pastoral availability and care. We are conscious of the challenge to go and 'feed the lambs and the sheep' to put our talents and abilities at the disposal of others so that the good news can be brought 'to the afflicted, liberty to captives, sight to the blind, freedom for the oppressed' (Luke 4: 18-19). Our hope is that the lives of staff and students can be enriched and enhanced in the service they provide to others.

CHAPLAINCY AND OUTREACH

The Assistant Chaplain was appointed in March 2004 with dual responsibility: 0.5 Assistant Chaplain and 0.5 Active Community Fund Co-ordinator. A grant was awarded to help develop outreach programmes and to administer the programme and it was allocated to increase the Assistant Chaplain's salary and to finance an adequate London living allowance. There remains an issue consistent with the report (Chapter One, 4:2.2) as to whether salary scales for Chaplains should be on an even par with academic staff. This issue is presently under discussion through the Common Pay Scale which will be introduced in August 2006. In real terms it means that Chaplaincy funding has fallen from where it was before the Assistant Chaplain was employed. We are also losing out in terms of the amount of hours the Assistant Chaplain spends working in the Chaplaincy.

The Assistant Chaplain works closely with the Director of Work Based Learning, the Widening Participation team, and our College Careers Department in looking for suitable placements for students. The Assistant Chaplain is also a member of the Innovation Development and Outreach Committee which oversees the entire programme.

OUTREACH PROGRAMMES – MAKING A DIFFERENCE

Outreach programmes complement the academic life of the students at St. Mary's. All the programmes encourage student leadership, community building and structured time for volunteering and reflecting on the service experience.

Students work with and service a large variety of people living on the margins of our society and they have the opportunity to work with young people, young adults, elderly, homeless and people with learning disabilities whose lives are enriched by their involvement. There are many reasons why students choose to volunteer; it is a great way to get involved on the College campus and get to know other students. It allows meeting and building relationships with people in our local community and beyond. Volunteering helps to create an awareness of social justice issues and will ensure that the students make a difference by helping other people. Students must complete a Criminal Records Bureau form which is administered by the College Registry and Induction days must be completed in the various voluntary programmes before the students begin their short or long term placement.

Opportunites for volunteering in 2005-2006 exist in the following areas:

KEEN (Kids Enjoy Exercise Now) - Students help to organise sports and recreational activities for children with special needs.
(www.keenlondon.org)

The Soho Family Centre - The Centre provides a formal daycare through a unique childminders scheme, pre-school education, family drop in centre and Chinese and Bengali community projects.
(www.sohofc@btclick.com)

The Shooting Star Trust - A local project based in Hampton to provide care and support for children with life limiting illnesses and for their family and friends.
(www.shootingstar.org.uk)

CARA - Provides a range of services to people living with HIV and Aids, helping them to manage the virus in order to live life as fully as possible.
(www.caratrust.freeserve.co.uk)

Richmond Housing Partnership - This is a vibrant housing association based in Twickenham. It is a pro-active organisation that aims to provide many fantastic opportunities for customers with a desire to improve their quality of life such as free IT training, Sports coaching sessions, Music therapy, Youth clubs, Dance clubs plus much more.
(www.rhp.org.uk)

Irish Centre Housing - An Irish led organisation providing accommodation and support to single homeless people. ICH is committed to 'providing quality housing, support and related services to disadvantaged Irish and others in housing need'.
(www.irishcentrehousing.org)

Breast Cancer Awareness - Helps raise awareness and funds for Breast Cancer throughout the academic year.

The Roy Kinnear Foundation is situated across from the main entrance of the College and its aim is to give quality of life to young adults with severe learning disabilities.
(www.roykinnear.com)

Feltham Young Offenders Institution - We have taken students to engage with the young men who are serving prison sentences at present, and our College teams have played rugby, football and hockey as well as taking part in athletics. In the past there has been a group taking part in faith sharing and a group of students were involved in presenting the radio station.

Simms Lourdes - Fundraising to raise money for children with learning and physical disabilities to travel with the HCPT Pilgrimage to Lourdes at Easter. Students are also available to help with major fundraising activities with HCPT and recently they were commended for their hard work and endeavour at a Race Night held in Wimbledon which raised £38,000.

PART THREE – SERVICE LEARNING:
WORK IN THE COMMUNITY

The Chaplaincy works closely with the Director of Work Based Learning to ensure that students can gain credits towards their final degree. The Leader of the Music group was successful in completing the service learning module and we encourage other students who are in leadership roles within the Chaplaincy groups to take the opportunity and make a formal commitment to the programme. As we have a good working relationship with voluntary organisations we are able to offer a 'market place' where students can successfully complete a service learning module and organisations are introduced to the College community.

WHY SERVICE LEARNING?

> Volunteering is one way of enabling students to experience at first hand the wider social issues facing communities. If Higher Education develops the whole person by contributing to the 'maturing process' then active citizenship is crucial to the wider goals of social inclusion and the creation of a more cohesive society (DfES Work Experience Group, 2001, p.11).

Service Learning:
- Enhances student learning by offering the opportunity to apply theory to practice
- Fills unmet needs in the community through direct service which is meaningful and necessary
- Enables students to help others, give of themselves and enter into caring relationships with others
- Assists students in seeing the relevance of the academic subject to the real world
- Enhances the self-esteem and self-confidence of students
- Increases the civic and citizenship skills of students
- Provides students with the valuable skills of reflection and articulation
- Enables students to develop a range of work based skills
- Assists agencies which benefit from enthusiastic volunteers
- Exposes students to societal inadequacies and injustices and empowers them to help to remedy these
- Develops a richer context for student learning
- Prepares students for their careers
- Impacts local issues and local needs
- Develops partnerships between the College and the community
- Enhances students' abilities and dispositions to become socially responsible professionals
- Enables the College to develop projects that serve the interests of the local community
- Offers an academic approach to fulfilling this aspect of the College mission
- Enables students to learn first hand about social issues that have significance in contemporary life and in the workplace

SERVICE LEARNING: WORK IN THE COMMUNITY

MODULE AIMS

This module aims to provide students with a practical, work-related experience by carrying out a placement in a local social, community, educational or charitable agency. The module will help prepare students for organised service activity by developing in them an awareness of wider social issues together with an appreciation of their relationship with the College and the local community. The module seeks to develop students' employability skills through the process of self-reflection and evaluation.

ELIGIBILITY

On successful completion of the module, students gain 15 credits at Level 2. The module is offered to all undergraduate students, whatever their degree programme.

LEARNING OUTCOMES

On completion of the Module, students should be able to:
- Appreciate the role of service agencies, in a diverse context
- Evaluate and sustain their own role in the community
- Critically review their own development in the areas of self-concept, confidence, competence, and awareness
- Evaluate and deploy transferable and employability skills such as: communication, time-management, teamwork and independent learning
- Demonstrate an ability to reflect on and appraise their own experience, performance and growth
- Understand the attributes required to become socially responsible professionals and the contribution that they can make through organised service activity

PLACEMENT COMPONENT

Students spend a minimum of 60 hours (part-time) in a local charitable, social, educational or community agency, carrying out various types of work. The choice of agency or work will usually be related to the student's academic studies and must be agreed in advance by the module tutor. The time spent in an agency is carefully monitored and assessed (according to professional criteria) by the student's placement supervisor.

MODULE CONTENT

In addition to the placement, students also attend lectures, seminars and tutorials which cover the following topics:

Introduction to Service Learning

Introduction to the module and the way it works. What is Service Learning? Terminology and definitions. Particular features of not for profit organisations.

Work Based Learning / Setting Goals

Purpose of Work Based Learning. Experiential Learning theory. Setting goals for the work experience element of the module and beyond.

Evaluating the need for not for profit organisations and their role in contemporary British society

Economic, social and political perspectives.

Mission led organisations

Researching and understanding the history, governance, structure and processes, funding, context, organisational culture, missions, goals, and community relationships of your chosen organisation.

Perceptions of community and of service activity

What is community? What makes communities work? The history and philosophy of community service. Identifying community issues with particular focus on London and the local area.

Reflection and Articulation

Approaches to reflection. Techniques for self reflection and completion of the log book.

Transferable Skills and adapting to the workplace

Identification and development of employability skills. Developing ways of working appropriate to an individual workplace. Skills assessment. Ethical issues in the workplace.

Managing Time and Stress

Guidelines for good time management. Dealing with stressful situations at work.

Outputs and outcomes in the not for profit sector

Managing impact. Measuring Success. Performance management information.

Summary of work experience and contribution to the community

FUNDRAISING

There are some students who would prefer not to volunteer for a short or long term placement but would rather involve themselves in fundraising activities for local and national charities each year. The organisations which we work with in the voluntary placements are benefactors of our fundraising and we also support local, national and international charities. Each year we have an Advent and Lenten Appeal and the money is distributed to a worthwhile project in the Third World. These projects usually involve a link with a former student and in the past we have refurbished a school in Zambia and built a Library in Ghana. This year we are raising money to construct an HIV/Aids Hospice in Guatemala which is run by Sr Dee, a former student, who recently returned to the College to receive an Honorary Fellowship. We also have students who take a gap year working with our contacts in the projects we have sponsored abroad and this has been very successful, again students can obtain degree credits for the voluntary placement if it takes place during their course of study. Since I started as College Chaplain in 1996 we have raised, with the help of students, over £200,000 for worthwhile causes at home and abroad. We also have a College organisation called Strawberry Hill Overseas Concern which works together with the Chaplaincy and, over the past year, we have raised nearly £100,000 to support projects in the UK and overseas. We are trying to engage the staff in donating a regular amount of their salary each month to support the projects that we propose each year and some which will run for a longer term. The 'Give as You Earn' scheme provides regular funding and also allows staff the opportunity to donate to other chosen charities, it has provided regular funds for SHOC projects in Guatemala, Sierra Leone and Kenya.

In 1997 we founded our own HCPT group and it is successfully led and organised by students and former students. The group fundraise each year and are supported by the Chaplaincy, once again it provides an opportunity for students to develop their skills as group leaders and through the service learning module obtain degree credits.

COMMUNITY SCHOLARSHIPS

As part of St. Mary's agreement with the Office for Fair Access, entry scholarships are being offered to undergraduate students who are entering higher education in September 2006. The aim of the College is to attract students who are gifted and talented, to encourage and enable their talent to develop during their course of study. There are 75 scholarships available each year and 25 have been designated in the area of community and applications will be dealt with by the Chaplaincy team, Director of Work Based Learning and the Administrator of the Strawberry Hill Overseas Concern fund. The scholarships are open to people of all faiths, traditions and beliefs. The scholarships are available to students who can contribute to the Mission of the College through their involvement in voluntary work, participation in service opportunities or fundraising locally, nationally or internationally. By doing so the prospective students will have demonstrated that they have offered their skills, resources and gifts for the purpose of creating a more just world. Applicants should demonstrate an ongoing regular commitment to community work over a period of time and be able to provide evidence for this. They will be asked to indicate how they propose to continue their engagement in community work during their course of study. The scholarship rewards will be renewed for each year of the course, up to a maximum of three or four years, depending upon the length of the programme being followed and subject to performance against the scholarship criteria. There are fifty scholarships available in two other areas, sport and creativity. I felt that it was important that the Chaplaincy have an input and ensure that students will be financially rewarded for taking part in working with local, national and international voluntary organisations.

THE WAY FORWARD

As a Chaplaincy we will continue to build up our own community and encourage students to be outward looking as well. In developing the outreach programmes we are mindful of the differences and similarities of the partners involved. It is important to acknowledge that in the field of service learning two of the main players, the College and the placement/voluntary agency, may have different goals. With the close working relationship of the Chaplaincy, the centre for service learning has a function to provide an educational experience also for the students who take part. A voluntary organisation exists to serve those in the larger community with unmet needs, often the most basic ones of food, clothing and shelter. Part of the vision of St. Mary's typically includes developing students into socially responsible citizens, and voluntary organisations need individuals committed to the welfare of society as a whole.

Listening to the voices of the partners means engaging them in dialogue about the programmes from beginning to end. In cases where the goal of the

College is placed at the forefront, the result may be more critical thinking on the part of the student but less direct service that benefits the community. In the programmes where the service need is emphasised as more important, the students may find themselves actively engaged in the operations of the voluntary agency but lacking the reflection and relevant coursework to make the experience educational. True service learning and outreach must be reciprocal, with equal weight being given to service and learning and the roles of all parties as educators and learners. Our aim is to create an environment that will be conducive to a productive partnership.

The programme for service learning is taking time to grow at St. Mary's although we are pleased with the number of students who volunteer during their course of study without receiving any credits towards their final degree. There are always many willing helpers and our task is to open up new areas of involvement and continue working with our present partners. I would agree with the report (Chapter One, 1:2.2) that there are greater demands on students in terms of paid employment and my fear is that this will increase with the introduction of tuition fees in September 2006. We also have an increased number of mature and part time students (ibid, 2:2.3) as well as students travelling to the College from a forty mile radius. This does limit the number of students who are willing to engage in outreach programmes and voluntary activity.

We have a group of American students who choose to study at St. Mary's for one or two semesters each academic year. It is interesting that many would like to take part in our outreach programme as it is part of their 'own University culture' back home. In the University they attend there is a well-established programme which has been running for many years and they are willing participants in our College programme in order that they may secure credits.

There is no doubt that the present patterns of student and College life have eroded the traditional model of Chaplaincy (Chapter One, 1:6) but I am ever hopeful and encouraged that we can always be proactive in engaging students. Each new academic year the goal of developing potential at St. Mary's is not confined to academic work, the Chaplaincy complements the work of the academic schools and will continue to work closely with students in developing their skills and talents creatively in serving each other and the wider needs of our world. My continued hope is that in the years ahead students will go on to assume active leadership roles within the Church and society, benefiting from taking part in Chaplaincy groups and activities knowing that 'we are called to act justly, love tenderly, serve one another and walk humbly with God' (Micah 6:8).

St Mary's College Management Structure
(as at February 2006)

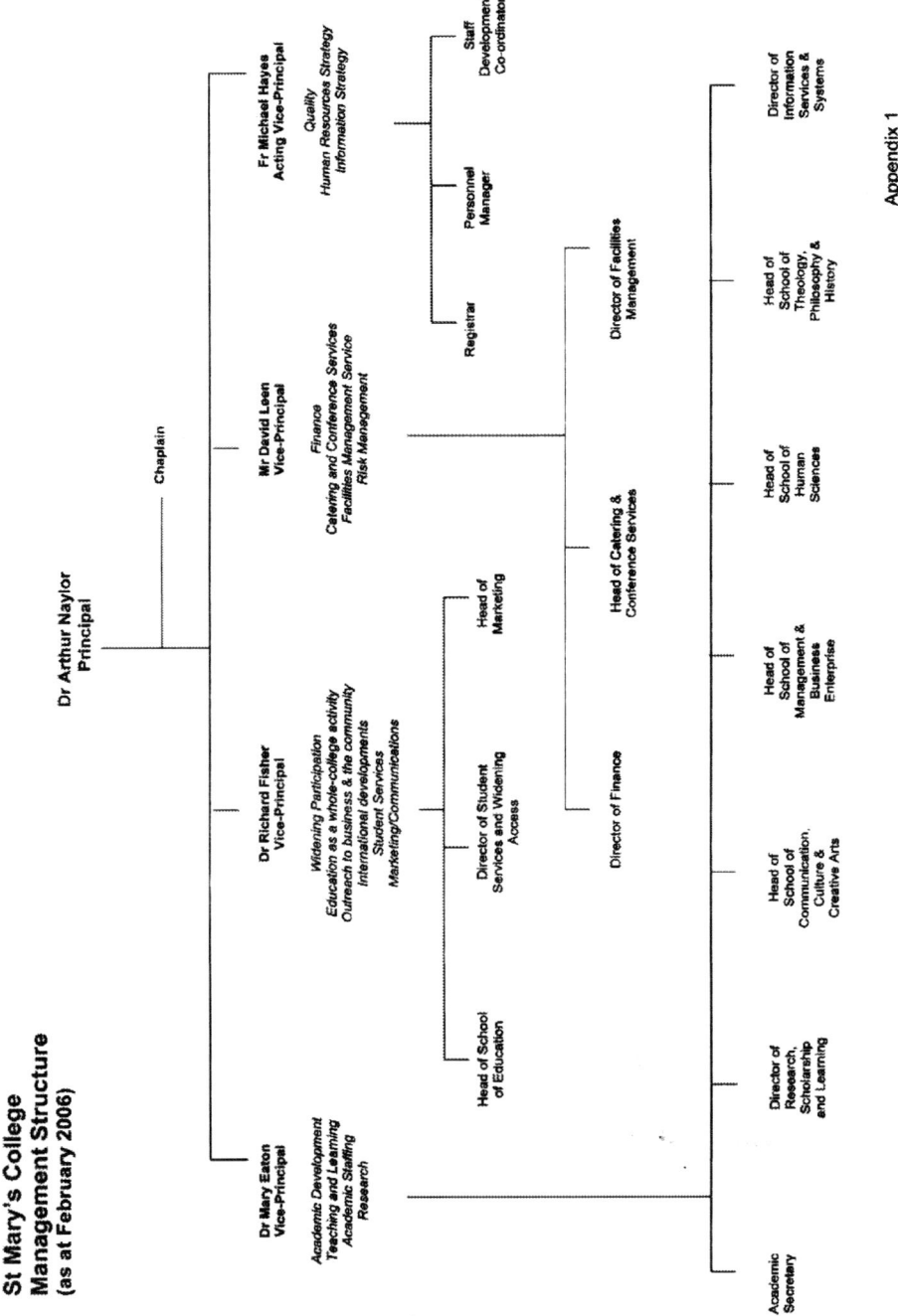

Appendix 1

REFERENCES:

Arthur, James (Ed), (2000) *The Church Dimension in Higher Education*, Council of Church and Associated Colleges, Canterbury: Church House Publishing.

Bishops' Conference of England and Wales: Working Party on Collaborative Ministry, (1995) *The Sign We Give*, Chelmsford: Matthew James Publishing.

Dearing, R (2001) *The Way Ahead: Church of England Schools in the new millennium*, London, Church House Publishing.

Department for Education and Skills (DfES) Work Experience Group, (2001) *The Work Related Learning Report*, London: DfES.

Doohan, Leonard, (1989) *Grass Roots Pastors. A Handbook for Career Lay Ministries*, San Francisco: Harper & Row.

Flannery Austin (Ed), (1995) *The Conciliar and Post Conciliar Documents*, New York: Costello Publishing Company; Dublin: Dominican Publications.

Hollis, Bishop Crispian, (2004) *Growing Together in Christ*: Diocese of Portsmouth.

Hollis, Bishop Crispian, (2005) *Go Out and Bear Fruit*: A Pastoral Plan for the Diocese of Portsmouth.

Hollis, Bishop Crispian, (2006) *Signs of Hope: A Journey of Faith into Communion and Mission*, The Pastoral Review, Volume 2 issue 1, Jan-Feb.

Intercom (2006) : *A Pastoral and Liturgical Resource for People in Ministry*, Maynooth: Catholic Communications Office, March.

Legood, Giles (Ed), (1999) *The Church's Sector Ministries*, London: Cassell.

Lubich, Chiara, (1991) *From Scripture to Life*, New York: New City Press.

McGrail, Peter & Sullivan John (Eds), (2005) *Dancing on the Edge: A Report into Catholic Chaplaincy in Higher Education*, Liverpool Hope University.

Norman, James (Ed), (2004) *At the Heart of Chaplaincy*, Dublin: Veritas.

Olivier, Clement, (1995) *Three Prayers*, St. Valdimir Press, Paris.

Pope Paul VI *Decree on the Apostlate of Lay People* (Apostolican Actuositatem) Catholic Truth Society, London.

Pope John Paul II, (1988) *The Vocation and Mission of the Lay Faithful in the Church and in the World*, (Christifideles Laici), London: Catholic Truth Society.

Chapter Ten

CHAPLAINCY IN ECUMENICAL AND INTER-FAITH CONTEXTS

STEPHEN WILLIAMS

INTRODUCTION

UNIVERSITY OF POPPLETON

> Once again, it's time for some of the university's movers and shakers to select their Books of the Year.
>
> **The Revd Tom Spacey, University Chaplain**
>
> I enjoyed *Religious Multi-skilling* by Jeff Harcourt. Mr Harcourt courageously wonders why, in an age of multi-skilling, it is still thought appropriate to retain a strict division of labour between priests, mullahs and rabbis. He looks forward to the day when "progressive ecumenism" allows "all-purpose pastors" to ring communion bells for Catholics as readily as they give the early morning Islamic call to prayer or make up the tenth person for Jewish ritual prayers. A sign, as John the Baptist might have said, of things to come! (Taylor, 2005).

Laurie Taylor's weekly parody of life at the fictitious, if all too recognisable, University of Poppleton, playfully identifies operational trends and ideological currents which he satirises as 'emergent practice' in higher education institutions. The above quotation from his regular column in the Times Higher Education Supplement neatly evokes the management-speak 'blue sky thinking' which could envisage such a 'rationalisation of chaplaincy service delivery.' Mr Taylor deals in caricatures which have just enough of the truth in them to make them seem plausible.

This Paper's intention is to recover the story behind the current level of ecumenical and inter-faith chaplaincy which is generally held to represent received good practice. Just how near are we to Laurie Taylor's multi-skilling chaplain? I hope to offer a reality check on the true degree of ecumenical and inter-faith collaboration which is found within the Higher Education institutions which are the limited focus of this study. Namely, those HE institutions found within the Greater London region. That is an area roughly bounded by the M25 orbital motorway within which are found some 14 universities, including the federal University of London with its 32 constituent colleges, schools and institutes. Just how far have we travelled along the road of *'progressive ecumenism'*? How uneven was the climbing path that led us here? Have we reached a high plateau or merely pitched a provisional camp on the slope? Is there further to go? Up? Or down?

This paper draws on the observed experience of myself, as Senior Anglican University Chaplain in the Diocese of London, since 1991, and before that as Anglican Chaplain to the London School of Economics and Political Science from 1981–1991. I have also conducted semi-structured interviews with my predecessor, The Revd Prebendary Dr Eric Tinker, (Senior Anglican University Chaplain from 1969- 1990), and with The Revd Dr Martin Eggleton, who between 1976 and 2000 was severally Free Church Chaplain to Brunel University, Senior Methodist University Chaplain, and Ecumenical Chaplain to Middlesex University. I have also conferred with my Senior Denominational Chaplain colleagues, and noted the experience of the 36 Anglican university chaplains who are my direct reports.

In the second part of this paper I draw on the shared observations of my university chaplaincy Jewish and Muslim colleagues, Rabbi Gavin Broder and Sheik Musa Admani.

THE EARLY DAYS

The early days of HE chaplaincy in London were the heady days of the 1960's. Suddenly everything seemed re-negotiable. The 'Old Dispensation', which included 'The Church', in its various institutional incarnations, was at best under critical attack, at worst, overlooked as irrelevant. The spirit of enquiry was the spirit of the age, and determined the terms of reference given to Lord Robbin's National Committee of Inquiry into Higher Education (1963).

> 'There should be maximum participation in initial higher education by young and mature students and in lifetime learning by adults, having regard to the needs of individuals, the nation and the future labour market. . .'

The Report recommended immediate expansion of universities, and that all Colleges of Advanced Technology should be given the status of universities. Consequently, the number of full-time university students was to rise from 197,000 in 1967-68 to 217,000 in the academic year of 1973-74 with 'further big expansion' thereafter.

Apart from these potent secular and educational market forces, other forces were at work. Within the Church(es) a self-critical awareness was emerging, too. The spirit of reform and modernisation that flowed into the Roman Catholic Church from the Ecumenical Council, popularly known as Vatican II, was a timely complement. In London the initiative to reach out to the buoyant and expanding 'university and polytechnic' sector was initiated by the Archdiocese of Westminster's University Chaplaincy under the charismatic leadership of Monsignor Bruce Kent. In 1966, the acquisition of a property, 111 Gower Street, directly opposite the 'Godless institution' of University College, London was the first clear statement of intent to place the Church within the sphere of university life, rather than simply invite 'Catholics' to step outside to join in traditional parochial congregational patterns. The Roman Catholic Church was able to offer residential accommodation to some 60 students as well as have a base from which develop a more proactive ministry.

The Anglican Church's initial sortie into the sector came a little later. The Revd. Gordon Philips, Rector of St George's, Bloomsbury developed a small team of university chaplains concentrating on the major, central colleges of the University of London. By the late 1960's it became clear to the Senior Staff of the Diocese of London that ministry to the HE sector could not simply be a 'bolt on' to existing local parochial provision. From 1969, under the leadership of the newly appointed Senior University Chaplain, Prebendary Eric Tinker, the leasing of two Georgian houses from the University of London in Woburn Square, and later the leasing of the Catholic Apostolic Church, in Gordon Square, gave an independent, non-parochial infrastructure to the Bloomsbury based Anglican Chaplaincy, now expanded to all the universities and polytechnics in London. The 1970's saw a piecemeal expansion of HE chaplaincy across the Archdiocese of Westminster and the Diocese of London, which was mirrored in dioceses south of the Thames. In most cases deployment of dedicated and specifically recruited chaplaincy staff was dictated by the scale and relative strategic significance of the university, college or polytechnic which was prepared to allow chaplaincy activity on its campus.

In conversation with Dr Eggleton and Dr Tinker it was made quite clear that an "ecumenical spirit of collaboration and co-operation" characterised those early days of HE Chaplaincy in London. Centrally, in Bloomsbury, the Roman Catholic Chaplains based at 111 Gower Street got on extremely well with their local Anglican counterparts. I also believe it is significant that coincidentally they were all drawn from the liberal traditions within their respective Churches. In East London, the local Roman Catholic and Anglican Bishops were very ecumenically minded; as were the various denominational clergy working at Queen Mary College. A happy modus operandi soon evolved. A similar ecumenical chaplaincy working pattern was found in South Kensington, clustered around Imperial College, the Royal College of Music and the Royal College of Art campus sites. In order to 'formalise' these spontaneous, harmonious ecumenical working practices, 'covenants' were designed to further strengthen and enshrine the good practice - a practice which had developed out of the mutual respect and affection enjoyed by those pioneer HE chaplains from different Christian traditions.

The initial 'ecumenical chaplaincies' grew organically and were not imposed from above by ecclesiastical dictat. The institutional church benedictions came later: official 'Management Committees' came in the wake of personal friendships. Of course those first HE chaplains realised that what had emerged as 'good practice' within a favorable climate needed to be 'officially ratified' in order to 'institutionalise' those gains for future chaplains. You could not presume that 'positive personal chemistry' would always exist between later HE chaplaincy colleagues.

THE 1980'S

The 1980's saw further expressions of formalised ecumenical cooperation in the North and West of London. In 1982 the Anglican College of Education, All Saint's College, Tottenham was absorbed by the vigorously developing Middlesex Polytechnic, now Middlesex University. The advantageous sale of the property by the Church of England to the local LEA realised a sum which was held in Trust. As a prime object of the Trust was to support 'ecumenical chaplaincy', this provided the first part of a financial package which later included substantial donations from the Polytechnic, as well as the Anglican, Roman Catholic and Free Churches. The emergent Middlesex University Ecumenical Chaplaincy Trust managed the project until it was wound up in 2000. The end of the partnership, and effectively organised chaplaincy provision, was precipitated by funding partners being forced to withdraw due to the then current economic downturn.

However, while the sun shone through the 1980's and 90's, the Middlesex Ecumenical Chaplaincy had Methodist, Anglican and Roman Catholic

Chaplains working collaboratively, under the leadership of a Senior Chaplain. They all reported to the ecumenical Management Committee which had officially nominated representatives from the University, the All Saint's Educational Trust, and the contributing denominations.

On looking back it becomes clear that many of the ecumenical, inter-faith and pastoral strategies we now take for granted were pioneered by the Middlesex Polytechnic/University Ecumenical Chaplaincy. The Middlesex University model offers a departure from the earlier, organic, 'bottom up' ecumenical experiments of the 1960's and 70's as it was specifically initiated, sponsored and monitored by a legally constituted ecumenical body.

Brunel University, at Uxbridge, West London, offers the final example of an ecumenical Chaplaincy which warrants both attention and celebration. Again it was the product of the early 1980's and the prevailing winds of ecclesiastical change and collaboration which blew on from the 1970's. Once again the impetus for an ecumenical project was prompted by a Roman Catholic initiative. The sale of the house used by the Catholic Chaplaincy, off campus, provided the core of the financial package which made possible the erection of purpose built premises, described as an 'Inter-denominational Chaplaincy' on an as yet undeveloped part of the extensive 'green field' Brunel University campus site. The 'Meeting House' was built on land generously set aside by Brunel University and demonstrated a recognition by Senior University Staff that the provision of facilities for religious groups was part of their overall welfare and student support responsibility.

The project was financed by the Archdiocese of Westminster (2/3rds of construction costs) and the Diocese of London (1/3 of construction costs). On completion the furnishing of the Meeting House was paid for by the Methodist Church. In 2004, after twenty years, the building reverted, under the terms of the original licence, to legal ownership by the University, but remains the hub of a Chaplaincy which continues to go from strength to strength.

Both Brunel University's Inter-denominational Chaplaincy and Middlesex University's Ecumenical Chaplaincy were early examples of HE Institutions undertaking formal, legal partnerships with an ecumenical consortium. In both cases the allocation of dedicated premises, and in Middlesex's case, the part-funding of the chaplains' stipend, are illustrative of a high level of ownership by the host institution.

By the mid 1980's a pattern had been established across the northern part of the region which is the focus of this study. Almost at its cardinal compass points one found a formally constituted 'ecumenical' chaplaincy team, often with shared chaplaincy premises: namely, at Brunel University, Middlesex University, Queen Mary College, and Imperial College.

By then a range of other London HE Institutions had also developed some form of chaplaincy provision after being approached by the main stream Christian denominations. By 1985 four more 'Senior Chaplains' had been appointed by The United Reformed Church, the Baptist Union, the Methodist Church and the Orthodox Church. Although these representative 'Senior Chaplains' did not have teams of their own denominational chaplains to directly deploy or manage, they did add a further ecumenical dimension to an already established Anglican and Roman Catholic hegemony. By 1986 the Diocese of London budgeted for 15 full-time HE chaplaincy posts and dedicated a proportional share of the Diocesan property portfolio to house them. The Archdiocese of Westminster was able to deploy somewhat fewer priests and nuns, who were primarily based in Bloomsbury and West London, but who each had a number of HE institutions to which they ministered as visiting Chaplains.

THE 1990'S

By 1992, and the end of the binary divide in HE , the so called 'New Universities' had begun to develop their student support services in line with the new funding council expectations and in response to the competitive HE market place.

Over the next ten years HE institutions like the University of North London, London Guildhall University, University of Westminster and City University contracted financial partnerships with the Diocese of London to deliver chaplaincy provision. Other HE institutions like The Royal Veterinary College, The Royal Free, Imperial College, and University College Hospital Schools of Medicine, The School of Pharmacy, The Guildhall School of Music and Drama, The Royal Academy of Music, The University of the Arts, Chelsea College of Art and Design, the Royal College of Art and Thames Valley University also established financial partnerships with the Diocese of London to deliver chaplaincy provision. These strategic decisions by HE Senior Staff reflected the understanding quoted in *Dancing on the Edge*.

> (The Anglican approach to parish ministry) 'is a territorial, rather than a congregational, strategy. And by extensions that's the same attitude and same understanding that Anglican Chaplains have in a university setting. They're there for everybody, whether they're of faith or no faith. They're there for everybody – staff, support staff, administrators, teachers, caterers – whoever it may be; it's a holistic and entire stance towards ministry.'

This position was echoed by the institution

> 'Now when it comes to the institution, how do they perceive us?
> They see the Anglican Church as the recognized Church, and they recognize that we offer a service to the whole community, not just to a tendency within it' (Chapter One, 3:2.1).

Although these instances of HE institutions allocating scarce financial resources for what could appear to be 'Anglican' Chaplaincy provision, the reality is more complex. The 'paid' chaplain is usually charged, or at least tacitly understood to be, the 'lead' chaplain for a team of ecumenical, denominational visiting chaplains. Increasingly a 'mission statement' or 'policy document' is commissioned and accredited by the host institution. Some care is gone into to ensure that all such 'statements of chaplaincy provision' is in accord with equal opportunities, diversity and anti-discrimination legislation and peer review best practice.

The general commissioning context could be summarised as this. The Diocese of London is recognised by many HE institutions senior staff as the tried and tested preferred provider. Nevertheless, it is on the understanding that the Anglican Chaplain facilitates the constellation of denominational visiting chaplains who may not be full-time.

In *Dancing on the Edge*,' Peter McGrail and John Sullivan go to some lengths to evaluate both the positive and negative outcomes for these arrangements. They are not just a metropolitan phenomenon but can be found replicated throughout the United Kingdom. I will not rehearse them again here, but restrict myself to one observation. It will always be the personal relationships between chaplains which sets the temper of life within an HE chaplaincy, whether it be a long established ecumenical venture with a pedigree of 'covenanted' agreed practice, or a more recently convened, loose association aspiring to collaborative best practice. I could offer no better aspirational call to chaplains working together as that encapsulated in *Dancing on the Edge*.

> 'However, if ecumenism is truly constructed on the basis of bringing together the best of the different traditions, then they must be built upon the establishment of shared space within which all can be authentically themselves, but with real friendship, mutual respect and a willingness to learn from each other. A genuinely ecumenical chaplaincy, therefore, would build positively on the strengths of all the participants: it would in effect, hold a vision and a mode of working that embraced unity and diversity' (Chapter One, 3:2.2).

If it was the personal friendships which developed between the pioneer HE chaplains that drove the initial ecumenical chaplaincy experiments - then it will have to be an equally congenial, collegial spirit that underpins chaplaincies that evolve to face the future challenges in our post modern, secularised HE institutions. When questioned about the different demands faced by parochial and sector ministries I used to answer, "We cannot afford the luxury of denominationalism in university chaplaincy." I now appreciate that there are areas of chaplaincy life where an honest recognition of divergence and even conflict are healthy signs. There will inevitably be flash points ignited by deeply held and long established theological beliefs. A veneer of politeness does not do justice to big issues such as gender and ministry, sacramental integrity, individual church traditions of order and discipline. Nor the complexity of having complementary or conflicting lines of accountability where a Chaplain is appointed jointly by a denomination and a university. Nevertheless, the day to day experience of HE Chaplaincy in the London region is testimony to the overriding imperative that where it is possible, we do all that we are able to do together.

2006: THE VIEW FROM THE BRIDGE

So where are we now? What does the contemporary 'ecumenical' context look like? It has to be admitted that in some ways the 'rosy glow' of yester year has faded. I have to acknowledge that the barometer measuring the ecumenical climate makes puzzling reading. For example, let us look at the four formally constituted ecumenical chaplaincies identified earlier in this paper. They are Middlesex University, Queen Mary-University of London, Imperial College, and Brunel University.

First, Middlesex University: As noted earlier, the Ecumenical Trust which employed and managed the Chaplaincy Team was formally wound up in

2002. This was a drawn out legal procedure, dictated by the terms of the Trust and the requirements of the Charity Commission. The decision to do so was driven by financial constraints on the two main funding partners, Middlesex University and the All Saints Educational Trust. Vigorous attempts were made by myself, as Chairman of the Trust, and others to find alternative provision. Sadly, 'Chaplaincy' is now reduced to a page on the Middlesex University Website listing local church and clergy contacts to which students with religious queries are now referred. Until recently, the Baptist Union was being encouraged to explore the possibility of appointing a Senior Baptist University Chaplain who might have responsibility for reviving the Chaplaincy at Middlesex University as a major part of his/her role.

This has now been abandoned. In its place, stop gap chaplaincy provision is occasionally provided by local clergy who may have part of the five MU campus sites within their parochial boundaries. This is a vastly unsatisfactory arrangement and is in stark contrast to the earlier ecumenical Chaplaincy Team which delivered high quality care and innovative programmes for some 20 years.

However, the Free Churches Higher Education Group, comprising of representatives from the Baptist Union, the Methodist Church and the United Reformed Church, covenanted in 1999, has promised to keep the situation at Middlesex University under review.

The situations at Brunel University, Queen Mary College and Imperial College have similarities and can be described collectively. Brunel and Queen Mary still have 'Management Committees' which hark back to the days of their formal inception. At Brunel the Management Committee meets once a term. It reviews the finances, infrastructure, and programmes of the Meeting House. It is a Committee which represents the various stakeholders in the Chaplaincy, most prominently university senior officers who have an overall brief for estate/facility management and welfare provision. It needs to be remembered that ownership of the Meeting House is now held by the University. The 'ecumenical team' at Brunel is much reduced from its former complement. There is a full-time Anglican Chaplain and a local Baptist Minister who nominally acts as 'Free Church Chaplain'. There is currently no Roman Catholic Chaplain after the death of the former chaplain who worked part-time for two days per week in term time. An Anglican member of the Brunel University staff has trained as an Assistant Chaplain and is accredited to the team by the University. Also Brunel University generously funds the provision of a part-time lay Administrator for the Meeting House. The Meeting House is increasingly used as a popular venue by local and university groups and societies. A consequence is that the level of work has dramatically expanded while the size of the ecumenical team has been reduced. To all effects and circumstances the former model of a formally constituted 'inter-denominational' chaplaincy ended some years ago.

Queen Mary's Management Committee, after a long period of ineffectuality, has not met since 2001. The day to day management of 'Saint Benet's', the extensive and well equipped QM Chaplaincy Centre, is left to the full-time Anglican Chaplain. After suffering a long period of infrequent Free Church and Roman Catholic visiting chaplain provision, two more regular Methodist and Roman Catholic Clergy have now been appointed to augment the team. Funding to refurbish and modernise the building has been provided from Anglican funding sources. The Diocese of London has undertaken to fund repairs to the fabric of the Chapel and residential accommodation. Both former 'beacons of ecumenical chaplaincy' have reverted to operating on a par with the more dispersed model found in the majority of HE institutions. That is a loose association of interdenominational chaplains with the only full-time member being Anglican.

The situation at Imperial College is similarly reduced from its former high level. The team has one full-time Anglican Chaplain and a part-time Roman Catholic Chaplain. Free Church provision is via referral. There is a full-time Chaplaincy Assistant who is usually an Anglican ordinand.

Why has there been such a diminution? I suggest there are three primary reasons. Firstly, the issue of 'ecumenism' has slipped down the agenda because the initial gains of the 1960's have bedded down and become the assumed state. Ecumenism is no longer perceived as a 'big issue', but rather as the received, common practice. In some ways this period of stagnation and regression resembles the cautions levelled at a long and complacent marriage. You have to keep working on the relationship to ensure it is not taken for granted or else it can atrophy and die.

Secondly, financial and personnel deployment constraints have reduced the number of clergy who can be recruited and paid to maintain the former high levels of ecumenical team work. The United Reformed Church and Baptist

Union have not had a full-time Senior HE Chaplain in post in London for the last four years. The Methodist Church is in the process of reviewing its operational structure in the region and is having difficulty finding a funding package for its Senior HE Chaplain. It must be remembered that, in the three Free Churches cases reported here, the nomenclature of 'Senior' Chaplain indicates the one full-time and representative role of the post holder. They have a subsidiary role in attempting to identify and encouraging a network of congregational clergy who might be able to act as local Free Church clergy to whom HE staff and students might be referred. The Roman Catholic HE Chaplaincy has experienced similar funding and recruitment difficulties, but managed to maintain a wide provision of visiting chaplains who hope to encourage the sacramental life of gathered staff and students, and nurture Students' Union recognised Catholic Societies where they exist. In contrast the Anglican Diocese of London has expanded its HE Chaplaincy Team extensively by developing financial partnerships with a range of HE institutions, educational charities and parishes. The regular recruitment of many highly qualified clergy, particularly well suited to this sector ministry, has been one of the appreciable trends in London Diocesan life over the last decade.

Thirdly, the notable downturn in the membership of many denominations means that executive operational decisions have to be made about deployment of scarce resources. In my view, the mistaken decision is often made to retrench the parochial/congregational base at the expense of investing in the strategic missionary endeavour which is HE chaplaincy. The timing is unfavourable. There are fewer resources to spread across a widening sector. Many churches have suffered loss of income and lower rates of clerical recruitment at a time when HE was expanding and therefore the HE market demands increasing.

Now for the good news! It must also be reported that there is still one, formally constituted 'HE Ecumenical Chaplaincy' within the Greater London region. That is Kingston University Ecumenical Chaplaincy. The Kingston University Ecumenical Chaplaincy is ecumenical in one particular respect in that it recruits its 'Chaplain' from a broad range of denominations i.e. Anglican, URC and Methodist. The current post holder is a Methodist minister. Representatives of these Churches are on the Management Committee alongside university and student representatives. The Roman Catholic and Jewish 'Honorary' Chaplains, and a Baptist minister are 'observers' on the Management Committee. In 2002

I acted as the external member of the second Quinquennial Review Group and was delighted with the health of what I saw.

The aims of the Kingston University Ecumenical Chaplaincy are:
- To offer care and confidential guidance to all students and staff.
- To meet, where possible, the diverse needs of members of the University.
- To encourage discussion about Christian faith and to promote inter-faith dialogue.

This last aim will lead us on to the inter-faith contextual analysis offered later in this chapter.

Although I lamented the popular perception that the 'steam has run out' of the ecumenical movement, we can celebrate the fact that working ecumenically is now simply taken as read! Despite the occasional 'local difficulty', HE chaplaincy automatically operates on an integrated and inclusive ecumenical front across the region. This is still 'good news.'

If the early ecumenical endeavours were the product of 'bottom up' initiative, it needs to be recognised that the last decade has seen formal ecumenical agreements ratified between various National Churches which have prompted 'top down' collaborative projects. By 1995 four Anglican and five Lutheran National Churches signed the Porvoo Common Statement. In 2003 the Anglican and Methodist Churches signed a covenant. Both these institutional statements of agreed commonality have had direct bearing on HE Chaplaincy practice in London. For example, The Lutheran Senior Chaplain was able to secure funding for a half-time Lutheran Student Chaplain. However, he recognised that the relatively limited number of ordained Lutheran clergy in the UK could significantly reduce the possibility of recruiting a suitable person. He therefore asked me, as his Anglican opposite number, to let him have details of any Anglican priests who might consider the post. Contacts were made, advertisements placed, completed applications received, and a short list of three candidates was drawn up. The preferred candidate was an Anglican priest. She was duly appointed and has been successfully in post for three years.

Most recently another 'sector ministry' post was advertised for a Chaplain to the Deaf within the Anglican Diocese of London. This time the successful candidate was a Methodist Minister. I offer these two examples of local practical collaboration for ecumenical chaplaincy which are direct outcomes from national ecumenical agreements.

The example of ecumenical collaboration on a national and institutional level is paralleled on the ground in London. The Senior University Chaplains of the Anglican, Baptist, Lutheran, Methodist, Orthodox, Roman Catholic and United Reformed Churches meet regularly as the London Chaplaincies Liaison Group. The Group discusses current developments, reflects on deployment issues, and plans ecumenical events and services which are offered to the HE community within the Greater London region. Two events are particularly appreciated. Every year a Service of Thanksgiving is held for those who have given their bodies for medical education and research. Each year some two hundred and fifty cadavers are donated, for use by the medical and dental schools in the region. The service takes place at Southwark Cathedral and is attended by upwards of one thousand people. It needs to be realised that the family and friends who attend this service will not have had a funeral for their loved one. Therefore we offer an opportunity to express all those thoughts and emotions usually given a focus at a funeral or memorial service for the deceased. It is also an opportunity for medical students to realise and show their appreciation for the gift of the donors.

The Liaison Group also organises a one-day workshop on an issue of interest to personal tutors, student welfare and counselling staff, and residential hall wardens. A topic is identified which will help these key HE support workers understand some of the religious implications around an issue: for example the dimension of religious belief in mental health. Since 2000 it has been agreed that the functions of the Liaison Group should include mutual consultation when new denominational HE chaplains are appointed. When a new Senior Chaplain is recruited, wherever possible, a member of the Liaison Group is invited to be part of the interviewing process.

Perhaps the most telling example of all is the ecumenical spirit which animates the termly Chaplaincy Team Meetings which I organise as Senior Anglican Chaplain. As such I am charged with the professional training and personal development of Anglican HE Chaplains in the Diocese of London. These events have proved very popular and appreciated. So much so that Anglican HE Chaplains in four adjacent dioceses asked if they may attend. Soon the Anglican Chaplains were asking if their ecumenical colleagues could come too. We now invite over 70 different denominational HE chaplains from within the M25 region, with attendance rates averaging around 40.

To end the first section of this paper I will offer one anecdote from a recent Team Meeting. The training topic was 'The Chaplain's Response to Death and Other Serious Incidents on Campus.' The venue, appropriately enough, was Her Majesty's Tower of London, no stranger to incidents of sudden death! These Team Meetings always supplement 'professional training inputs' with times for informal networking, relaxing and eating together, and of course, worship. On this occasion we were delighted to be invited by the Chaplain of the Tower to a celebration of Holy Communion, according to the 1662 Book of Common Prayer in the Norman Chapel of St John, in the White Tower. This was a powerful and privileged occasion - made the more so by the consecrated wine being administered by my colleagues the Senior Lutheran and Methodist Chaplains. It is a story which I trust illustrates both the tenor and the depth of the current best ecumenical spirit of those HE chaplains who work in the London region.

THE INTER-FAITH CONTEXT

I am conscious that giving separate and secondary billing to an analysis of the inter-faith context after first describing the ecumenical context might reinforce the impression that any inter-faith dimension is a recent and relatively less significant aspect of HE chaplaincy experience. Close attention to the history of HE chaplaincy within the region over the last 25 years challenges that notion.

For example, the Jewish Chaplaincy to Students has been active since 1970 with a full-time Rabbinical Chaplain based in Bloomsbury. The post holders have always proved to be friendly, open and reliable colleagues for the Christian denominational chaplains.

The aim of the Jewish Student Chaplaincy is:
- to retain, strengthen and inspire Jewish identity amongst all Jewish students
- to increase the number, quality and diversity of Jewish activities on campus
- to increase students' participation in Jewish activities of some kind
- to provide high quality education in Judaism to as many students as possible

- student welfare
- practical support
- educational resources
- spiritual guidance.

A further example of the longstanding 'inter-faith' context for HE chaplaincy work is found at Brunel University. From its completion in 1984 the 'interdenominational' Meeting House was used by Muslim students for daily and Friday prayers. Washing facilities were included in the original design specification. Indeed it is only relatively recently that a larger hall needed to be booked on campus to accommodate the increased number of Muslim students who wished to attend Friday prayers. Individuals and smaller groups of Muslim students still use the Meeting House for prayer and speaker meetings.

Another example of early Muslim prayer room provision comes from my personal experience when I was appointed Anglican Chaplain to the London School of Economics in 1981. The room which was allocated for Christian Chaplaincy use soon proved unsuitable. It was far too small and did not guarantee an assured level of privacy when confidential counselling was required. The LSE had recently set aside a dedicated Muslim prayer room. This I felt set a precedent for also enhancing the provision of the Christian Chaplaincy's accommodation. I duly took advantage of this supportive climate of opinion and asked for improved facilities. Consequently the chaplaincy was moved into a suite of rooms which offered separate spaces for meeting, counselling and catering. The new chaplaincy rooms were located in the same building as the Muslim prayer room. This 'accident' of geography proved to be a happy one. It meant that Christian and Muslim students and staff saw each other publicly expressing their faith and offered insights into our mutual devotional practices. The premises were also more centrally situated on the LSE campus, which gave the chaplaincy's profile a boost and strengthened our strategic encounter with the LSE community. I feel this experience offers a parallel with what I sometimes imagine were the benefits enjoyed by the early Christians - in that the first generations of Christians were seen by the Roman authorities as a subset of Judaism and thereby enjoyed the same legal and social privileges afford Jews. Just as the early Christian communities evolved, perched on the back of the Jewish precedent, so, at LSE at least, the Christian Chaplaincy gained a positive resource due, in part, to the earlier resources given to enable the Muslim community to perform their daily prayers. It helped establish a sort of parity in the religious ecology of the School.

The inter-faith interdependence of the ecumenical Chaplaincy at Middlesex University was even more developed. It may be recalled that the All Saints College of Education had been merged with the Middlesex Polytechnic and other institutions to form the newly constituted Middlesex University. The year1992 saw the launch of the 'New University's' Tottenham campus site with a series of high profile events. A special inter-faith and ecumenical service took place to mark the opening of the All Saints Chaplaincy Centre. As part of the infrastructural developments the former college chapel had been imaginatively remodelled and refurbished to become a multi purpose space that lent itself for use as a place for worship, a stage for the performing arts, or as a teaching and key note lecture venue. To further underline the openness of the Centre many faith groups took a part in the opening service. There was a Hindu Choir, readings from the Buddhist scriptures by a Buddhist monk, a local Rabbi read from the Torah, and a local Imam recited verses from the Qur'an. The ecumenical Christian Chaplains represented the Anglican, Methodist and Roman Catholic traditions. The vitality and importance of Middlesex University's commitment to rejuvenating this rather neglected area of North London was given national coverage when the BBC broadcast a special outdoor 'Songs of Praise' from a giant marquee erected on the campus car park. No internal venue would have been large enough to host this hugely popular event. The University recognized the multi-cultural significance of what was happening within it. There was a wave of mutual religious respect and cooperation amongst the ethnically diverse population surrounding the University's five campus sites which ran like an elongated archipelago across 70 miles of North London. An academic expression of this recognition of its particular cultural context led Middlesex University to establish a Centre for Inter-Faith Studies within the Department of Religious Studies. The example of Middlesex University's pioneering recognition of ecumenical and inter-faith collaboration was to a great extent prompted by the multi-cultural and socially diverse areas of London within which its constituent educational institutions had been established and from which they recruited a significant proportion of their students.

The merging of the University of North London and London Guildhall University to become London Metropolitan University (2002) offers another example of one of London's so called 'new universities' responding innovatively to the religious character of its 'client base'. London Metropolitan University became the first HE institution within the region to appoint a full-time University Imam. When he joined the Chaplaincy it was doubly significant because all the other members of the team were women. That is two full-time Anglican Priests and two part-time Roman Catholic Chaplains, one lay and one Sister. The Imam took part in the services at which each of the Anglican Chaplains was licensed by the Bishop of Stepney. These were powerful public demonstrations of the two faiths' commitment to find innovative ways forward through collaborative patterns of ministry within modern secular HE institutions.

In 2005 Brunel University also accredited a part-time Muslim Chaplain. He visits the Uxbridge campus site to attend and lead Friday prayers. He also makes the point of walking around the campus with his full-time Anglican colleague to visibly demonstrate that here at least Muslims and Christians are working harmoniously together. The Anglican Chaplain says these weekly walkabouts "present a united face of pastoral and spiritual care." In each case the two HE Muslim chaplains mentioned here are both keen to be described as 'Chaplains'. This helps make the term not exclusively 'Christian' but rather descriptive of a broader pastoral and religious role.

A final example of this growing trend is a Muslim woman joining the University of Westminster Chaplaincy Team as a voluntary Muslim chaplain. This trend is to be welcomed. The identification and accreditation of bona fide and suitable people to act as Muslim chaplains would enhance the breadth of chaplaincy provision and act as a positive force influencing the climate of opinion within HE communities. However, one practical difficulty hampers the wider rolling out of such inter-faith provision; Namely, the absence of a local or national infrastructure for training Muslim HE chaplains. There are a number of Muslim chaplains who have received specific training for work within the National Health Service. Also some induction training is given for Muslims chaplains working within the Prison Service. I understand that this issue is now under urgent review within the UK's Muslim community.

My own experience of inter-faith interaction on the ground has been mixed. Occasionally international political events have triggered dangerous situations. Most critically in my experience was the shock which affected the School of Oriental and African Studies after the 1994 massacre of 27 Muslim worshippers in the Abraham Mosque in Hebron. I literally had to physically position myself between a provocative Hasidic Zionist and a group of Muslim students who were tracing out the number 27 in votive candles on the floor of the Students' Union. In heart warming contrast I have celebrated a lunchtime Eucharist for a small group of SOAS staff and students in one part of the L shaped inter-faith prayer room while a group of female Muslim students performed their mid-day prayers in the other. We can only hope and work for increased inter-faith chaplaincy provision to cultivate a climate of tolerance, mutual respect and dialogue; a climate in which it will be taken as the norm that just as Christian chaplains work ecumenically, so the nomenclature of 'Chaplain' is conscientiously and automatically extended to include Jewish and Muslim colleagues.

CONTEXTS WITHIN CONTEXTS

Higher Education in the London region is both a reflector and setter of social trends. Pluralism, multi-culturalism and secularism are all alive and well within its colleges and universities. It is almost impossible to chart the various philosophical and social currents which swirl outside these institutions. It is equally treacherous trying to steer a credible intellectual course without fear of capsizing at the confluences of theory, belief and practice which eddy within their seminar, lecture and common rooms, bars, laboratories and virtual intranets. One great claim for the British liberal tradition is that our universities were the 'engines of enlightenment'. Seeing themselves as champions of such progressive ideals, the evangelistic secularists of the post war period thought they had more or less seen off the vestiges of a religious world view. It is therefore to be expected that it comes as a surprise to many senior academics and HE administrators that their students and staff are now as likely to be petitioning for dedicated prayer facilities as they are for cheaper residential accommodation. It is equally to be expected that an upturn in overtly religious behavior and attitudes might excite apprehension given the dual association in many people's minds between religious fanaticism and political violence. Indeed the college chaplain is often unofficially regarded as the 'religious gate keeper' for the institution. So any leafleting, proselytising, evangelising or uninvited interest from a range of so called cults, new religious movements, or the more fundamentalist and fervent tendencies of the main line religious faiths often triggers a call from the Registry to the Chaplaincy.

The recent radicalisation of some elements of the UK Muslim community has once again aroused a latent suspicion of religious zeal in some academic quarters. The fear is that the street conflicts we see reported daily in the media will translate to unrest on our campuses. More positively, innovative ways of providing for growing numbers of ethnic and religious minority groups are seen to be the proper concern of HE institutions. This is in line with the government's policy of moving from the post Second World War (2.5 % of the 18 years of age cohort) elitist model of education to the mass model (50% of the 18 years of age cohort) aspired to in Britain today. It is now seen as imperative to offer an academic setting in which the 'client/customer/student' is able to express their religious, ethnic and cultural identity. Thus access and participation are widened. To this end a number of universities are formally exploring ways in which the chaplaincy can help deliver these services and add value to the university experience. Senior HE staff are sensitive to the findings of polls and league tables which might influence their recruitment numbers. It is interesting to note that the city campus of London Metropolitan University, formerly London Guildhall University, recruits over 75% of its students from the adjacent Boroughs of Islington, Stepney, Hackney and Tower Hamlets. The local high preponderance of immigrants and second generation young people of Asian backgrounds made the decision to appoint London's first University Imam inevitable, as much as it is creditable.

The authors of the report *Dancing on the Edge* cite the growth in numbers of students with non-Christian faith allegiances at one particular university as due, largely, to the recruitment of international students (Chapter One, 2:3.2). I would like to supplement this observations with a number of my own which are specific to the London regional experience.

Firstly, in some ways, 'twas ever thus'. In other words the larger colleges of the University of London have traditionally had a notably high proportion of international students. They also recruited locally from within a cosmopolitan area. For example the London School of Economics had a 50% international/home student ratio in 1980. It has since risen to 66% of the student body being international. This is due to LSE's deliberate policy of recruiting such a high percentage to guarantee a tranche of funding which is not dependent on UK central government. Now the charging of home student fee rates for European Union students makes the LSE and other UK colleges even more attractive and financially viable for continental would-be students. Also, the global brand which is LSE demands a definable international identity for both students and staff. The prime place of the English language as the lingua franca of the business and commercial world can only further increase the UK HE international market share.

The recruitment of higher numbers of international students and staff also has a positive outcome for conventional university chaplaincies. It needs to be recognised that the proportion of international students who are 'church goers' is often considerably higher than that of their UK home based counterparts. African, North and South American, Asian, Australia, European and Caribbean students often come from cultures which boast much more energetic and popular churches. It has been my experience that the enthusiastic core of any HE chaplaincy may often predominately comprise of international students. A warm and welcoming chaplaincy can offer the possibility of a 'home from home' for international students and staff who may feel the university to be a large and inhospitable institution set in an intimidating and anonymous metropolis. So the greater recruitment of international students can benefit all religious groupings within the HE sector.

CONCLUSION

At the beginning of the second part of this report I noted my observation that there has been a longstanding 'inter-faith' context to HE chaplaincy within the London region. It is not a recent phenomenon to be 'bolted on' to the dominant ecumenical mode - not least because of London's sociological nature as a vibrant, cosmopolitan and multi-cultural conurbation which is home to over six million, let alone London being the historic destination of choice for tens of thousands of international students, academics, HE support and ancillary staff. However, I think social trends are also at work. An apparently invisible social group or class may grow in numbers until it reaches a critical mass which brings it to the notice of the otherwise oblivious majority. This recognition might take longer in a highly populated area with a high turnover in sizable, transient sectors. The moment of public recognition might also be sparked by a political flashpoint or climactic event. A number of social commentators identify the 1988 demonstrations against the publication of Salman Rushdie's novel, The Satanic Verses, as being the occasion when British Muslims found their own political, social and cultural voice. Formerly, marches which focused on some issue which had a racial aspect were generally organised by political parties and trade unions. The anti-Rushdie demonstration was the first time that Muslims came onto the streets and into the British conscious as an identifiable cohesive national community.

The 9/11 terrorist attacks in New York, in 2001, and the 7/7 bombings in London, in 2005, were more recent events which prompted a wider social and religious awareness of Islam. One consequence for US society has been a notable increase in interest in Islam and conversions to the Muslim faith. A consequence for London HE institutions has been a drive to foster initiatives which would nurture better inter-faith relations. Here are some recent examples.

The University of London Union (the London University wide Students' Union) approached the University Chaplaincy to forge a new partnership. ULU asked us to help plan and deliver a dedicated 'Chaplaincy and Inter-Faith Centre' in the Union Building which was about to undergo radical refurbishment. Also, the London School of Economics has forged a partnership with the Diocese of London whereby the Anglican Chaplain will be paid to act as the official Inter-Faith Advisor to the School. Certainly the issue of being better informed about the various faith communities which comprise the greater HE community is on the student radar, too. The University of London Union recently organized a Multi-Faith Question Time entitled, 'Faith in Student Life'. Inter-Faith training events for HE chaplains are now given a high profile. For example the 2006 Lent Term London Chaplains' Team Meeting focused on Inter-Faith Issues on Campus. While, further afield, the Diocese of Leicester sets a fine example with the St Peter's Centre for Study and Engagement in a Multi-Faith Society, by offering a four day study course for those working in a multi-faith context in colleges and universities in the East Midlands and nearby.

It is increasingly recognised by HE Senior Staff that their institutions reflect the diversity and belief of both British and international society. Increasingly, the provision of prayer space is accepted as a service that universities and colleges need to provide as much as internet access and child care facilities. Nevertheless, a climate of positive opinion which seeks to embrace religious and social diversity is tempered by a cautious approach to managing such inter-faith prayer facilities on campus. For example, clear ground rules and regulations are laid down for prayer room users. All external speakers who are invited to address any faith group must have their names submitted to the HE authorities for checking before they are allowed on campus. All notices in prayer rooms must be written in English. Any preaching at Friday prayers must be on theological and not political subjects. 'Faith Awareness Weeks' must be sensitive to the feelings of other faith groups. They must not become 'faith conversion' events. Chaplains often act as honest brokers between the faith groups and college authorities. For example by discussing the choice of which books on Jesus can be sold on the Islamic Society book stall; or by discovering that the Islamic Society which has been tasked with the management of the Muslim Prayer Room is exclusively Sunni and deliberately excludes any Shia Muslims. This is despite the College's express intention that no single school of thought should dominate Friday prayers.

It has been humbly ceded by both Jewish and Muslim HE Chaplains that their role is extremely demanding. They feel poorly prepared for campus ministry as the formation given to Rabbis and Imams is training best fitted for teaching and liturgical leadership roles within gathered communities of Jews and Muslims. The need to adopt a pastoral and proactive engaged ministry within a secular environment is often acquired by learning from the example of their Christian colleagues.

Although the immediate HE 'context' may seem like a minefield for inter-faith chaplaincy, several examples of good practice are being developed. Often innovative and ingenious ways forward are found to help chaplaincy develop despite serious obstacles. For example the issues of gender and sexual orientation can appear potentially divisive. However, people make their own arrangements. Many 'Muslim Sisters' find it easier to talk to a female Christian chaplain than a male Imam. On the other hand conservative evangelical men can feel more comfortable with the firm line on homosexual practice taught by the Imam. They may then be surprised when the Imam seizes the pastoral opportunity to teach them that while believers may hate the sin they must love the sinner!

My Muslim colleague has a disarming way of describing his HE ministry as, 'Sanitization'. This he defines as trying to help wilder, zealous students become more 'sane'. He boldly maintains that moving people from a fundamentalist position to a moderate approach is not a 'pragmatic moderation': a mere tactical response to a serious situation which might get out of control. Rather he sees it as being a Quranic, scripturally instructed 'conviction moderation'. He firmly believes that the public example of chaplains from the 'Abrahamic Block' working together, as he describes inter-faith chaplaincy, can only help foster shared aspirations for hope and peace. Also he points out that a great deal of ignorant stereotyping needs to be challenged. We need to make clear the diversity *within* the various religious faith traditions as well as the diversity *between* them.

Perhaps the overarching contextual challenge which faces all faith chaplains was articulated in a recent lecture at the London School of Economics (03.11.05). His All Holiness, The Ecumenical Patriarch Bartholomew, gave the London Hellenic Society Annual Lecture on 'The Role of Religion in a Changing Europe.' He identified secularism and pluralism as the broader cultural currents into which we are cast. He concentrated on emphasising the positive contribution religion can make to society. How it can be a stabilising factor and counter nationalism. How it is critical that we find ways to promote dialogue and rapprochement. To this end he demonstrated the importance of the 1994 Bosphorus Declaration which sought to encourage faith leaders to commit their communities to encouraging tolerance, dialogue and peace building. Most significantly The Patriarch gave a European imperative to establish good inter-faith relations as a mediating bridge between the East and the West. He only had to hint at the shadow of global conflict to hasten and chasten us.

The challenge of continuing to develop ecumenical and inter-faith models of chaplaincy best practice is demanded by the HE environment. If universities ever were ivory towers, they are certainly not today. Perhaps once seen as liberal 'engines of enlightenment' they are now more often viewed as qualification factories for clients who need to enhance their employment prospects.

The 2001 British Census was the first to ask for the religious background of respondents. It was interesting, even surprising to learn that 72% of the population described themselves as Christian, 3% Muslim, 0.5% Hindu, 0.5 % Sikh, and 0.5% Jewish. Whatever the legal secular status of modern national and educational institutions, it still remains true that the majority of the British population maintain a 'religious' outlook at some level or other. Perhaps the apparent credibility gap between the broadly believing society and the secular world of HE can now be bridged with confidence.

I suggested earlier that the first generations of Christians prospered under the Roman dispensation because they were viewed as a Jewish subset. Equally today I wonder if the resurgence of popular religious belief, in some ways championed by Muslim activism, might lead to a future HE 'context' where 'faith' will no longer be viewed with tired, intellectual disdain but rather recognised for the credible system it can be and the power for good that it ought to be.

Perhaps, another historical parallel can be drawn? It was Islamic and Jewish scholars who sustained the philosophical, mathematical and scientific tradition of the Greek and Roman eras whilst Western Europe lost its way in the 'Dark Ages' and early medieval period. Perhaps today the example of confidence in their faith shown by British Muslims might encourage a climate of inter-faith religious endeavor which can help Christians, Jews, Muslims and other faith adherents to vigorously explore the issues on which they agree and respectfully acknowledge the differences which distinguish them. Perhaps, in such a rejuvenating and mutually enriching context, British HE institutions can regain a degree of being beacons of values, rather than merely be reduced to educational establishments where society trains the highly skilled workforce its economic base demands?

REFERENCES:

McGrail, Peter and Sullivan, John (2005) *Dancing on the Edge: A Report into Catholic Chaplaincy in Higher Education*, Liverpool Hope University.

Taylor, Laurie (2005) 'University of Poppleton,' *Times Higher Educational Supplement*, 16th December.

Chapter Eleven

REIMAGINING THE CHAPLAINCY FOR THE 21ST CENTURY AN AMERICAN PERSPECTIVE

MONICA M MANNING

I arrived on a major public research university campus in the mid-sixties on the "cutting edge" of the baby boom generation. I was excited to have four years of living amidst this immense resource of knowledge. The possibilities for exploration and learning, thinking and pondering, and growing and *becoming educated* seemed unlimited. I trust many of the faculty and administrators wanted those experiences for me, too. But they were overwhelmed by the arrival of the boomer generation. Suddenly students were sleeping on cots in hallways of dorms. Classes were standing room only. There were not enough sections of courses to meet the number of freshmen enrolled. Possibilities of a liberating education dimmed as administrators became preoccupied with numbers and faculty were stretched to adapt to much larger classes. In some ways, my experience is not unlike what British students may confront today with the government's commitment to rapidly expand the numbers of university-educated people.

Fortunately, during the most tumultuous era in American higher education, two places on campus provided me the opportunity to reflect on what I was learning, invited me to explore the bigger questions of life, and encouraged me to try out new ways of thinking – experiences hard to come by in crowded classrooms. The first place was the university's debate team; the second was the campus Newman Center, the Catholic chaplaincy.[1] In those years immediately following Vatican II, the Newman Center was an intellectually exciting place to gather. John XXIII's window opening was felt even on the American prairie. We learned about issues the church was debating. We read, talked about, and explored the varying perspectives emerging from the Council. What we learned helped us form our own, deeper, moral and theological framing of the critical issues we confronted not only in society but also in our daily lives: Vietnam, civil rights, and the rights of women.

Those years of campus and indeed personal turmoil for students and faculty alike also shaped my calling as an educator. As teacher, administrator, public official, and now as an entrepreneur, my continuing sense of vocation is that of educator. I have been privileged to work with all types of higher education institutions (HE institutions), from community colleges to major research universities. Always, the core of my work has been supporting colleges and universities in fulfilling their potential of providing access to higher learning. These experiences are foundational for me as I look at higher education chaplaincies today.

The challenges we face in today's world demand both intellectual rigor and spiritual grounding for clear understanding and productive living. I firmly believe there is opportunity for chaplaincies at UK HE Institutions to play a unique role in fostering the needed integration of this intellectual rigor and spiritual grounding because chaplaincy spans the boundaries of the academic and faith communities. The challenge these chaplaincies face is captured well in the title of the Report, *Dancing on the Edge*. The response to this challenge may require rethinking and reimagining the chaplaincy today. It will require stronger, deeper relationships with multiple stakeholders to change the experience from the precariousness of dancing to the strength of being centered on the edge[2] – being what Kevin Egan described in an earlier chapter as a spiritual presence on the frontier. It is an exciting place, a place that calls for a new kind of leadership in campus ministry. This challenge compels the work of more clearly articulating the spirit of chaplaincies as they seek to serve today's students, staff, and universities. In a world of bewildering choices and disruptive changes, chaplaincies have the opportunity to create the space where people can engage in a spiritually-grounded fashion with both personal and global dilemmas.

Dancing on the Edge captured my attention because I have particular interest in what happens at the boundaries of institutions. I'm intrigued by what new forms of organization and new areas of knowledge are emerging. It is the boundary areas that have been demonstrated to be the ones with the greatest potential for providing new value to the world (Starbuck, 1993). At the same time I am intrigued by the dimensions of organizations that we have not called on, that is, their potential for collective intelligence and collective wisdom. My work has included exploring the spiritual dimension of education itself as well as the spiritual dimension of institutions, primarily academic institutions. Lest you think that my perspective is solely theoretical, I am constantly engaged with colleges and universities, helping them from a pragmatic perspective provide service to an increasingly complex and fast-changing society. My focus is practical – but practice that is based on research and theory in organizational systems, higher education, and the religious and wisdom traditions to foster life-giving academic institutions.

Let me recognize the limits of speaking from an American perspective: The American religious landscape is quite different from that of the UK in the percent who self-describe as church-goers. Nearly 44% of Americans claim to attend church weekly, though pastors would be pleasantly surprised if their personal experience confirmed this. (The comparable figure for Britain is 27%.)[3] And while our countries appear more similar in the growth of the Islamic, Buddhist, and Hindu traditions, a notable difference is the number of Christian denominations of significant size in America. Another significant difference is that there is no established church in the US, so I may not be aware of sensitivities around this aspect of the cultures of England and of Wales.

The thesis of this chapter is that greater strength for chaplaincies will come, not from a formal university appointment or location within the academic structure, but rather by becoming more 'centered at the edge' of both the university and church worlds. I will begin with some observations about the higher education landscape in terms of religion and spirituality. That will be followed by a specific focus on the challenges inherent in the HE chaplaincy today. I will then outline a pathway for chaplaincies to consider that could reap benefits in terms of a deeper, spiritual grounding for the chaplaincy itself as well as the capacity to provide a prophetic voice for higher education institutions, for faith communities, and for the larger society. My first hope for this chapter is that it will be seen as a way to develop clarity of purpose and deeper spiritual grounding in the chaplaincy's relationships at the boundaries in order to offset the precariousness of living at the edge. My second hope is to help chaplaincies incorporate new, fresh thinking about today's challenges, opportunities, and resources from the diverse perspectives of people who care about the chaplaincy but who are not necessarily involved directly in its daily work.

RELIGION AND THE HIGHER EDUCATION LANDSCAPE

The Report laid out the challenges facing chaplains today: changing student profiles, ambiguous and uncertain relationship with academic institutions, expanding ecumenical and inter-faith environments amid shifting conditions within the Catholic Church community.

It is tempting to address each of these factors separately, but a response that would support a vital chaplaincy needs to take a broader and more integrated approach. One danger in trying to address the factors separately is the potential of finding that responses to one factor create unanticipated problems *vis a vis* another factor. Perhaps the greater danger is that a piecemeal approach accepts the status quo as a given and attempts to make adaptations within it. This could lead to changes that are based on assumptions no longer relevant and that foster even more unproductive conditions.

According to the Report, a key driver of the configurations of current chaplaincies was "the prevailing attitudes of the very different eras in which they were founded and in which their statutes and basic ethos were set down" (Report, p. 35). It cautions that these "arrangements once put in place tend to remain as relics of bygone times, without review or updating." The ambiguity of the role of the chaplaincy likely stems both from the impact of this historical formation and the decisions of diverse occupants in the ensuing years. Whoever has held the chaplaincy has shaped it by their responses to changing institutional expectations and denominational experience as well as by their personal gifts and their understanding of their role. The relationships established and the quality of those relationships continued to shape the chaplaincy long after the people directly involved were gone. Paraphrasing theologian Walter Wink, they have shaped not only its exteriority but the interiority -- the spirituality at the core of the chaplaincy (Wink, 1996 p. 3).

The Report laid out the changing demographics and patterns of student life. In addition to rapid expansion and increased fees, the imposition of quality audits has preoccupied university administrations. The arrival of older and increasingly part-time students with different patterns of course progression and varying involvement with campus activities has pressed educators and challenged long-time modes of operation. Finally, the expansion of enrollment of students from other countries has brought new meaning to diversity on campus.

Complicating these factors are the changing attitudes students carry toward religion. A bifurcated population is emerging. While many students show little interest in religion, others are aggressively seeking greater understanding of the religious and wisdom traditions. Writing in *The Tablet* Peter Vardy noted that "Religious studies is increasingly popular as an examination subject with sixth-formers in Britain's schools" (Vardy, 2005). But he added an insightful caveat, "Higher intellectual rigour among young people will require a similar level of engagement from the clergy." As these students arrive at HE institutions they may bring more sophistication than previous generations. Christopher Lamb, writing a year earlier, reported that theology was "undergoing something of a renaissance among undergraduates. The Universities and Colleges Admissions Service says that applications to study religious studies and theology increased by 7 per cent. Many universities are receiving their highest intakes of theology students in years" (Lamb, 2004). Professor Douglas Davies, head of Durham's theology department, commented about the impact of September 11 2001 on these students: "There are many young people who ponder the 'meaning of life' and now, more than ever, are bombarded by media-based opinion, fact and fiction, about the state of the world (Lamb, 2004). Interestingly, Lamb learned that students reading theology have often had no religious upbringing.

In the U.S., we are learning more about students' attitudes toward religion and spirituality through new research from UCLA of over 112,000 American freshman (Astin and Astin, 2005). Commenting in the *Chronicle of Higher Education*, Professor Alexander Astin, the director of the research project expressed a view similar to Professor Davies, "There are large numbers of students who are involved in spiritual and religious issues and who are trying to figure out what life is all about and what matters to them...We need to be much more creative in finding ways to encourage that exploration" (Bartlett, 2005, p. A1)." The *Chronicle* report continued, "Most [American] college freshmen believe in God, but fewer than half follow religious teachings in their daily lives." A majority of first-year students (69 percent) say their beliefs provide guidance, but many (48 percent) describe themselves as "doubting," "seeking," or "conflicted."

A Religious Studies Colloquium at Carleton College (a highly selective, non-sectarian, liberal arts college in the Midwest) bore out this conclusion. Members of the panel, all graduates of the department, described how they had not planned on majoring in religious studies in college. They found, however, that courses in religious studies were the place in the college that invited them to ask the "big questions:" Who am I? Why am I here? How do I relate to the universe? What do I want from my life?[4] Mark Wallace, associate professor of religion at Swarthmore College, knows these students well. While he recognizes that many professors are uncomfortable engaging with questions about the meaning of life, he advises "Meaning is exactly what students are looking for. They hunger and crave that sort of conversation in a college environment" (Bartlett, 2005, p A1).

It would be a mistake to assume that these questions come only from students fortunate to attend traditional, private, residential colleges. Among community colleges (the closest American counterpart of Further Education Institutions), the fastest growing curricular area is Religion and Philosophy. Writing about Bergen Community College (New Jersey) with an enrollment of 14,000 students, another *Chronicle* article noted that with eight full-time faculty, philosophy and religion courses enroll more than 2,000 students in about 50 sections each semester. This is despite the fact that credits in these disciplines are not required in any of the college's degree programs (Evelyn, 2004, p. A12).

Arthur Chickering, who with his co-authors, has the most recent in-depth publication on this subject, *Encouraging Authenticity and Spirituality in Higher Education*, captured well some of the places where American students find themselves. Observing that students coming to college often have their childhood faith challenged for the first time, he described the number of alternative responses that ensue: "One is to seek out guidance and grounding within the faith. Another is to bifurcate faith and knowledge. A third is to seek understanding in other faiths, and a fourth is to reject faith entirely."[5] Chickering emphasized that what is key here is that there is a core learning/development process happening that most of their college experience totally ignores.

Often educators even at religiously-affiliated institutions are chary of questions that incorporate or border on the spiritual or religious (Braskamp, et al, 2005). A national study on spirituality and the American professoriate released in March 2006 found that only 30 percent of those surveyed believed that colleges should be concerned with facilitating students' spiritual development. Still, over half believed that the goals of a college education include enhancing students' self-understanding, developing moral character, and helping students develop personal values (Astin and Astin, 2006). The researchers specifically defined spiritual development as about making sense and meaning out of our lives. This was an attempt to separate spirituality from religion in order to increase the pool of responses. But while spirituality may be a more acceptable term than religion, much of what we understand about spirituality is a consequence of our religious and wisdom traditions. No other area of study or of life has for so long maintained a focus on development of the spiritual life.

Evangelical writer and activist Jim Wallis provided a pan-Atlantic observation reporting on his January 2006 book tour for *God's Politics* in England:

> (T)he most heartening aspect of the trip to me was the turnout at the speaking venues. Not only were the crowds large, but they were also full of young people, which is especially unusual for events in Britain having to do with faith. Many of the event sponsors were astounded and grateful to see so many young Britons coming out for serious discussions of spirituality and politics. Just as we have found all over America, a new generation is looking for an agenda worthy of their gifts, energy, commitment, and lives. The best conversations I had in the U.K. were with talented young men and women who really want to make a difference in their world - just like in the U.S (Jim Wallis, 2006).

While much of the attention has so far been on traditional-aged students, it's wrong to assume that mid-career adults are only seeking marketable skills when they return to college. When triggering events such as changes in work, personal life, health, etc., drive an adult to seek additional learning, they are often seeking learning to make sense (and meaning) of their lives (Noone, 1999). These are spiritual questions, but most higher education institutions do not offer space for their exploration.

American colleges and universities organize to provide religious and/or spiritual resources for students in at least as many diverse ways as their counterparts in England and Wales. The office of chaplain occurs only in the structure of private colleges (religiously-affiliated and some non-sectarian, private institutions). At public institutions where religious resources are available, the range of faith communities, especially Protestant denominations, may be much wider than found in Britain. In *Religion on Campus*, Conrad Cherry listed more than fifteen denominations and/or centers affiliated with a major public research university.[6] Often organized into a ministerial alliance with a communication link to a public institution's Student Life Office, these services are paid for wholly with private resources, a consequence of the historical separation of church and state in America. Noting that very few undergraduates at this particular university were involved with religion at all, Cherry summed up the situation of religion on campus as "healthy in supply but weak in demand" (Cherry, DeBerg, and Porterfield, 2001, p. 46).

This lack of student engagement in traditional chaplaincies on campus has led some institutions such as American University (a private university) to pursue innovative approaches. The popular Kay Spiritual Life Center at AU has attracted the interest of a number of private colleges and universities as a new way to provide a center on campus for religious life and spiritual growth. The change here is significant. While worship services are available through the Kay Center, what attracts students is that it describes itself as a place where "people of conscience, intellect, and spirit find a place for their questions and life struggles" (www.american.edu/ocl/kay).

While the literature indicates that British chaplaincies serve Further Education Institutions, the American counterparts of these institutions, community and technical colleges (almost exclusively public institutions) are essentially devoid of any kind of religious or faith community services. As their students are primarily commuters, the assumption is that if they are interested in religious services, they can seek them in their local communities of residence. Based on current enrollments, that means that nearly 50% of American undergraduates attend HE institutions that have no chaplaincy services available.

Another difference worth noting is that in America a rich conversation about spirituality in higher education (as well as elsewhere in society) has developed amidst an increasing politicization of religion. Desiring to stimulate this conversation in a responsible way, in 1998 Wellesley College hosted a national conference on spirituality and higher education. President Diana Chapman Walsh described the surprising attendance by over 800 students, faculty, staff, and chaplains as an indication that there "was a yearning among many in the academy that hadn't found a place to settle" (Walsh, 2005). The Education as Transformation Project emerged from the conference. Its director, Peter Laurence explained its intent to challenge "the academic orthodoxies that dismiss religious identity and religious insight as extraneous to learning and community life. . .(and challenging) conventional patterns of organization in higher education that maintain fragmentation, disconnection, competition, and ecological irresponsibility" (Laurence, 2005). Other initiatives such as the Spirituality in Higher Education research projects at UCLA cited earlier, the Community for Integrative Learning and Action Institute (people.umass.edu/dkscott/CILA) started by David K. Scott, former President of the University of Massachusetts, and the Center for Formation in the Community College (www.league.org/league/projects/formation) based on the formation programming of author/educator/activist Parker J. Palmer have introduced explicitly spiritual language and exploration for interested faculty and staff at public as well as private institutions.

It's little wonder, though, that even these intriguing explorations of spirituality, teaching, and learning are seen with concern by some faculty. With religion becoming a more contentious issue in American political and social spheres, these faculty would prefer that the academy be an oasis where the destructive nature of some religiously-oriented conversations is not welcome.

CORE CHALLENGES AND QUESTIONS

As in the US, amidst dwindling numbers of church goers in England and Wales (BBC News, 2004), especially among young people, and, despite increased interest in religious studies by students, some HE chaplaincies find such little demand for services that they have to go out and find students (Report, p. 46). The challenge to the chaplaincy is then: Are there new ways to reach out to students seeking deeper meaning and purpose in their lives and to support those young men and women who want to use their talents to make a difference?

This challenge is not new for many chaplaincy staff. The Report conveys many efforts and intentions on the part of chaplain staff to try to determine how best to carry forward their ministry. However, the sense of precariousness, the small numbers of students engaged, the challenges of ecumenical and inter-faith collaborations all indicate the need for new approaches. A number of questions are embedded in this challenge: How can chaplaincy best serve students today? Is it possible – and productive – to develop a shared, interfaith vision of HE chaplaincy? How could the great diversity of partners and stakeholders in the chaplaincy be engaged in developing a shared vision to deepen the commitment and expand the resources to achieve it? What would an inclusive discernment process look like? Could such an approach of engaging partners and stakeholders in the chaplaincy help create a stronger foundation based, not on structural change, but on a shared commitment to its purpose?

AN INSTITUTIONAL FORMATION APPROACH

The complexity of the chaplaincy situation described in the Report is even greater than that experienced by American higher education. However, creating the kind of collective discernment process that could strengthen the chaplaincy is similar to work we are leading with American colleges and universities. Drawing on the works of Peter Senge on systems thinking (Senge, 1990), Margaret Wheatley on self-organizing entities (Wheatley, 1996), and Michael Sheeran SJ on communal discernment (Sheeran, 1983), we began in the nineties to create the space for campuses to engage in processes of collective enquiry and collaborative learning to explore their spiritual dimension. Our focus is on drawing on the best of the institution's past while recognizing that its changing environment is creating new challenges – but also new opportunities to serve the world. The goal is to create a vital, meaningful, fulfilling future for the university and for those who comprise it. While we were initially creating our own models based on the ideas of Senge, Wheatley, and Sheeran, our approach was bolstered by the theory and practice that James Surowieckie described in *The Wisdom of Crowds*. Importantly, he points out that not just any large gathering is likely to yield wisdom. The conditions he found essential to fostering good decision-making in large groups are diversity of perspectives, independence of thinking, and decentralization of work that still provides for aggregation of ideas (Surowiecki, 2004).[7] I have come to call this work *institutional formation*. It is about creating institutions that serve society well and that foster productive and rewarding professional and personal lives. Institutional formation is a recognition of the spiritual dimension – the interiority or the inner landscape – of HE institutions. It focuses on the collective experiences through which the members of an institution shape its meaning, identity and purpose.

BRINGING PEOPLE TOGETHER

Two lines of work come together for me in institutional formation. The first line – or tributary – is that of whole system planning processes. When invited to work with campuses on strategic planning, we sought to draw on the incredible resources, insight, knowledge and perspective that we knew were embedded in the faculty and staff. Instead of the traditional top-down approach to planning, we suggested bringing 80 to 100 people from across the university together to imagine its right future. We experimented with ways to bring people together in convenings that provided for productive conversations about what was most important, most meaningful to them and to their institutions. With experience and with the discovery that something unusual and hopeful was happening in these gatherings, we have become comfortable with our ability to invite as many as 500 or 1000 people to gather to reflect together and to bring their collective capacity to create the right future.

EXPLORING THE COLLECTIVE SPIRIT

The second tributary of the work of institutional formation comes from Walter Wink, a New Testament theologian whose study has produced a radical, yet compelling understanding of institutional uses and abuses of power (Wink, 1984). I'm hesitant to try to distill his analysis into a few lines, but I want to give you a sense of what he has written to show where I first began to find hope for understanding institutions at a deeper level. Wink believed that any attempt to face the problem of evil in society from a New Testament perspective could only be productive with an understanding of what the bible calls the "Principalities and Powers." As he conducted his research, he found that in the biblical era, these Powers were visible and invisible, earthly and heavenly, spiritual and institutional. The spirituality of an institution exists as a real aspect of the institution even when it is not perceived as such. Institutions have an actual spiritual ethos, and, he warns, "We neglect this aspect of institutional life to our peril" (Wink, 1984, 3)

I was drawn to his idea of a corporate spirit as not just the sum total of its parts. It bears the institutions' divine vocation, the message of what it ought to be. When institutions turn their back on their vocation to serve the general welfare, they become "demonic" (Wink, 1986, p. 78). Attempts to transform a social system without addressing both its spirituality as well as its outer forms are doomed to failure. According to Wink, the Powers are good because they help us organize human life; they are fallen when they put self-interest ahead of the long-term interests of the whole; and they can be redeemed by recalling them to their vocation. (Wink, 1999, p. 3)

The more I worked with diverse campuses, the more the concept of collective spirit or interiority spoke to the fact that a university is more than a collection of individuals. It is the collective expression of what is in the hearts of those who created it, who passed through it, as well as those who work in the university today. I began to ask how we might call the university back to its highest vocation.

INSTITUTIONAL FORMATION AND VOCATION

Discerning the vocation of an institution means asking what it is being called by society to do today. As in Britain, American colleges and universities are confronted by far more expectations by their diverse stakeholders than any single institution can begin to address. Some institutions try to respond to all and find themselves overwhelmed. Other have tried to ignore all expectations and discovered society losing faith in them. Amidst many and often conflicting demands, it is essential for an academic institution to discern its own unique, life-giving path to serving society.

Similarly, the range of expectations of the chaplaincy is daunting. In *Campus Ministry*, Simon Robinson listed the remit of the chaplaincy across three pages, covering eighteen forms of pastoral care, eleven kinds of spirituality work, six areas of ethical contributions and three kinds of community building (Robinson, 2004, pp. 36-38). What seems to be missing is an organizing principle, a compelling vision, a clear sense of purpose. While Robinson may not intend for all chaplains to take up the whole load alone, his list indicates the range of expectations others may have of the chaplaincy. Chaplaincies, like universities, need to find ways to set priorities and to clearly communicate those priorities among the many expectations. The challenge is how best to identify the most meaningful priorities. The danger is in trying to do it alone.

An institutional vocation process provides for a spiritually-grounded communal discernment consistent with Frederick Buechner's description of a calling: "Where your heart's deep gladness and the world's deep hunger meet" (Buechner, 1993, p. 119). The work is about creating the space where people in HE institutions – or in chaplaincies – discover their collective heart's deep gladness and can discern from among the many deep hungers of the world which ones they hope to meet. It is about deciding the right risks and actions to take to pursue their shared sense of a collective calling. Addressing the challenge of guiding organizational change during turbulent times, Rebecca Chan Allen describes call as "an invitation to a new course of (self-) organization. . .People and organizations are called to change when they have outgrown their knowledge base and are in need of new learning and development. Call is a signal that there is more creative potential in a system than is being used" (Chan, 2002, pp. 63-64). Institutional formation with its process for discerning institutional vocation is a way to acquire the new knowledge, provide for the new learning, and take the steps to develop the full potential of the institution.

FORMATION CYCLE

The basic model of this process is a three-part cycle of reflection, fulfillment, and risk-taking (Manning, 1998, p. 2). Inviting key stakeholders to join in exploration of core questions starts the process. In the complex, interdependent world we live in and our institutions, whether large universities or small chaplaincies, must survive in, it is no longer possible for a leader or a small group of people to have all the knowledge, insight, and perspective needed to discern right direction or to acquire sufficient resources.

Clearly, it would be important for a chaplaincy that chose to explore an institutional vocation process to identify its right partners or stakeholders to invite into discernment. Creating an environment that welcomes diversity and independent thinking is essential. The Report's findings suggest a gathering should include students, university personnel including perhaps some from the religious studies faculty, local clergy and faith community leaders as well leaders from the sponsoring denominations including those in national positions. With the expansion from ecumenical work to inter-faith work, engaging leaders from other faith communities is important. Bringing people face-to-face in real time is necessary to fostering the kinds of conversations and learning required. A collective discernment process is more than just a "pooling" of perspectives. It begins by asking open and honest questions of those who care about the chaplaincy. It then draws on their memories of what is most important from the past that they want to carry into the future. Questions follow that engage their imaginations of the most exciting and fulfilling future for the chaplaincy.

A caring, spiritually-grounded approach is essential. Some of the questions that arise about the chaplaincy may be difficult. But these questions need to be answered if there is going to be a viable future for the chaplaincy. Some questions that might be considered:

What does it mean to be a learner and how does this relate to faith, religion, spirituality, and the wisdom traditions?

- How might the chaplaincy help students integrate their fragmented lives, inviting the big questions about life and its meaning as they make course and program choices?

- Is the pastoral model the best approach in an educational environment where people learn to ask questions, to challenge conventional wisdom, to think for themselves?
- Is the reliance on a parish or congregational model appropriate in an academic setting?
- What are the implications of living in a global society where religious traditions are having increasing impact on the economy and the political order?
- Other valuable questions can be found in Appendix 1 of the Report.

Taking time for *reflection* provides for discovering what we individually and collectively know about the past and present of the institution. Establishing a better understanding about what gives people a sense of *fulfillment* provides a basis to begin to imagine the possibilities for the institution. With this shared knowledge and understanding comes a greater willingness and commitment on the part of all participants to take more productive *risks* to capture the potential of the institution.

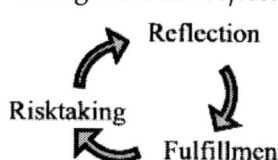

What we know as well as our sense of what gives fulfillment changes over time. That suggests that the process needs to be on-going. Most important is that there is an opportunity for the people who care about an institution – in this case, the chaplaincy – to ask: What is it we are here to do? What is it we care most about accomplishing together? What are we willing to do together to serve society and to support each other in our service to society?

A compelling purpose is needed to give chaplains, university administrators, and associated denominational and faith community partners reason to work together to address the challenges inherent in present arrangements. The question here is: What is the larger purpose to be served? This is not unlike the "big questions" that students carry, even if they don't articulate them. Just as students too often end up in jobs and careers they don't like because they haven't figured out what is important to them, chaplains, universities, and denominations are likely to end up in arrangements they don't like because they haven't been clear about what is at the heart of these arrangements. An institutional vocation process draws on the spiritual dimension of the gathered group by asking the deeper questions about life together and shared hopes for the world.

Hard data is also important to an institutional vocation process. If the UK has no comparable research effort to that of the Higher Education Research Institute of UCLA, then this is an important area for development. American colleges and universities used the data in several ways:

- For religiously-affiliated institutions already collecting information about enrolled students' interest in spirituality and religion, it provided a national baseline;
- For some of these same institutions, it demonstrated that their assumptions about the impact of the institution on students' spiritual development were less significant than they had hoped; and,
- For some institutions not collecting such data, it compelled them to realign their basic assumptions about students' interests (UCLA Division of Student Affairs, 2006).

Certainly this information would be even more related to the core of the work of chaplaincies in higher education. Leadership for such research efforts might come from a collaboration of religious studies professors, student life staff, and chaplaincy staff.

A PROPHETIC VOICE FOR PARTNERS

The UK chaplaincy has a wider expectation for service than that of its American counterpart. Throughout the literature, calls for it to play a prophetic role recur. Its purpose is not only to serve students but also to serve the university, the church, and society. The Report makes clear that HE institutions are challenged by changes in their world. Increasing numbers of foreign students arrive with different expectations about accommodations as well as worship. Though not addressed in the Report, professors in Britain, like most American faculty are likely discomforted by engaging with topics of religion. Even religious studies faculty may be challenged by students who want to go beyond the academic study of religions and ask questions about faith and meaning in their own lives. Too often these enquiries are dismissed with the assertion that talk about religion doesn't belong in the academy. This only demonstrates the aptness of Walter Wink's observation that one of the best ways to discern the weakness of a social system is to discover what it excludes from conversation (Wink, 1986, p. 1).

By extending hospitality to those in the academy to engage with the deeper questions of life's meaning, especially life in the academy, the chaplaincy creates the space for prophetic voice(s) to emerge. Consistent with the universities' core focus on learning, the chaplaincies could become centers that promote spiritual and religious understanding around these questions that explore issues of authenticity and values (Chickering, Dalton, and Stamm, 2005, p. 103).

Prophetic voice(s) for sponsoring denominations and other faith communities, too, could emerge in this collaborative approach. Many are seeking better engagement not just with young people but with an educated populace. This looms as a major challenge throughout all faith communities as more societies advance the learning of their people. Declining church attendance attests to the lack of fulfillment people experience in churches today. The Report cautions that reaching young people while at university may well be the last chance for faith communities to bring the resources of their tradition and practice to help people find meaning in life (Report, p. 68). Chaplaincies can be much more than simply a venue for those who choose to stay connected to their tradition. The chaplaincy may become the one place where the wisdom and religious traditions can be intellectually and faithfully explored by those students and staff who are searching for meaning in their lives. They can provide models for sponsoring denominations and faith communities to bring a deeper, more intellectually rigorous approach to the practice of their faith tradition.

The declining numbers of church-goers are often attributed to the academy's low regard or hostility toward religion. The danger in this line of thinking is that the churches may miss how their own action or inaction undermines their ability to serve an educated society. A pastoral approach with its association of a congregation to a flock of sheep tended by a shepherd may no longer be helpful in an educated society. The HE chaplaincy could illumine for churches new ways of engaging people whose education has taught them to be questioning. Bringing the best and deepest of their religious traditions to those who seek deeper spiritual meaning in life may require wholly new forms.

Finally, the chaplaincy could be the place where a safe, open environment is maintained for students and staff to explore the increasing impact of religions on a global society. If we are to have the sophisticated citizenry that is conversant with the role of religion in world issues, that understands the importance of tolerance for religious pluralism, the chaplaincy with its inter-faith partnerships may open the prophetic space for these conversations to begin. The chaplaincy may well stand in what educator and activist Parker

Palmer calls the tragic gap between reality and possibility. "Democracy," he says, "depends on our capacity to stand in the tragic gap with hearts of hope – which means hearts that can hold the pain to which hope exposes us – refusing to abdicate our citizenship by collapsing into either resigned cynicism or irrelevant utopianism" (Palmer, 2005, p. 25). An educated society will need the sustenance of the religious and wisdom traditions to hold the tension of that tragic gap of our world's reality and its possibility. Finding right ways to bring the world of learning and the world of faith traditions together, chaplaincies can begin to create the possibility that our choices and actions can be both intellectually rigorous and spiritually-grounded.

It may be a lot to put on a chaplaincy: finding new ways to engage with students on their terms, creating hospitable space in the academy for productive conversation about faith and meaning, and engaging with the issues of religious pluralism in a global society. The challenges are immense. But so is the potential of British chaplaincies where the numbers of university students enrolled will continue to grow for at least the remainder of this decade.

CENTERED LEADERSHIP

Religion on campus is in flux because campuses are in flux and so too are religions in society. It is not surprising that chaplains find themselves dancing on the edge of the HE institution as well, perhaps frequently, on the edge of their respective faith communities. The image captures their predicament. The Report as well captured the accompanying ambiguity which brings its own benefits. Rather than seeking a more formal organizational position in the HE institutions, chaplaincies may be better served by creating firmer ground through more sustaining patterns of interconnection and deeper relationships that weave together their unique nexus between the purposes of both universities and of faith communities. A collective discernment process could provide the path to finding clarity about the chaplaincy as it relates to both these worlds while not ceding a useful independence. By bringing the right people together and giving them the opportunity to articulate what the chaplaincy could do that is in their shared interest, those in the chaplaincy could construct a stronger foundation and strengthen support for their work.

Both tradition and innovation are essential to reimagining the chaplaincy that will serve our fast-changing society. A discernment process that engages the people to be served and draws on the spiritual dimension of the institution provides a way to discover which traditions are life-giving and what innovations will be life-enhancing. The opportunity is to go beyond being a shared satellite of the university and the church. This approach provides the chaplaincy a way to fashion itself as a center for living the integration of faith and learning.

REFERENCES

Allen, R.C. (2002) Guiding Change Journeys, San Francisco: Jossey-Bass/Pfeiffer.

Astin, A. W. & Astin, H.S. (2006) "Spirituality and the Professoriate," UCLA Higher Education Research Institute.

Astin, A. W. & Astin, H.S. (2005) "The Spiritual Life of College Students," http:spirituality.ucla.edu/spirituality/reports

BBC News (2004) "We Believe But Not In Church, 18 May.

Bartlett, T (2005) "Most Freshman Say Religion Guides Them," Chronicle of Higher Education, Vol 51, Issue 33, p. A1

Braskamp, L.A., Trautvetteer, L.C., & Ward, K. (2005) "How College Fosters Faith Development in Students," Spirituality in Higher Education Newsletter, Vol 2, Issue 3. http://spirituality.ucla.edu/newsletter/past

Briskin, A., and Frenier, C. (2005) "Declaration of Intent," The Collective Wisdom Initiative.

Buechner, F. (1993) Wishful Thinking: A Seeker's ABC, San Francisco: HarperSanFrancisco.

Cherry, C., DeBerg, B, & Porterfield, A. (2001) Religion on Campus, Chapel Hill & London, The University of North Carolina Press.

Chickering, A., Dalton, J. & Stamm, L. (2006) Encouraging Authenticity & Spirituality in Higher Education, San Francisco: Jossey-Bass.

Evelyn, J. (2004) "Can Philosophy Exist?" The Chronicle of Higher Education, 21 May 2004, Vol 50, Issue 37, A12.

Lamb, C. (2004) "The Theology Generation," The Tablet, 10 February.

Laurence, P. (2005) "Teaching, Learning, and Spirituality," Spirituality in Higher Education Newsletter, Vol 2, Issue 2. http://spirituality.ucla.edu/newsletter/past

McGrail, P. & Sullivan, J. (2005) Dancing on the Edge: A Report into Catholic Chaplaincy in Higher Education. Conference of Catholic Chaplains in Higher Education.

Manning, M. M. (2004) "Institutional Formation: Agreements of Belonging, available at www.novalearning.com.

Manning, M. M. (1998) "The Music Inside," available at www.novalearning.com.

Noone, L.P. (1999) "The Competitive Environment," American Association of Higher Education National Conference, Washington DC.

Palmer. P. J. (2005) "The Politics of the Brokenhearted," Kalamazoo: Fetzer Institute.

Parks, S. D. (2000) Big questions, worthy dreams: mentoring young adults in their search for meaning, purpose, and faith, San Francisco: Jossey-Bass.

Robinson, S. (2004) Ministry Among Students, Norwich: Canterbury Press.

Senge, P. M. (1990) The Fifth Discipline, New York: Doubleday.

Sheeran, M. (1983) Beyond Majority Rule, Philadelphia Yearly Meeting of the Religious Society of Friends.

Starbuck, E. (1993) "Biological model for technology transfer in university-industry-government partnerships," Technology Management, Vol 8, Nos 6/7/8.

Surowiecki, J. (2004) The Wisdom of Crowds, New York: Doubleday.

UCLA Division of Student Affairs (2006) "Institutional Use of Spirituality Data," Spirituality In Higher Education Newsletter, Vol 2, Issue 4. http://spirituality.ucla.edu

Vardy, P. (2005) "A New level of Interest," The Tablet, 9 March.

Wallis, J. (2006) "God's Politics in the UK, " Sojomail, 22 February.

Walsh, D. C. (2005) "An Interview with Diana Chapman Walsh," Spirituality in Higher Education Newsletter, Vol 2, Issue 3. http://spirituality.ucla.edu/newsletter/past

Wheatley, M. J. (1996) A Simpler Way, San Francisco: Berrett-Koehler Publishers.

Wink, W (1984) Naming the Powers: The Language of Power in the New Testament (The Powers : Vol 1), Minneapolis: Augsburg/Fortress Press.

Wink, W. (1996) The Spirit of Institutions, unpublished paper presented at Fetzer Institute.

Wink, W. (1999) The Powers That Be, New York: Galilee Trade (a division of Random House).

Wink, W. (1986) Unmasking the Powers: The Invisible Forces That Determine Human Existence (The Powers, Vol 2), Minneapolis: Augsburg/Fortress Press.

ENDNOTES:

1. Newman Centers are Catholic chaplaincies on public campuses, operated independently of the college and usually administered by the local diocese. These centers are not affiliated with the Cardinal Newman Society founded in 1993 to renew the Catholic identity in Catholic higher education according to a highly conservative agenda.

2. This phrase comes from "Centered on the Edge," a publication of the Fetzer Institute's Collective Wisdom Initiative www.collectivewisdominitiative.org
3. Institute for Social Research, University of Michigan 1997. The figures may have declined in both countries since this research was completed. http://www.umich.edu/news/index.html?Releases/1997/Dec97/chr121097a
4. Religious Studies Colloquium, Carleton College, attended by author, January 14 2006,
5. Arthur Chickering, personal communication with author, January 6 2006
6. A Campus Ministry Alliance at a major public research university includes: Newman, Hillel, Inter-Varsity Christian Fellowship, the Greek Orthodox Church, Christian Reformed, Episcopal, Society of Friends, United Methodists, Evangelical Lutheran Church in America. Baptist, Church of the Brethren, Disciples of Christ, Presbyterian, and the United Church of Christ and non-denominational para-church groups, such as Campus Crusade for Christ according to Cherry, et al, in Religion on Campus, pp 76 – 77.
7. Another explorations on collective intelligence and collective wisdom has been funded by the Fetzer Institute through the Collective Wisdom Initiative. This initiative operates on the premise that the investigation of group and collective consciousness requires a "partnership of both scientific processes and wisdom traditions – a quest for knowledge, understanding, and comprehension. For when these strands are woven as one, we are better able to perceive what binds things together, to grasp at deeper levels a potential that involves each of us in an attraction and instinct for life (Declaration of Intent, 2005)." What binds things together, what emerges at the deeper levels, what compels the instinct for life all speak to a spiritual dimension in groups and in institutions.

APPENDIX

REFLECTING ON UNIVERSITY CHAPLAINCY

The following questions are intended, first, to offer prompts for personal reflection for chaplains already in post, perhaps enabling them to take stock and to prepare for appraisal. Second, since many chaplains work as members of a team, these questions might be useful for such teams as they jointly evaluate their context, the issues facing them, their strategies, their needs and the needs of students and the institution. Third, the questions might be helpful for people considering applying for university chaplaincy posts, those who serve on selection committees for such posts and those responsible for deploying, supporting, overseeing or evaluating chaplains. Fourth, as a part of this particular research report, the questions below, together with the annotated bibliography that follows them, are intended to offer further lines of enquiry, both for chaplains themselves and for other researchers.

Who does a university chaplain belong to? Is she or he part of the church or part of the university, or a hybrid who belongs comfortably with neither? How important is belonging (and comfort)? Is the liminal status of the university chaplain, partly to be identified with the church and partly to be identified with the university, inevitable and indeed part of his or her particularity, special calling and source of grace? How do chaplains relate to the university authorities: is their work promoted, permitted or prevented? What is the relationship between university chaplains and the wider church community: are they ignored and isolated, if their work promoted, supported and encouraged, or is it inhibited and constrained?

What are the main priorities that take up the time of university chaplains? How could we describe the 'curriculum' of university chaplaincy: the explicit curriculum, that is, what is announced as happening, the hidden curriculum, the less obvious messages that get conveyed in the way things are done and the null curriculum, those things that are omitted, left out, do not happen, get ignored? What are the major challenges they face in their work? What are the principal sources of satisfaction to be enjoyed in their diverse tasks and encounters?

How are chaplains prepared for their roles? How are they appointed, provided for financially and materially, professionally supported and evaluated and by whom? What are the training – or consciousness-raising – needs of managers with respect to chaplains? Who provides training for chaplains and in what ways and how effective is this?

Where are chaplains located in the complex and dynamic nexus of communications in the university? Who communicates what to them and how? What access do they have to the principal channels of communication in the university? Similarly, where do university chaplains fit in with regard to ecclesial communication? How does the flow of information about church matters and events feed into and flow out from the university?

What might chaplains need to know about students – their interests, development, personal needs and the pressures upon them? What do chaplains need to know about liaising with other professionals who provide pastoral support to students? How well informed should they be about wider church affairs, ecumenical perspectives and other religions? Which concerns of the academics should be familiar to them? What about the perspectives of senior administrators, who so often frame the work and set the agenda for members of the university?

What will be the basis of or the foundation for the personal credibility, authority and leverage of university chaplains? Why should people listen to them? What is the right balance to be struck between a highly personal (and perhaps idiosyncratic) approach, relying heavily on the special gifts and talents and interests of the chaplain, as opposed to a more detached, impersonal style?

How is the work of university chaplains to be conceived? Are they appointed to accompany people in their journey while at university? Are chaplains there to help people to pray, to become disciples, to cope, to belong, to relax, to think, to grow, to become politically and prophetically conscious? Is their role in showing how faith might be related to university culture and academic life? Are they promoting theological literacy, that is, intelligence about faith? Are they encouraging institutions to live up to the ethical dimensions of their mission and alerting people to shortcoming, temptations and distortions? Is their role to keep open the channels of communication between the university and the church? Are they guardians against conflict between groups and individuals? Is their work high-jacked in service of student retention? Is their task to interweave the Christian narrative into the other narratives enacted on campus? Do they find themselves acting as a filter for expressions of religious faith, authorising some voices and sidelining others?

What kind of ecclesiology is being embodied, proclaimed and facilitated in the work of chaplains?

What kinds of obstacles and enemies are identified to the optimal working of chaplaincies: are these obstacles material, spiritual, personal, institutional? Is the enemy fundamentalism, liberalism, selfishness, indifference and apathy, or relativism? Is a major cause of concern an over-bearing, intrusive and uncaring managerialism? Are aggressive forms of evangelism and proselytism a source of embarrassment? Or is narrow rationalism and a hyper-critical hermeneutics of suspicion eroding faith positions? Is the problem that for many the church lacks credibility? Is the lack of a sense of community or a pervading anonymity a major issue? What is the right blend of representing and conveying in its integrity, as an elder, a religious tradition and being at the cutting edge of that tradition, bringing it into question and offering a safe space for risk-taking and experimentation with regard to it?

ANNOTATED BIBLIOGRAPHY

ARTHUR, James (2006) *Faith and Secularisation in Religious Colleges and Universities*, London, Routledge, ISBN 0415359406.

Though based in the UK, Arthur offers a wide-ranging international perspective of issues currently facing Christian, Jewish and Muslim higher education institutions. Critical of many of the settlements made with dominating secular norms, he provides a clear and helpful analysis of the challenges posed by secularisation as this process impacts upon institutional identity and mission, governance, curriculum, academic freedom and prospects for the future.

ANDERSON, Charles (1993) *Prescribing The Life of the Mind*, Madison, Wisconsin, The University of Wisconsin Press. ISBN 0299138348.

A sane, balanced, constructive essay outlining what is at the heart of the main business of a university, liberal education, developing the competence of citizens and cultivating the capacity to reason carefully and to question critically and responsibly.

ASTLEY, Jeff, FRANCIS, Leslie, SULLIVAN, John and WALKER, Andrew (eds) (2004) *The Idea of a Christian University*, Carlisle, Paternoster Press. ISBN 1842272608.

Theologians from Anglican, Catholic, Orthodox and Protestant traditions engage both with the historic roots from which the idea of the Christian university emerges and with contemporary challenges and opportunities faced higher education today.

BARNETT, Ronald (2003) *Beyond All Reason*, Buckingham , Open University Press. ISBN 0335208932.

One of a whole series of works by this shrewd observer of the university world in the UK (and beyond), this book explores the ideologies that permeate higher education and how they exert influence (by no means always benignly) on priorities and practices.

BENNE, Robert (2001) *Quality With Soul*, Grand Rapids, Eerdmans. ISBN 0802847048.

A landmark study of how six universities and colleges combined fidelity to their sponsoring faith traditions with high provision in secular terms. Extremely valuable exploration of factors at work across several different Christian denominations, including Roman Catholic. Penetrating and constructive diagnosis of past and present and prognosis for the future.

BLUMHOFER, Edith (ed) (2002 *Religion, Education, and the American Experience* Tuscaloosa, The University of Alabama Press. ISBN 0817311467.

Contains useful chapters on the view from the university chapel, the role of faculty in maintaining Catholic identity, spiritual leadership in the university and the relationship between the study of religion and other disciplines.

BORAN, George (1999) *The pastoral challenges of a new age*, Dublin, Veritas. ISBN 1853904775.

Sub-titled 'Helping young people and adults to understand and meet the challenges to faith in a changing world.' Accessible and intelligent commentary on various features of contemporary culture such as freedom, secularisation, sexual revolution and pluralism. Relates these to questions of identity, meaning, ideals and motivation.

BUCKLEY, Michael (1998) *The Catholic University as Promise and Project*, Washington, D.C., Georgetown University Press. ISBN 0878407103.

These elegant, perceptive and penetrating reflections in a Jesuit idiom critically and creatively retrieve historical and contemporary perspectives on the mutual bearing on each other of theology, philosophy, education, culture and the university context.

BUDDE, Michael and WRIGHT, John (eds) (2004) *Conflicting Allegiances The Church-Based University in a Liberal Democratic Society*, Grand Rapids, Brazos Press. ISBN 1587430630.

A particular strength of this book is the way it brings out the difference between being led by the imperatives of the Gospel in decision-making and priorities and having one's agenda directed by the market and state. Challenging chapters raise questions about the kind of hospitality offered at a university – more like that of a hotel or a home? – how different disciplines may be understood and approached by Christians, addressing the vocation of students and the role of chaplaincy.

BUFORD, Thomas (1995) *In Search of a Calling: The College's Role in Shaping Identity*, Macon, Georgia, Mercer University Press. ISBN 0865544662.

A positive and humane analysis (drawing inspiration from both the biblical and the wider humanist tradition) of how universities can promote self-knowledge and educate whole people to identify their calling in life how to and to equip themselves to follow this.

CERNERA, Anthony and MORGAN, Oliver (eds) (2002) *Examining the Catholic Intellectual Tradition, Volume 2*, Fairfield, Connecticut, Sacred Heart University Press, ISBN 1888112018.

An advanced level conversation about Catholic intellectual life in the academy, emphasising notions of stewardship of the tradition, developing the tradition, and handing on the tradition, with extended treatment of teaching as a vocation. A fine concluding chapter usefully clarifies six elements of learning in a Catholic university.

CERNERA, Anthony (ed) (2005) *Lay Leaders in Catholic Higher Education*, Fairfield, Connecticut, Sacred Heart University Press, ISBN 1888112107.

Blend of research report and responses from leaders from many USA higher education institutions. Directly address key aspects of Catholic lay leadership: mission, theological foundations, contextual realities, spirituality, as well as brief treatments of trusteeship, sponsorship, promoting Catholic identity.

CHERRY, Conrad, DeBERG, Betty, and PORTERFIELD, Amanda (2001) *Religion on Campus*, Chapel Hill & London, The University of North Carolina Press. ISBN 0807855006.

Sub-titled 'what religion really means to today's undergraduates' this is a fascinating exploration that really gets under the skin of four universities (one a Catholic university) in different regions of the USA. It investigates factors inhibiting and enhancing the ethos of these institutions, religious practice of students and faculty, the teaching of religion, the shadow side of university life, tensions and signs of hope. Provides much food for thought about chaplains need to situate themselves in relation to the workings of their environment.

CHICKERING, Arthur, DALTON, Jon & STAMM, Liesa (2006) *Encouraging Authenticity & Spirituality in Higher Education*, San Francisco, Jossey-Bass, ISBN 0787974439.

This major, well-researched study takes a broader-than-any-specific-religion approach to spirituality. It explores ways to integrate authenticity and spiritual growth in curriculum, student services, community partnerships, assessment, policy issues and institutional life. Built up from theoretical inquiry, court cases, practical examples and the views of students, academics and administrators. Full of relevance for chaplains and for senior staff responsible for institutional mission and values.

CHRISTENSON, Tom (2004) *The Gift and Task of Lutheran Higher Education*, Minneapolis, Augsburg Press. ISBN 0806650230.

An impressive examination of how Lutheran theology and anthropology can influence approaches to curriculum, pedagogy and community building.

CLAERBAUT, David (2004) *Faith and Learning on the Edge*, Grand Rapids, Zondervan. ISBN 0310253179.

After several chapters that critique how Christian faith has become situated in relationship to academic developments and ethos, the author indicates faith and learning may be related in the physical sciences, the arts and humanities and in the behavioural sciences.

D'COSTA, Gavin (2005) *Theology in the Public Square*, Oxford, Blackwell, ISBN 1405135107.

The author of this highly controversial book, Head of Theology & Religious Studies at the University of Bristol, has something thought-provoking to say to church, academy and nation, especially in the UK and in the USA. Makes a strong case for a Christian, and specifically a Catholic, university within public provision, addressing equally the call to citizenship, discipleship and scholarship. Brings out styles of thinking prevalent in universities that are alien to a Christian worldview. Re-establishes theology's link with the church (and worship) and its role in the circle of disciplines.

DOVRE, Paul (ed) (2002) *The Future of Religious Colleges*, Grand Rapids, Eerdmans. ISBN 0802849555.

Considers the role of religious scholars in the academy, whether the religious college is dying or facing a new dawn, analyses the relationship between various religious traditions (including Catholicism) and the university, provides reflections on *Ex Corde Ecclesiae*, and examines how academic freedom fits into a religiously affiliated university.

ELFORD, R. John (2003) *The Foundation of Hope*, Liverpool, Liverpool University Press. ISBN 0853235198.

The story of Liverpool Hope University College and how its mission as a church college relates to many features of its life and work, including student experience and support services, widening participation, urban renewal, teaching theology, research, chaplaincy, ecumenism, teacher education.

ESTANEK, Sandra (ed) (2002) *Student Affairs at Catholic Colleges and Universities*, Franklin, Wisconsin, Sheed & Ward. ISBN 1580511163.

Many of these chapters have insights useful to university chaplains who outside of Catholic institutions. Topics covered include student development,, conscience formation, controversial issues, embracing diversity, and managing crises.

GARBER, Steven (1996) *The Fabric of Faithfulness*, Downers Grove, Inter-Varsity Press. ISBN 0830819940.

Sub-titled 'weaving together belief & behaviour during the university years,' this work shows how Christians can relate effectively the university context to the questions, temptations, aspirations and needs of students. It considers the types of example, mentoring and support strategies required to address all these.

GILLIAT-RAY, Sophie (2000) *Religion in Higher Education*, Aldershot, Ashgate. ISBN 0754615626.

Sub-titled 'The politics of the multi-faith campus,' this one of very few works devoted to religion in UK universities. It investigates the changing composition of university faith communities, student needs, religion and the corporate life of universities. Chaplaincy organization, funding and staffing receive careful attention.

GRAFF, Gerald (2003) *Clueless in Academe*, New Haven and London, Yale University Press. ISBN 0300095589.

Sub-titled 'How Schooling Obscures the Life of the Mind,' this wonderfully insightful book shows how to bring out the best in students by helping them to join academic conversations and to relate these to their own experiences. Obstacles to effective communication between lecturers and students are clearly mapped out and improvements suggested.

GUTHRIE, David (ed) (1997) *Student Affairs Reconsidered*, Lanham, Maryland, University Press of America. ISBN 0761807950.

Co-published with the Calvin Center, this set of essays by Christians from the Reformed tradition provide a framework for considering the spectrum of issues relating to managing student life on campus from a a clearly Christian perspective.

HAUGHEY, John (ed) (2004) *Revisiting the Idea of Vocation*, Washington D.C., Catholic University of America Press. ISBN0813213614.

This collection of theological explorations on a topic that should be central to the work of chaplains' work with students draws on Lonergan, John's Gospel, Judaism, Islam, St Ignatius, *Pilgrim's Progress*, psychological dimensions and Protestant perspectives.

HAYNES, Stephen (ed) 2002) *Professing in the Postmodern Academy*, Waco, Texas, Baylor University Press. ISBN 0918954827.

Sub-titled 'Faculty and the Future of Church-Related Colleges,' this collection contains insightful essays on postmodernity, curriculum, the Catholic academy, the faith-knowledge dichotomy, Eucharistic accompaniment and the dynamics of religious commitment among students and their families.

HEFT, James (ed) (2005) *Believing Scholars,* New York, Fordham University Press, ISBN 0823225267.

Ten Catholic intellectuals – five men and five women – from different disciplines – reflect on what being a Catholic means for their scholarship, its orientation and nature. They include anthropologist Mary Douglas, theologian Gustavo Gutierrez, philosopher Charles Taylor, historian Marcia Colish and journalist Margaret O'Brien Steinfels.

HOGE, Dean (et al, eds) (2001) *Young Adult Catholics*, Notre Dame, University of Notre Dame Press. ISBN 0268044759.

An in-depth study of USA Catholics in their 20s and 30s, their affiliations with, relationship to and distance from the church and the factors that help and inhibit a sense of belonging.

HOLMES, Arthur (2001) *Building the Christian Academy*, Grand Rapids, Eerdmans. ISBN 0802847447.

Slim, succinct, accessible and eloquent historical perspective on the task of developing Christian higher education over two thousand years.

HUGHES, Richard and ADRIAN, William (eds) (1997) *Models For Christian Higher Education*, Grand Rapids, Eerdmans. ISBN 180284121X.

Building on good practice in the past, these essays suggest strategies for success in the 21st century drawn from detailed explorations of Catholic, Lutheran, Reformed and several other Christian traditions, blending theory with practical examples from universities and colleges representing these traditions.

HUNT, Thomas, NUZZI, Ronald, ELLIS, Joseph & GEIGER, John (eds) (2003) *Handbook of Research on Catholic Higher Education*, Greenwich, Connecticut, Information Age Publishing. ISBN 1593110588.

An extremely valuable guide to a vast range of studies, covering Catholic identity and mission, governance, curriculum, faculty, campus ministry, the changing composition of the student body, student support services, religious orders and university-community partnerships.

JACOBSEN, Douglas and JACOBSEN, Rhonda Hustedt, (eds) (2004) *Scholarship & Christian Faith*, Oxford & New York, Oxford University Press. ISBN 0195170385.

Positive and constructive essays illustrating the bearing of Christian faith on scholarship in a few disciplines, paying attention to contemporary contexts and campus climate.

LANDY, Thomas (ed) (2001) *As Leaven in the World*, Franklin, Wisconsin, Sheed & Ward. ISBN 1580510892.

Sub-titled 'Catholic Perspectives on faith, Vocation, and the Intellectual Life,' these essays grew out of a decade of conferences for staff working in American Catholic universities intended to assist them in understanding better the interaction between faith and work. Apart from the range of disciplines referred to, a particular feature of this work is its treatment of six different streams of spirituality within the Catholic tradition. A wonderful mixture of personal stories, theological analysis, spiritual insights and the educational implications flowing from all these.

LITFIN, Duane (2004) *Conceiving the Christian College,* Grand Rapids, Eerdmans, ISBN 0802827837.

President of Wheaton College, in Illinois, for the past eleven years, Litfin provides a systematic set of challenges for forms of higher education that claim the label 'Christian.' These challenges are: to understand more clearly our own identity; to see more fully whom we serve; to keep the Centre at the Centre; to strengthen the foundations of Christian thought; to preserve the idea of truth; to understand the integrative mandate; to sustain our commitment to the integrative task; to reinforce our commitment to revealed truth; to reconcile institutional commitments with individual freedoms; to appreciate our institutional uniqueness; and to engender a more congenial academic environment.

LOUW, Daniel (1999) *A Mature Faith Spiritual Direction and Anthropology in a Theology of Pastoral Care and Counseling* Louvain, Peeters. ISBN 080284670X.

A heavyweight, highly theoretical and theologically based interpretation of personhood, pastoral theology, maturity, healthy growth and the development of faith.

MANNOIA, James (2000) *Christian Liberal Arts*, Lanham, Maryland, Rowman & Littlefield. ISBN 0847699595.

Brings some of the key elements in a Christian approach to developing the qualities to be sought from a liberal education, in particular, a critical commitment that avoids dogmatism and scepticism, together with a sense of integration that avoids both dabbling and over-specialisation.

MARSDEN, George (1997) *The Outrageous Idea of Christian Scholarship*, New York, Oxford University Press. ISBN 0195105656.

This has now become a landmark work, much discussed in the literature about the degree to which the ethos of the academy is hostile or hospitable to faith among scholars. Forthright, accessible, stimulating set of arguments about how the rules of the academic game are not neutral but engaged in constraining Christian voices and perspectives and suggestive of ways that Christian faith might make a positive contribution in university scholarship.

McDONALD, William (et al) (2002) *Creating Campus Community*, San Francisco, Jossey-Bass. ISBN 0787957003.

Explores a wide range of ways of building a sense of community on campus, taking into account leadership, academic ethos and priorities, team work, service and students' perceptions.

MIGLIAZZO, Arlin (ed) (2002) *Teaching As An Act Of Faith*, New York, Fordham University Press. ISBN 082322209.

Sub-titled 'Theory and Practice in Church-Related Higher Education' this collection complements that of Sterk in its analysis of the bearing of Christian faith on many different academic disciplines in the social sciences, the natural sciences, the arts and the humanities. The editor offers a thorough, even magisterial overview of the literature on Christianity and Higher Education.

MILWARD, Peter (2006) *What is a University?* London, Shephaerd-Walwyn, ISBN 0856832332.

A small, beautifully produced (and very accessible to non-specialists) collection of succinct reflections from a Catholic priest with many years of teaching in a Catholic university in Japan. There are thirty-seven short chapters addressing questions about the university and philosophy, as What is a university? What is knowledge? What is wisdom? What is science? (language, literature, art, law, music, etc) What is man/woman/sex/food/clothes/food/life/death?

MOORE, Steve (ed) (1998) *The University Through the Eyes of Faith*, Indianapolis, Light and Life Communications. ISBN 0893672289.

Drawn from Reformed Christian perspectives, these essays examine the relationship between Christian faith and university (and the wider) culture at the turn of the millennium.

MOREY, Melanie and PIDERIT, JOHN (2006) *Catholic Higher Education*, Oxford, Oxford University Press, ISBN 0195305515.

This substantial (450 pages) book is based on extensive research in the USA, although many of its findings would resonate in other parts of the world. An invaluable resource for those concerned with the future of Catholic higher education, with implications for colleagues from other Christian denominations and from other faiths. Exposes a huge variety of factors that inhibit or enhance how Catholic identity, mission and culture are put into practice. The interplay between the wider culture, student culture, academic culture and religious culture, and that between leadership, governance, faculty, curriculum, policy and practice – all are critically analysed and evaluated, with a thorough grounding in data that has been carefully assembled and interpreted.

O'BRIEN, George Dennis (2002) *The Idea of a Catholic University*, Chicago and London, The University of Chicago Press. ISBN 0226616614.

A subtle and sophisticated exploration of issues that cast light of the nature, purpose, sense of direction and ethos of a university in harmony with a Catholic sensibility. O'Brien analyses biblical foundations, science and art, truth, freedom, fallibility and the place of religion and the church in the university context.

O'KEEFE, Joe (ed) (1997) *Catholic Higher Education at the Turn of the New Century*, Boston College together with Garland Publishing. ISBN 0815326602.

Brings together wide range of official documents and academic essays on many aspects of Catholic Higher Education, principally, but not entirely, from USA.

PARKS, Sharon, Daloz (2000) *Big Questions, Worthy Dreams: Mentoring Young People in Their Search for Meaning, Purpose & Truth*, San Francisco, Jossey-Bass. ISBN 0787941719.

Suggestions for how to read insightfully the situations facing young people in the 20s and for strategic interventions by mentors wishing to support for this age group in their search to find their way. Goes well beyond, but includes higher education.

PEPERZAK, Adriaan (2005) *Philosophy Between Faith and Theology*, Notre Dame, University of Notre Dame Press, ISBN 0268038872.

Very useful for staff reflecting on the relationship between faith and scholarship, Christianity and the academic life and the connections between prayer and thinking. Very good on the vocation of *scientia* to become *sapientia*, and on the fostering of qualities such as humility, generosity and patience in the academy. .

PETERSEN, Rodney (ed) (2002) *Theological Literacy for the Twenty-First Century*, Grand Rapids, Eerdmans. ISBN 0802849644.

Offers wide range of ways of understanding education in theology, from diverse Christian traditions, taking into account changes in the cultural context of universities today, both secular and church-based.

RAMOS, Alice and GEORGE, Marie (eds) (2002) *Faith, Scholarship, and Culture in the 21st Century*, Washington, D.C., American Maritain Association, distributed by The Catholic University of America Press. ISBN 0966922654.

For chaplains involved in or supporting efforts to provide Catholic Studies in secular institutions, there is a sound overview of such attempts in a 30 page chapter from Frederick Erb.

REISER, William (ed) (1995) *Love of Learning, Desire for Justice*, Scranton, University of Scranton Press. ISBN 0940866412.

A collection of essays showing how undergraduate education might address and incorporate an option for the poor across several disciplines.

RHODES, Frank (2001) *The Creation of the Future*, Ithaca and London, Cornell University Press. ISBN 080143937X.

A magisterial and very clear analysis of the role of the American university (which so often leads the way for university trends in the UK). Covers professionalism, research, community, teaching, undergraduate and postgraduate education, service, governance and leadership.

ROBINSON, Simon (2004) *Ministry Among Students*, Norwich, Canterbury Press. ISBN 1853115827.

Based on substantial practical experience of chaplaincy work in a secular university, this work covers student culture, theology of chaplaincy, worship, building bridges, spiritual and pastoral care of students, working with staff, postgraduate, international and non-traditional students, as well as faith in the curriculum and the prophetic role of chaplains.

ROEBBEN, Bert and WARREN, Michael (eds) (2001) *Religious Education as Practical Theology*, Louvain, Peeters. ISBN 9042910321.

Although this collection of essays ranges beyond higher education, it includes well-informed analyses of the changing self-understanding of young people, their attitudes towards their responsibilities and contexts and towards religion.

SCHUURMAN, Douglas (2004) *Vocation*, Grand Rapids, Eerdmans. ISBN 0802801374.

Sub-titled 'Discerning our callings in life,' has in mind particularly college students. A useful study of a neglected theme, complementing Haughey (2004).

SCHWEHN, Mark (1993) *Exiles From Eden*, New York, Oxford University Press. ISBN 0195073436.

This seminal study, recently re-issued, has influenced much of the ensuing literature on religion and the academic vocation. Tackles false or distorting approaches to the separation of personal faith and academic rigour and demonstrates effectively the close links between the virtues and intellectual work.

SIMON, Caroline (et al) (2003) *Mentoring for Mission*, Grand Rapids, Eerdmans. ISBN 0802821243.

Shows the need for, potential of and ways to tackle the nurturing of new staff in the meaning and application of mission at college and university.

SIRE, James (2000) *Habits of the Mind*, Downers Grove, Inter-Varsity Press. ISBN 0830822739.

A crisp, carefully argued and persuasive exploration of the intellectual life as a Christian calling. Brings together effectively discussions about intellectual and moral virtues and provides guidance about avoiding both excessive rationalism and mindless fideism. Useful for lecturers and advanced level students.

STERK, Andrea (ed) (2002) *Religion, Scholarship, & Higher Education*, Notre Dame, University of Notre Dame Press. ISBN 0268040540.

A variety of perspectives on diverse models of relationship between religion and scholarship and future prospects, particularly useful for its treatment of potential links between religious faith and specific academic disciplines.

SULLIVAN, Robert (ed) (2001) *Higher Learning and Catholic Traditions*, Notre Dame, University of Notre Dame Press. ISBN 0268030537.

Seven powerful essays from the UK and from the USA reflect upon dangers, hopes and choices for Catholic universities (Alasdair MacIntyre) and consider the bearing of Christian faith on several areas of the curriculum.

TOTON, Suzanne (2006) *Justice Education: From Service to Solidarity*, Milwaukee, Marquette University Press, ISBN 0874627273.

The author, based at Villanova University, shows how a Catholic university should engage in a preferential option for the poor in the way it orients teaching, research and service. Provides practical examples of how a university can participate in the creation of justice and peace and teach compassion.

WEINGARTNER, Rudolph (1999) *The Moral Dimensions of Academic Administration*, Lanham, Maryland, Rowman & Littlefield. ISBN 0847690970.

Sometimes the chaplain has to be a critic of or utter a prophetic voice in relation to damaging policies and procedures conducted in the academy. This work gives an overview of some of the principal areas requiring moral evaluation in a university setting in terms of institutional practice.

WILCOX, John and KING, Irene (eds) (2000) *Enhancing Religious Identity Best Practices From Catholic Campuses,* Washington D.C., Georgetown University Press. ISBN 0878408142.

Very substantial volume with informative and thought-provoking chapters covering Catholic identity, leadership, trustees, academic disciplines, student life and strategies for change.

WILKENS, Steve; SHRIER, Paul; MARTIN, Ralph (eds) (2005) *Christian College, Christian Calling,* Lanham, Altamira Press, ISBN 0759109354.

Sub-titled 'Higher Education in the Service of the Church' this collection of twelve chapters, all but one contributed by faculty at Azusa Pacific University, has a special focus on showing a positive relationship between the academy and the congregation in church, a connection that is too often fragile, if not entirely severed. Teachers of philosophy, theology, church history, biblical studies and ministry explain their disciplines in terms of Christian life rather than academic achievement. They steer a path between secular neutrality that dilutes faith and uncritical transmission of Christian tradition.

WOLTERSTORFF, Nicholas (2004) *Educating for Shalom Essays on Christian Higher Education* Grand Rapids, Eerdmans. ISBN 0802827535.

A collection of essays over a 30 year period by an important and influential Christian philosopher.

INDEX

Appointment processes for chaplains: 66 -71, 140, 146, 196

Appraisal of chaplains: 72-75, 90, 203, 207, 269

Bangor (University of Wales): 191-205

Cambridge: 175-189

Ecumenical aspects of chaplaincy: 51-64, 66, 67, 84, 99, 113, 126-7, 140, 147, 178, 199-220, 224-238

Eucharist: 26, 30-31, 32, 33, 39, 59, 60, 63, 73, 79, 80, 82, 138, 158, 177, 178, 186, 187, 191 – 198 passim, 200, 203, 210-212,

Gender issues in chaplaincy: 176-187

Interfaith: 60-64, 87, 134, 158, 236, 240, 248, 264

Jewish/Judaism: 61, 62, 140, 146, 225, 235, 238, 239, 242, 246, 247

Islam/Muslims: 46, 60-64, 125, 141, 187, 199, 212, 225, 226, 239-242, 244, 246-248, 251

Hindu/ism: 212, 240, 247, 251

Heythrop: 175, 187-189

Hindu/ism: see Interfaith

Jewish: see Interfaith

Judaism: see Interfaith

Islam: see Interfaith

Leeds, University of: 165

Liverpool Hope University: 12, 16, 126-132

London, University of: 224-247

Management and supervision of chaplains: 71-84

Manchester Metropolitan University: 139-149

Mass: see Eucharist

Muslims: see Interfaith

Poppleton, University of: 225

St Mary's College: 205-223